THE MARKET FOR
POLITICAL ECONOMY

THE MARKET FOR POLITICAL ECONOMY

The advent of economics in British university culture, 1850–1905

Edited by
Alon Kadish and Keith Tribe

London and New York

First published 1993
by Routledge
11 New Fetter Lane, London EC4P 4EE

Simultaneously published in the USA and Canada
by Routledge Inc.
29 West 35th Street, New York, NY 10001

Typeset in Baskerville by
Ponting–Green Publishing Services, Chesham, Bucks
Printed and bound in Great Britain by
Mackays of Chatham PLC, Chatham, Kent

British Library Cataloguing in Publication Data
A catalogue record for this book is available from
the British Library.

ISBN 0–415–03874–X

Library of Congress Cataloging-in-Publication Data
The Market for political economy : the advent of
economics in British university culture, 1850–1905 /
edited by Alon Kadish, Keith Tribe.
p. cm.
Includes bibliographical references and index.
ISBN 0–415–03874–X
1. Economics–Study and teaching (Higher)–Great Britain–
History. 2. Universities and colleges–Great Britain–
Curricula–History. 3. Economics–Great Britain–History.
I. Kadish, Alon, 1950– II. Tribe, Keith, 1949–
HB74.9.G7M37 1993
330'.071'141–dc20 92-37258 CIP

CONTENTS

CONTENTS

CONTRIBUTORS

R. D. Collison Black is Emeritus Professor of Economics, Queen's University, Belfast.

Thomas A. Boylan is Professor of Economics, University College, Galway.

Gregory Claeys is Professor of the History of Political Thought, Royal Holloway and Bedford College, University of London.

Timothy P. Foley is Senior Lecturer in English Literature, University College, Galway.

Istvan Hont is Lecturer in History, University of Cambridge.

Alon Kadish is Senior Lecturer in History, Hebrew University, Jerusalem.

John Maloney is Lecturer in Economics, University of Exeter.

Keith Tribe is Senior Lecturer in Economics, Keele University.

EDITORIAL PREFACE

The institutionalization of political economy in Europe, the United States and Japan

Gregory Claeys, Istvan Hont, Alon Kadish and Keith Tribe

In July 1982 a meeting took place in the Research Centre, King's College Cambridge at which it was decided to launch an international comparative project on the development and institutionalization of political economy. Its purpose was to examine the pre-eminence gained by political economy in the emergence and development of the social sciences in the course of the nineteenth century. Hitherto this problem had usually been approached using the methods and procedures of the history of ideas,[1] whereas the new project was conceived from the outset as one which would move away from conventional intellectual history towards a social history of ideas. In place of the usual emphasis upon theoretical innovation and development, primacy was instead to be given to the process by which political economy became a discipline of study within the university context. By gaining a definite place within the university curriculum political economy was institutionalized: on the one hand, a body of knowledge was shaped by the pedagogic and administrative conditions of university education; while on the other, a new discipline of study was transmitted in this form to successive generations of students for whom certification in economics became an important vocational qualification.

The King's Research Centre was at this time engaged in a research project, under the direction of Istvan Hont, into 'Political Economy and Society, 1750–1850'. This project had been initiated in 1978, and

1 For Britain, an early important, but neglected, essay by Sidney Checkland is an exception to this – 'The advent of academic economics in England' *Manchester School*, Vol.19, (1951), pp.43–70. More recently A. W. Coats has charted aspects of the later history of British and American economics in a number of essays, now brought together as A. W. Coats, *The Sociology and Professionalisation of Economics. British and American Essays Vol. 2*, Routledge, London 1993.

had already staged a major conference that had formed the basis for a successful volume on the Scottish Enlightenment.[2] During the Spring of 1982 the Centre was approached by Piero Barucci, then Professor for the History of Economic Doctrines at the University of Florence, with a proposal for a joint project on the development of economics as a university discipline. This proposal originally envisaged the creation of an international database of departments, chairs, textbooks and personnel, but at the initial meeting in Cambridge in July 1982 the scope was immediately widened to a comparative historical treatment of the process of institutionalization.

On this basis a 'Call for papers' was drafted,[3] envisaging a programme of research, discussion and publication with a distinct structure and sequence. National research groups were to be established and made responsible for determining the parameters and chronologies of national histories.[4] These groups were to gather information on the national development of economics as a university discipline, taking in a period stretching from the first established chair in the subject to that point in time when the subject could be said to constitute an autonomous discipline within the university system. Due account was to be given to the fact that the university system was itself undergoing a process of change, and this would necessitate the study of institutional contexts other than universities; but the focus was to be primarily the university. Following on from this initial phase of work, essays could then be written providing an overview of significant aspects of national developments in the institutionalization of political economy. A pre-conference meeting was planned for the following year at King's College, where the initial results could be discussed and any deficiencies rectified before a concluding conference, to be held in Florence no earlier than the summer of 1984. The purpose of this concluding conference was to evaluate the national contributions within a cross-national comparative framework, providing a fresh insight into the development of the discipline of economics as an international phenomenon.

As it turned out, the concluding conference was not in fact held until April 1986, at San Miniato; and the preparations for the final conference turned out to be of greater significance than the conference itself. This followed from several modifications to the initial programme, most significantly the addition of many European countries

2 I. Hont, M. Ignatieff (eds) *Wealth and Virtue. The Shaping of Political Economy in the Scottish Enlightenment*, Cambridge: Cambridge University Press, 1983.

3 Signatories to this were Istvan Hont, Gregory Claeys and Biancamaria Fontana of the Research Centre; Keith Tribe of Keele University; and Piero Barucci and Gabriella Gioli of the University of Florence.

4 Originally the project covered only European and North American universities; Japan was included in late 1983.

not initially included, and the staging of a number of workshops and national pre-conferences. The 'Cambridge Pre-Conference' meeting was held as planned in July 1983, and discussed progress in the establishment of working groups in Germany[5] and the United States, together with preliminary results from the British and French groups. A one-day workshop was then held at the Sorbonne in July 1984,[6] enabling the organizers to review the progress in recruiting contributors for Sweden, Denmark, the Netherlands, Belgium, Italy and Japan.[7] At this meeting it was agreed that the final conference was to take place in 1986, preceded by a further preliminary conference in Paris in June 1985,[8] and as many national workshops as possible. These were considered important as 'opinion-forming' events preliminary to the final conference, at which the framework of a national summary paper could be established through discussion among individual contributors.

The British group had a successful meeting at Keele in March 1985, and it was here that an overall interpretation of political economy in English, Scottish and Irish universities emerged. Throughout the life of the project, non-British contributors had habitually referred to the English case as if it represented an 'early start' to the development of political economy in a university context. By now, it was clear that this was a quite unwarranted historical prejudice, and that, by contrast, one of the important discoveries of the project was the concurrence of institutional developments in Europe, North America and Japan. Taking account of variations in the pace and timing of individual national developments, the most striking aspect of these varied developments was that the period of consolidation (the terminal date originally identified) occurred within the last few years of the nineteenth century. Before this time, political economy was primarily a subject of public discussion; after this time, it began its transformation into an academic discipline.

Throughout this period the project had been co-ordinated and directed from Cambridge, in the latter stages hampered by the fact that the Research Centre project which had been such an important source of support ended in 1984, and Istvan Hont himself moved to Columbia University early in 1986. Neither Istvan Hont nor Keith Tribe, both of

---

5 At this stage Hans Erich Bödeker and Keith Tribe were reponsible for the German group; responsibility was later assumed by Klaus Hennings. On his death late in 1986 Norbert Waszek, his Research Assistant, completed preparation of the German papers for publication.

6 Organized by the French group's convenor, Lucette LeVan-Lemesle.

7 The organizers failed in their attempts to gain coverage of Russia, and that for Spain and Portugal remained extremely limited.

8 This meeting took place at the Institut National d'Etudes Démographiques in June 1985, whose facilities were made available by Jacqueline Hecht.

whom had been most closely associated with the work of international co-ordination, were able to attend the San Miniato conference in April 1986. At the second meeting in Paris a draft programme had been devised which emphasized a comparative chronological frame. However, at the San Miniato Conference it proved difficult to shift the focus away from national case-studies to comparative analysis, despite the efforts of some participants, including Alon Kadish and Gregory Claeys of the British group. Originally, the final conference had been viewed as a vehicle to draw diverse national contributions together into a synthesis for publication. The national workshops and pre-conferences, conceived as a means of moving the project towards the concluding conference, in the event turned out to be a more coherent reflection of the project's original objectives, and publication was therefore begun on an independent nation-by-nation basis.[9]

Cumulatively these volumes provide an overview of parallel national developments. The original aspiration of the project was that a new synthesis would follow the establishment of a comprehensive analytical framework, but this framework proved extremely difficult to elaborate within the constraints of a collaborative international project. The group based in Cambridge enjoyed the benefits of working together, and, as the core of the British group, it succeeded in developing the most ambitious and comprehensive coverage of a central part of the project's programme. Initial optimism concerning publication of a large-scale work on the history of political economy in Britain from 1750 to 1900 foundered on the difficulty of successfully co-ordinating a significant research effort without the kind of resources initially provided by King's College.[10] Consequently, the British contribution to the project now appears several years later, but with the advantage of insights developed by the editors from their continuing work in this area.

9 The French contributions were published under the editorship of Lucette LeVan-Lemesle as *Les problèmes de l'institutionnalisation de l'économie politique en France au XIXe siècle* in the series *Oeconomia*, 1986. Further national volumes that have appeared are C. Sugiyama, H. Mizuta (eds) *Enlightenment and Beyond. Political Economy comes to Japan*, University of Tokyo Press, Tokyo 1988; M. Augello, M. Bianchini, G. Gioli, P. Roggi (eds) *La cattedre politica in Italia. La diffusione di una disciplina [sospetta] (1750–1900)*, Franco Angeli, Milan 1988; N. Waszek (ed.) *Die Institutionalisierung der Nationalökonomie an den deutschen Universitäten*, Scripta Mercurae Verlag, St Katherinen 1988; W. J. Barber (ed.) *Breaking the Academic Mould. Economists and American Higher Learning in the Nineteenth Century*, Wesleyan University Press, Middletown 1988.

10 The British Academy provided the funds necessary to distribute papers to all other groups in preparation for the San Miniato Conference, and the Nuffield Foundation funded two meetings at Keele, that of March 1985, and one the following year to co-ordinate preparation of a volume for publication, in addition to funding for transfer of all the British papers to disk.

ACKNOWLEDGEMENTS

The editors would like to express their thanks to the British Academy and the Nuffield Foundation for grants which assisted in the preparation of this volume. We would also like to thank Nicola Pike for the careful and efficient manner in which she edited and transferred the original manuscripts to disk.

INTRODUCTION
The Supply of and Demand for Economics in late Victorian Britain

When, in the early 1980s, the contributors to this volume began their work on the institutional development of political economy in Britain, the lack of a reliable overview of this process appeared in itself sufficient justification for the undertaking. Relatively little was known about the history of academic institutionalization in Britain; and it also became evident in the course of our research that historical under-standing of the modern British university system as a whole was gravely defective. It was at first far from clear what sort of conclusions would result from the enterprise. The initial, seemingly modest, aim was therefore to reconstruct the process whereby economics became an academic discipline within the context of the development of higher education in Britain. Only in retrospect have certain distinct patterns become discernible, and the significance of specific institutional his-tories evident. The need for an overall synthetic survey remains; and these essays form a sound basis for such a synthesis. None the less, the broad outlines of the entry of political economy into British university institutions are now visible, and in many respects they modify, or even contradict, the general working assumptions of existing studies that deal with the history of economics within the framework of a more conventional history of ideas.

Whereas the institutionalization of economics as an autonomous discipline lagged some way behind the development of economic theory in the hands of non-academic and academic economists, throughout the nineteenth century political economy was widely recog-nized in Britain as a legitimate, if relatively minor, component of a general liberal education. The study of political economy in British universities around the middle of the century was not well developed, but no one seriously disputed the need to include some political economy in the curriculum, in one form or another. A number of professorial chairs, some founded in the early part of the century, remained as testimonials to the recognition accorded to political economy, even though these chairs might be tenanted by somewhat

1

lack-lustre scholars, or even left vacant as was often the case in London. As for the actual teaching of political economy, this was largely based on Adam Smith's *Wealth of Nations*, to which was later added John Stuart Mill's *Principles of Political Economy* – as befitted a system of learning largely consisting of the study of great texts. The standard of teaching was itself frequently indifferent, and occasionally eccentric. Students seeking a general education often enough came away with some knowledge of elementary economic principles, but it was not until Jevons, and to a greater extent Marshall, that any single academic economist achieved a level of pre-eminence which attracted able disciples to their institutions keen to expound and develop their work.

Political economy entered the British university curriculum as part of a general shift in university teaching away from a small number of traditional schools, consisting of a wide range of subjects, towards a broader range of distinct disciplinary divisions. Initially, economics was associated with two of these groupings: the moral sciences (i.e. mainly philosophy) and history. The subsequent course of institutionalization was mainly determined either by internal developments within the relevant departments and faculties, or by attempts to break the mould and establish new institutions based on different concepts of the social sciences and higher education in general – processes which resemble the political division between legislative reformism and constitutional change. However, so long as external demand for academically-trained economists remained limited, many of the internal institutional changes that were made have only a retrospective importance; they are significant not for their contemporary impact, but rather for the long-term evolution of political economy into the economics professed by twentieth-century academics.

This slow pace of development for a subject which had indeed existed, in a form readily recognizable today, since the early nineteenth century, and which has such practical relevance to the development of public and business administration, seems at first sight to contradict our natural assumptions about the relations between education, government and economic development. The expansion of government and business activity during the later nineteenth century, together with the frequently-aired concern over the extent and quality of technical and scientific educational provision, ostensibly furnished a natural constituency for political economy as an academic subject. From this, it is a short step to the presumption that regular teaching in economic subjects must have become established in response to the evident commercial and administrative needs of later nineteenth-century England. This presumption, although prevalent at the time, was not then, as now, necessarily valid. Efforts were repeatedly made in the later part of the century to secure a place for the teaching of political economy within new and established institutions, the argument being advanced on all sides that this was a science whose principles were of central importance to the progress of industrialized nations. It was not for want of trying that economic science did not become firmly rooted in the academic curriculum of the modern English university until after the First World War. The principal reason for the limited success of these efforts was that there were insufficient students to support the proposed programmes of study beyond the most elementary level.

The demand for teaching in a subject like economics is itself a response to demand from employers for graduates possessing the skills and qualifications that the study of the subject confers. The lack of demand from students for the new programmes of study reflected therefore, by extension, a lack of interest for such qualification in the market for university graduates. There is indeed a linkage between the labour market and the development of new subjects within universities, but in this case it was the organization of the labour market itself which slowed the adoption of political economy as an academic subject, not lack of response on the part of educational institutions.

To use a modern expression, political economy entered the curriculum of the modern university as a supply-side push which, over several decades, encountered no steady and reliable demand sufficient to promote it from a subject of general interest to a subject of specialized study. In Oxford and Cambridge, and to some extent London, this was not a serious difficulty for those few scholars interested in political economy, since such demand as there was sufficed to support their interests and activities. In addition to this, the perceived vocational relevance of political economy to the worlds of commerce and business made it necessarily part of the curriculum of the modern university, a broadly-based secular institution pioneered in Britain by University College, London. Moreover, as a vocational subject, with a potential constituency among managers, young clerks, teachers and civil servants, it also addressed those social groups whose modest wealth and background debarred them from the two ancient universities. From the 1850s, for those not fortunate enough to live in London with potential access to King's College and University College, there was little prospect of systematic tuition and certification in political economy, or related subjects within the moral sciences.

This broad picture can be reduced to four basic approaches to the study of political economy in the second half of the nineteenth century, approaches which are by no means mutually exclusive, and at some stages were complementary.

First, at the most general level, political economy was seen throughout the nineteenth century as an integral part of political discourse – its tropes and figures constantly recurred in the speeches, writings and

3

conversation of all social classes. A sound general education therefore included some acquaintance with political economy and its principles. Such widespread concurrence in the public significance of these elementary principles none the less carried no necessary implications for systematic teaching. If anything, this ready acceptance of political economy as a component of public political discourse itself hindered the development of systematic teaching, since it was considered to deal in truths, the validity of which was self-evident, or else required little more than common sense. Controversy among political economists over arcane theoretical issues had little implication for this level of understanding, since however the issues might be resolved, such resolution would not alter public understanding of elementary principles, such as free trade. A deeper understanding of the subject, such as might result from its systematic study, would not, it was thought, seriously modify generally-accepted theses.

Second, this public attitude provides a background against which some teaching did develop, a background which provides a constant parameter in the studies collected below. Popular political economy emerged and developed independently of what became mainstream theory. Its relevance to the history of institutionalization is through the history of the university extension movement. The nature of the demand for extension courses and the lecturers' and examiners' reports seem to indicate a popular view of economics little influenced by early nineteenth-century socialism, Owenism or Marxism. The extension teachers reported some rare confrontations with socialist students, but the majority of their listeners held the basic liberal tenets of free trade and market economics, and were receptive to the new liberal modifications of orthodox theory. Students often had some knowledge of elementary economics but little interest in advanced theory – an attitude that younger lecturers, pursuing their own specialized studies, found extremely frustrating. Most extension centres were content to order the occasional introductory course in economics, while demand for further courses was usually limited to applied subjects with clear practical implications, or to economic history. The younger lecturers' dissatisfaction with the nature of popular demand reflected the change within their own academic institutions. An older generation whose own training was itself elementary held views of political economy and its applications much more akin to that of their audiences. Political economy, as suggested in the previous paragraph, consisted of some clear and simple truths both practical and moral, with changing views of society, e.g. the value of collective self-help through co-operatives or trade unions, often modifying economic doctrines. Working-class audiences seemed intent on strengthening their own beliefs and acquiring some useful knowledge rather than embarking upon the study of a new theoretical discipline, whereas middle-class students, many of whom were either seeking vocational qualifications (e.g. teachers or clerks) or regarded the courses as an elevated form of leisure activity, had little intrinsic interest in the subject. Consequently, extension lecturers who offered courses in economics could not expect to draw a sufficient income from lecturing unless they added other subjects. This may have posed no problem to the first generation of extension teachers, but must have been quite frustrating to younger graduates who were committed to specialization whilst unable to accept a cut and dried view of economic principles. On the other hand, the younger lecturers, many of whom were new liberals, concerned in the 1880s and 1890s by the dangerous attractions of Henry George and the re-emergence of radical socialism, were anxious to reach working-class audiences and impress upon them the relevance of modified liberal economics, thereby preserving the existing alliance between working and middle classes. Indeed, the very existence of the extension movement was supposed to demonstrate the possibility of better inter-class relations, and the committment of the educated middle classes to the progress of the working classes. Hence it was the nature of demand, shaped by popular perceptions of economics, that largely shaped the supply of extension courses.[1]

Third, this tendency became more pronounced following the Technical Education Act (1889) and the Local Taxation Act (1890) which gave to local authorities the means to subsidize extension courses. Technical education was widely seen as a means of improving Britain's economic performance and international competitiveness, while at the same time contributing to the material prosperity of the working classes. If the initial aims of the extension movement included the creation of better citizens, it was now offered the additional purpose of directly assisting in the improvement of the employment prospects and productivity of the working and lower middle classes. In doing so, the extension movement was to supplement and extend the geographical base of local university colleges which, like the extension movement, sought to combine vocational training with a general education. Technical education was commonly understood to include commercial education, which while including technical subjects such as accounting or commercial statistics, usually included some elementary economics as well.

Fourth, the vocational imperative, in which the teaching of political economy was linked to questions of national efficiency, figured strongly in the arguments of those seeking to promote the regular study of

---

1 The fact that these courses were necessarily self-financing lends additional edge to this situation.

political economy at university level. Such arguments were of course based upon the assumption that the reason for the slow development of the teaching of political economy could be found in the want of supply, arguments that are of course predictable for those seeking to increase the supply. As has been suggested above, and is demonstrated at length below, it was the want of demand that was the real check on development, and so this particular line of argument was, and is, based on a false premise. In fact, what finally assisted political economy into the curricula of the modern British university as an autonomous academic discipline were those very changes which rendered the university 'modern': an intellectual fashion for specialized degrees, the emergence of structured three-year teaching programmes, and the subdivision of academic staff by department and seniority. These changes provided a dynamic which fragmented the moral sciences into constituent disciplines, while at the same time promoting a greater degree of definition in history as an academic subject. The joint effect of these pressures upon the accepted location of political economy within the existing educational structures led inexorably to the formation of political economy (or, as it became in this process, 'economics') as an autonomous discipline of study. Cambridge led the way with the economics tripos, but change elsewhere was much slower, corresponding, as it has been suggested, to the general development of external demand. Hence the tripos should be seen not only as an outcome of an internal development, but also as an 'heroic' achievement of Marshall's.

These distinct perspectives focus upon the various factors inhibiting the speedy translation of a wide public interest in political economy into systematic teaching of the subject in university-level institutions. The real deficiency is not to be found in the institutions themselves, but rather in the absence of a constant and rising demand on the part of students, for reasons touched upon above. This argument forms a persistent theme of the case-studies collected here. But this lack of demand for new courses and any qualification that they might confer is itself only the reflection of the actual or perceived need for qualification in the subject for specific forms of employment, and this aspect of the problem cannot be systematically addressed in these essays, directed as they are to individual institutions and their actual, rather than potential, constituencies. As noted above, it was generally supposed that the increasing complexity of industrial economies generated of itself a need for administrators and managers versed not only in elementary principles of economics, but trained in the analysis of statistics, market structures, taxation and finance. These assumptions shaped the proposals made by reformers seeking to secure political economy within the university curriculum, and are often today repeated without comment in historical surveys of the period. Indeed, the political and economic issues that educational reformers addressed in the later nineteenth century have, at the close of the twentieth century, themselves become incorporated into a vision of the decline of British industrial pre-eminence. From this cultural-critical perspective on later nineteenth-century Britain, educational reformers appear to be endowed with a particular presentiment of what was to come; their criticism of contemporary conditions is mobilized as unmediated commentary upon the causes of industrial decline.

However, if we turn to the foreign contemporaries of these reformers, in France, in the United States, in Japan, we discover local reformers voicing similar criticisms of their own educational systems – far from the Podsnapian invocation of 'foreign superiority' being a specifically English phenomenon, as E. P. Thompson so astutely noted many years ago,[2] in the field of educational reform, and particularly in the case of political economy, it turns out to be an international phenomenon. Everyone is claiming to be behind everyone else in some vital aspect of cultural and economic development. This is of course a normal condition of competition and innovation, and due allowance for this rhetorical feature has to be made in judging the analyses of contemporaries. Registration of this fact helps us to look beyond the rhetoric of educational reform to the actual linkages between economic development and educational innovation. The linkage between economic development, the labour market and educational provision appears of course to be self-evident, the assumption being that deficient development can be remedied by specific educational provision. But this apparent truth always was, and still is today, of doubtful validity. It is not clear, for example, whether economic development promotes educational provision, or the other way round. Even if we overlook this problem and accept that economic development is associated, in some indeterminate way, with educational reform, applied to the later nineteenth century this presumption overestimates the rate of bureaucratic evolution in the leading industrial economies of the period.

The United States and Germany were, for example, the most dynamic industrial powers at the close of the nineteenth century, with the most elaborated business and administrative structures. Advanced commercial education aimed at meeting the requirements of these structures for trained managers and officials did not however become significant phenomena until shortly before the First World War. For many years after the foundation of the Harvard Business School in 1908, for

2 In his critique of *New Left Review*'s posture with respect to Continental European theory and culture – 'The Pecularities of the English', *Socialist Register, 1965*, pp.311–62.

example, the course of study was for one year only; until 1914, 25 per cent of the first year students at most stayed on for a second year, which was itself not clearly distinct in level from the first.[3] In Germany, the Cologne Commercial College, which had opened in 1901, had 300 students on a two-year course by 1906, and a large new building in 1907.[4] The Berlin Commercial College opened in 1906, and likewise developed rapidly, both in terms of student numbers and courses. The period of vigorous development in the teaching of commercial and economic subjects in the United States and Germany begins towards the end of the first decade of the twentieth century – almost ten years after the foundation of the Faculties of Commerce in Manchester and Birmingham, and longer of course in the case of the London School of Economics. This 'late development' of commercial and economic teaching in the United States and Germany serves to place in perspective the apparently tardy and weak development of British foundations, serving an economy where industrial enterprises were comparatively small, and public administration only beginning its ascent as a distinct, specialized activity.

Significant 'demand' in Britain for graduates with a background in commerce and economics first developed in the context of teaching, public administration and business in the 1920s, and not before. The First World War had a major and irreversible impact on the development of central administration, while municipal administration gained new powers in the 1920s with respect to housing and urban development. Significant industrial combines in Britain likewise date from this period, providing a higher profile to graduate business education and the needs of management. Viewed from the later twentieth century, such developments might appear piecemeal and hesitant; but in respect of changes in the market for university graduates with specialized skills, such developments marked a qualitative change from the conditions

---

3 M. T. Copeland, *And Mark an Era. The Story of the Harvard Business School*, Boston: Little, Brown and Company, 1958, p.37. The first business school in the United States was of course the Wharton School at the University of Pennsylvania, but although this was founded in 1881, it did not develop a graduate programme until the 1890s, and its period of significant growth coincided with that of the Harvard Business School – S. A. Sass, *The Pragmatic Imagination. A History of the Wharton School 1881–1981*, Philadelphia: University of Pennsylvania Press, 1982, pp.50, 98.

4 It should be noted in this context that the present Soldiers' Field complex of the Harvard Business School was built in the mid-1920s, the Baker Library not being completed until 1927. Until that date the School operated from makeshift office and teaching accomodation provided by Harvard University. Before the 1930s German business education was arguably the best organized, had the best facilities, with more numerous and better-educated students than anywhere else in the industrial world.

prevailing before 1914 By this time, of course, teaching in economics and commerce was a routine part of the university curriculum, and so universities were able to develop and adapt to the demands placed upon them. The arguments advanced by educational reformers of the 1890s concerning the 'needs of industry' first began to come true in the 1920s, but since their arguments had been generally accepted in the meantime, universities were in a position to turn out appropriate numbers and types of graduates. The fortuitousness of this development should not deflect our attention from the fact that the rhetoric of the 1890s was untimely, and the reasons for this can be briefly examined here.

The Civil Service reforms of the 1850s occupy a central place in our understanding of the relationship of educational reform and the development of public and private bureaucracies. A leading feature of these reforms was the progressive rationalization and standardization of the educational background of recruits. The introduction of a formal process of examination and qualification for recruits in turn had a great influence on the diffusion of public examination and certification in the later nineteenth century. In Germany, the teaching of economics in the University had always been closely linked to the administrative requirements of state and principality; with the extension of central and local government activity in mid-Victorian Britain it would seem logical that some kind of vocational qualification in economics and commerce would become *de rigueur* for the aspiring state official. A closer examination of the structure of administration and the nature of reform activity around the middle of the century fails to bear this out. The pedagogical model developed by the East India Company in the first decade of the nineteenth century for the training of administrators – a training in history, political economy, law and languages – was not imitated with the reform of recruitment and qualification for the Home Civil Service.

The most famous statement of mid-century administrative reform was the 'Report on the Organisation of the Permanent Civil Service' (1854), commonly known under the names of its signatories as the Northcote–Trevelyan Report. This brief document was in part a summary of themes broached in a number of previous departmental investigations and reports, all of which emphasized problems of corruption and inefficiency arising from the patronage system of recruitment and promotion. The report recommended that some form of qualifying examination be introduced, that promotion be solely on grounds of merit, and that the work of the Service itself be systematically arranged in terms of a division between routine clerical work, and work which involved a higher degree of responsibility. Admission to the Civil Service, argued Trevelyan and Northcote in their Report, was sought after not because it provided an opportunity to serve the state, but because it provided a haven for the indolent. They furthermore argued that promotion was likewise a matter of patronage, to the general detriment of the efficiency of government. The solution proposed envisaged the introduction of a general qualifying examination, coupled with the standardization of qualifications across departments. This work of standardization was to be facilitated by the creation of a central board, which through a system of annual reports would establish general standards for recruitment and promotion within the Service:

> we need hardly allude to the important effect which would be produced upon the general education of the country, if proficiency in history, jurisprudence, political economy, modern languages, political and physical geography, and other matters, besides the staple of classics and mathematics, were made directly conducive to the success of young men desirous of entering into the public service.[5]

While the primary purpose of the Report was to alter recruitment procedures and introduce general criteria into the promotion process, this subsidiary objective of exercising influence on the general content of 'secondary' education[6] became important in the marshalling of support for reform. Trevelyan involved a number of educational figures in the discussions of 1854. In fact a letter from Jowett, Master of Balliol and a key figure in the mid-century debates on educational reform, was appended to the Report in its first published form. The most interesting issue raised in this letter concerned the difficulty of assessing moral character on the basis of examination performance – for if the system of patronage was to be abandoned some alternative form of 'character reference' became necessary. Jowett suggested the substitution of a system of testimonials, following this with a preliminary examination in

5 'Report on the organisation of the permanent Civil Service', British Parliamentary Papers (BPP) (1854) Vol.XXVII, p.14.

6 Secondary education in Britain, i.e. compulsory post-elementary education with a school-leaving age of from thirteen to sixteen, was not clearly defined until the Education Act of 1902. A corollary of the consequent division of the educational system into primary, secondary and tertiary sectors was that a point of transition between school and university was finally unambiguously defined. Hitherto there had been constant alterations in the age limits for sitting Civil Service examinations, and also with the permitted age of entry into the Indian Civil Service. This was also a point of issue in the controversy over Scottish education, in which pupils transferred direct from parish schools to university, where they subsequently followed a general course of study. The length of time spent at university was also variable, quite apart from the issue of full- and part-time students in the case of the provincial colleges. The question of appropriate age of entry for examinations and colleges was a constant one throughout the nineteenth century.

writing, composition, book keeping and arithmetic. Successful candidates could then move on to a higher examination, the difficulty being that this meant, *de facto*, examination in classics and mathematics, since this was what it was reasonable to assume that candidates had been taught. As many were to point out in the ensuing months, distinction in these subjects was of little relevance in the recruitment of diligent and worthy servants of the state; but if the higher examination was to be introduced there was precious little else that it could examine, given the nature of contemporary English education. Jowett presumed that more specialized knowledge would be required in some departments,

> viz., a knowledge of the principles of commerce, taxation and political economy in the Treasury, Board of Trade, etc.; of modern languages and modern history, under which last may be included international law, in the Foreign Office.[7]

This presumption was as we shall see ill-founded, and pre-supposed educational resources which were in fact barely existent. Nevertheless, the Civil Service Commission was brought into existence as the 'examining board' for Civil Service candidates, thereby creating a central instance to establish qualification and educational attainment among potential candidates, and thus introduce a reviewing instance into the question of qualification and attainment. Accordingly, in its first report it considered the general qualifications required of the junior clerk, the entry-level of all but very few recruits. They were four:

To write a good hand.
To be able to spell correctly.
To be able to write a simple letter grammatically.
To be conversant with the elementary portions of arithmetic.[8]

Appended to the Report was a listing of the standards of qualification required by most significant government departments; among them only the Factory Inspectors' Department required 'Elements of political economy' as the seventh of eight areas of qualification.[9] The Poor Law Board required no more than the basic qualifications, while an ordinary

---

7 Letter from Jowett to Trevelyan, January 1854, BPP (1854) Vol.XXVII, p.27. Jowett followed this remark with suggestions for the reorganization of school education in which 'political economy, law and moral philosophy' formed the third of four groups (p.28). (Jowett occasionally taught political economy at Balliol.)

8 'First Report of Her Majesty's Civil Service Commissioners', BPP (1856) Vol.XXII, p.xix.

9 'First Report', Appendix I Table B, p.4. The qualifications for Ceylon Writerships also made mention of political economy, but this is simply the continuation of the syllabus established at Haileybury for recruits to the East India Company.

clerk in the Board of Trade was expected to be able to write from dictation, perform elementary arithmetical operations, write a précis, show some geographical knowledge and make a translation from one ancient or modern language.[10] The purpose of the Commission at this time was to screen candidates who had been recommended to them – it was not until 1870 that a system of open examination was introduced. During the first 18 months of its operation it examined 3,004 candidates, recording a failure rate of 29.5 per cent in 1855 and 38.8 per cent in 1856.[11] The constant complaint which runs through these early reports concerns the low standard of spelling, composition and handwriting encountered, emphasizing the preoccupation of those in control of the recruitment process with elementary educational standards, rather than with the relevance of various subjects for future state officials.

These observations relate of course to the reorganization of the 'lower reaches' of the Civil Service, an area which embraced messengers, copyists, tide-waiters and postmen among several other categories. The distinction promoted by Trevelyan between 'mechanical' and 'intellectual' labour in the Civil Service would place this heterogeneous group in the former so far as there was any clerical content to their work at all. What then of the recruitment pattern to the 'intellectual' level? With the establishment of Class I Clerkships as a high-level entry point Trevelyan's 'division of labour' was given form; and when the first competition took place in 1872 there were twenty-two candidates for ten vacancies. In 1876, thirty-eight candidates competed for four places; in 1877, sixty-one for eleven. By comparison, during the period 1876–81 1,270 men and 416 boy clerks were appointed at the lower level after competition – and in fact for the whole of the later nineteenth century there were never more than an average of ten high-level appointments per year.[12] While the number of those employed in the 'Civil Establishments of the Crown (excluding Law Courts and Law Offices)' was 104,884 in 1859–60, only 13,629 came under the heading of clerks of all descriptions, there being in addition 1,485 sub-heads

10 'First Report', Appendix I Table B, p.6. The Treasury added '1. Exercises designed to test Handwriting and Orthography. Good Handwriting to consist in the clear formation of the letters of the alphabet' (p.6). The 'First Report' also includes all the examination papers set under its jurisdiction, from which it can be judged what kind of abilities were being assessed. No questions in political economy were included until the 'Sixth Report' in 1861, where they are included in the Irish Department (BPP 1861 Vol.XIX).
11 'Second Report of Her Majesty's Civil Service Commissioners', BPP (1857) Vol.III, p.xiii.
12 W. J. Reader, *Professional Men: The Rise of the Professional Classes in Nineteenth-Century England*, London: Weidenfeld and Nicolson, 1966, p.96.

and 156 non political heads of departments.[13] There were nineteen clerks in the Factory Inspectorate; nine in the central office of the Board of Trade; nine in the Treasury Exchequer; seventy-eight in the Audit Office. During the period 1856–70 twenty-two recruits entered the Treasury under the system of limited competition.[14]

Leaving aside the merits or otherwise of the pattern of reform introduced in the middle of the century, the requirement of the central administrative apparatus of the state for general clerical labour was quite small, and for this kind of employment diligence and 'a good hand' (besides 'good character') were all that was required. For the overwhelming majority of Civil Servants the work demanded of them was routine and required no specific academic training beyond that which was already supplied by school or private tutor. At the higher level, the number of places was so limited that it was not worth while to establish any specific course of tuition for potential recruits.

None the less, a key element in the Civil Service reforms of the 1850s was the conception that recruits at all levels should enter on the basis of examined and certified capacities, not by personal recommendation or by patronage. Two linked factors are required for this to become a reality: first, public examinations accessible to potential candidates must exist; and second, courses of study that will prepare them for such examinations should be widely available. In the first half of the century, popular educational initiatives had focussed upon the diffusion of knowledge of the sciences and the arts in lectures and classes. Knowledge accumulated in this way could not be examined, or certified, since there were no national public examinations available.[15] The University of London had been chartered as an examining body in 1836, but it only set examinations for the students of affiliated institutions. This was altered in 1858 and for the first time a university degree could in principle be gained by someone who was not a member of any educational establishment.[16] The examinations of the Society of Arts were first held in 1857; in the following year Oxford and Cambridge began

---

13 'Report from the Select Committee on Civil Service Appointments' BPP (1860) Vol.IX Appendix 5, p.362.

14 H. Roseveare, *The Treasury*, London: Allen Lane, 1969, p.172. Nine of these entrants had graduated from Oxford, six from Cambridge, and nearly all of them were products of major public schools, eight being from Eton.

15 The diffusion of such knowledge was conceived as a civilizing process, rather than preparation for any specific occupation. It was not appropriate that knowledge assimilated for this end should form the subject of formal examination.

16 J. Roach, *Public Examinations in England, 1850–1900*, London: Cambridge University Press, 1971, p.259. The degree of Bachelor of Science was introduced in 1860, and in 1878 degrees were opened to women for the first time.

their Local Examinations. By the early 1860s, therefore, there was a structure of public examinations in place that provided a route from impromptu engagement with the arts and sciences, through a systematic intermediate syllabus to matriculation and completion of degree-level work. This chronology predates the early development of the University Extension movement. Without such a structure the extension movement would have had both to organize teaching and determine syllabi and examinations. Instead, since the extension movement was not financially independent, its teaching was confined to the actual demands of provincial students, who were themselves able to define their objectives and courses of study by reference to existing national public examinations.

The University Extension movement can likewise be dated from the 1850s, when it was noted that there were numerous institutions of different kinds up and down the country propagating scientific and literary knowledge, but serviced by a number of paid lecturers of uneven quality. In the context of reforms at Oxford and Cambridge it was considered that such teaching would be better performed by lecturers from the established universities in the form of 'rural' or 'circuit' professors in natural philosophy, geology, astronomy and literature.[17] This pattern of 'peripatetic' lecturing using facilities hired from local institutes did later come to be the dominant form in which university teaching was 'extended'; but it is worth noting in passing that in Oxford this conception was initially interpreted primarily as a means for enlarging the student body by doing away with the requirement for collegiate residence at Oxford, and all the associated costs. This was the path outlined by Mark Pattison in his *Suggestions on Academical Organisation*, where he compared the existing system as a 'social luxury, like the first-class carriage in a railway, for those whose fortune warrants their having the indulgence'. But, he continued, 'the lecture-rooms, examinations, and degrees of the university, should be as open to all comers as a London hospital.'[18] This implied a development of the university, rather than the college, as a teaching institution, a development which turned reformers to the German system which, throughout the second half of the century, became the model around which debate turned. In this respect, however, Pattison emphasized the academic,

17 Lord Arthur Hervey, *A Suggestion for Supplying the Literary, Scientific, and Mechanics' Institutes of Great Britain and Ireland with Lecturers from the Universities*, Cambridge: Macmillan, 1855, pp.5, 13–14.
18 M. Pattison, *Suggestions on Academical Organisation*, Edinburgh: Edmonston and Douglas, 1868, p.77. See also p.68: 'We all understand by "University Extension", not merely an addition to the numbers attending Oxford, but the admission to its benefits of a class which has been hitherto excluded by social position or income.'

rather than the organizational, aspects of the German university – the German university was a model as a 'central association of men of science' and not as a particular tutorial and pastoral arrangement.[19] The simple geographical extension of teaching to the provinces was in this perspective of dubious value; it was more important to enhance Oxford as a seat of learning, restore faculties to their previous prominence and expose a greater number of residential students to them.

The issue re-emerged in the 1880s when M. E. Sadler, Secretary of the Oxford extension, questioned the policy whereby Cambridge and London extension courses were constructed as an approximation of a university's term's work in a particular subject. Sadler perceived the extension's role as providing popular adult education by the most effective means available. The emphasis was on popularity, rather than a strict university-like structure. Hence extension courses reflected two different concepts of education. The issue was apparently determined through negotiations between the extension organizations, forcing Sadler to modify his free-market approach, but in fact the matter was decided by the nature of demand and the attitude of local government to the financing of technical education.

Extension lectures and classes required a local demand and sufficient finance to pay for the lecturer and the hire of rooms (often those of a local Mechanics' or Literary institute). Developing this constituency of interest in higher education, once registered, into a more permanent local institution was a large and complicated step – buildings, equipment and endowment of departments and chairs were necessary, and the simple proposition of founding a local college also implied long argument over the range of subjects to be taught. Many of the University Colleges that were founded in the 1870s were initially restricted to the sciences – Newcastle, for example, began lectures in 1871 with four professors, in mathematics, chemistry, physics and geology.[20] This pattern was followed at the Yorkshire College of Science, Leeds (1874); Firth College, Sheffield (1879); and Mason College, Birmingham (1880). Sooner or later in all of these foundations pressure was exerted to widen the spectrum of tuition to include the arts. Since this translated into preparation of students for the London BA degree, it necessarily meant some tuition in philosophy and history, and hence some elementary political economy. Expansion of the new

---

19 Pattison, *Suggestions*, pp.163, 162. The cheapness of German university education to the individual student, and the opportunity it afforded of gaining professional qualification, was later emphasized by Bryce in his 'Preface' to J. Conrad, *The German Universities for the Last Fifty Years*, Glasgow: David Bryce & Son, 1885, pp.xix–xx.
20 E. M. Bettenson, *The University of Newcastle upon Tyne*, Newcastle: University of Newcastle upon Tyne, 1971, p.22.

civic university colleges towards a broadly-based curriculum therefore brought with it some teaching in political economy, although everywhere the demand for such teaching remained very limited until the later 1890s.

In the older Scottish universities some political economy had long been taught as part of moral philosophy, and indeed many of those who, later in the century, taught philosophy and political economy in the new English colleges had a Scottish educational background. When a separate chair in the subject was created in Edinburgh in 1871, it at once became primarily a vehicle for commercial education – the official title was that of a 'Chair of Commercial and Political Economy and Mercantile Law' and, given its endowment by the Merchant Company of Edinburgh, the great proportion of the students that it attracted were already engaged in commercial and legal careers.[21] In Glasgow, a lectureship in political economy was established in 1892 and held by William Smart, who was subsequently appointed to the Adam Smith Chair of Political Economy on its foundation in 1896. Teaching only moved beyond an elementary first year class in 1898, and up to 1914 there were only three members of staff: one professor and two lecturers.[22] At the two other older universities, St Andrews and Aberdeen, chairs in economics were not established until after the First World War. Development of the teaching of economics in Scottish universities as an autonomous activity properly belongs to the period of consolidation after 1920, and for this reason no case-study of the Scottish universities is included in this collection.

Manchester, Liverpool and Leeds are dealt with below as constituent members of the Victoria University, a federal body that rendered the northern colleges autonomous of the University of London degrees. Some mention should be made here of two other institutions whose developments are illustrative of the advent of higher education in the provinces during the later nineteenth century: Nottingham and Bristol. The former built directly on regular teaching in the Mechanics' Institute which had in 1862 gained some financial support from the Department of Science and Art. An assessment made in April 1871 of the local demand for adult education suggested that an audience existed for teaching in political economy, the science of health, constitutional history and English literature; and subsequently teaching began in literature, political economy and 'force and motion' in the

21 Hodgson held the chair until his death in 1880, when he was succeeded by J. S. Nicholson, who in turn held it until 1925.
22 Indeed, in the early 1950s there were only two professors and four lecturers (including one assistant lecturer) in the Political Economy Department: A. L. Macfie, 'Notes on the growth of political economy', *Fortuna Domus*, Glasgow 1951, p.128.

autumn of 1873, 1,832 students being registered for the session.[23] When the question of a permanent building was raised an anonymous donor offered £10,000 and after some discussion it was decided that this donation should be used to endow extension lectureships in a building provided by the Corporation, which was duly constructed and completed in 1881. Four professors were then appointed, plus six lecturers and demonstrators, and twelve teachers from the science classes transferred from the Mechanics' Institute.[24] During the first session the 381 day students were, as was usual for the time, out-numbered by the 623 evening students; moreover the day students were predominantly female, there being 94 men to 287 women.

In 1885 efforts were made to establish a commercial department in the college, based upon an endowment of £200 p.a. from a group of local businessmen. A lecturer was hired to equip students with the 'requirements of a merchant's office' and a course in commercial history and geography, political economy, mercantile law, book keep-ing, shorthand and modern languages laid out over three consecutive terms.[25] Little came of this, however, and a second attempt with a similar coverage was made in 1888 in collaboration with the Chamber of Commerce. This time the course survived, due perhaps to it having a definite three-year duration. As was the pattern elsewhere, the teaching of political economy in provincial institutions emerged as part of a wider attempt to provide higher commercial education, which included the elementary principles of political economy.

In Bristol, proposals in 1873 that a Technical School of Science should be created led to the involvement of Benjamin Jowett of Balliol College, Oxford, who offered support to the initiative so long as literary instruction was included alongside scientific. He in addition stipulated that the requirements of adult education had to be given especial con-sideration, and that classes be made available to women as far as possible. On these terms Balliol would subscribe £300 a year for five years. Teaching began in 1876 with lectures on mathematics, modern history, applied mechanics, modern literature, geology and Greek. Later in the opening week lectures were given in chemistry, experimental physics, French, zoology, German, Latin, and political economy.[26]

---

23 A. C. Wood, *A History of University College, Nottingham, 1881–1948*, Oxford: Basil Blackwell, 1953, pp.6–14.
24 Wood, *History*, p.25. Lecturing on political economy was carried out by the Revd. J. E. Symes, Professor of Language and Literature. The other chairs were in physics, mathematics and mechanics; chemistry and metallurgy; and natural sciences.
25 Wood, *History*, p.31.
26 J. W. Sherborne, *University College, Bristol 1876–1909*, Bristol: Bristol Branch of the Historical Association, 1977, p.5.

In the absence of specialized teachers to cover all these subjects the provision of tuition was naturally somewhat haphazard, but as far as political economy went the situation was improved in 1877 by the appointment of Alfred Marshall as Principal of the new college, with the additional title of Professor of Political Economy. Marshall's teaching was confined chiefly to evening classes of young business men; Mrs Marshall took the daytime classes, mostly made up of young women. It cannot be said that Marshall was happy in this post, for he suffered from ill-health and in 1879 tendered his resignation. It was not until 1881 that he succeeded in surrendering the position of Principal, and he continued in his academic position during 1882–3, moving to Balliol in the same year, and then, in 1885, to the chair in Cambridge.

The gradual academic shift towards greater early specialization in university studies facilitated the single most important institutional development in late Victorian political economy – the foundation of the Cambridge economics tripos. Marshall was not the only academic economist who was eager to ensure such early specialization but he was the most important, and widely recognized by his contemporaries as the doyen of British economics. His success in Cambridge is in addition due to his skills as a university politician, and the significance of his achievement can be in part attributed to the place which Cambridge occupied in the national system of higher education.

The actual course of the reforms initiated by Marshall in the Cambridge curricula was not linear. Marshall did not have a clear vision of the eventual outcome, and it was only in 1901, following resistance on the part of the historians to yet another reform of their tripos, that Marshall was prompted to propose an entirely new tripos for economics. The creation of an autonomous tripos in economics with an emphasis on theory and analysis, while at the same time excluding economic history, directed the course of future developments well away from the traditional inclusion of economics in curricula dominated by other subjects analytical and empirical. Elsewhere, some degree of specialization in economics was permitted, but for some years not to anything like the degree practised in Cambridge. Indeed the principle of early specialization was only partly supported by Marshall's students, whose views on the matter often reflected the time at which they had come under Marshall's influence – Flux, Chapman and Pigou for example all represent quite distinct stages of the evolutionary path trod by Marshall from the later 1880s.

The final supremacy of Marshall's conception of economics as an autonomous discipline lies some years beyond the chronological scope of this volume. It was the exogenous shift in demand for university-trained economists that facilitated the consolidation of this new discipline, a shift which began in the 1920s but did not gather real pace until the 1940s. This slow pace of development in the demand for university-trained economists had a serious impact on the development of the discipline as a whole, but represents issues and problems that have, until now, been rarely raised in histories of economics and the social sciences. One of the main aims of this volume is to establish the need for such an enquiry, and to identify some of the main issues requiring investigation.

1

THE TEACHING OF POLITICAL ECONOMY IN THE UNIVERSITY OF LONDON

John Maloney

Like many an economic theory, the idea of giving London its own university cropped up regularly across the years until the time was right for it to take hold. It was proposed by Sir Humphrey Gilbert in the sixteenth century; by Abraham Cowley in the seventeenth; and by Defoe, in a tract ambitiously entitled *Augusta Triumphans: Or, the Way to Make London the Most Flourishing City in the Universe*, in 1728. It was, however, a minor literary light who succeeded where Cowley and Defoe had failed: the poet Thomas Campbell, who in 1820 visited Bonn in the course of collecting material for a general survey of European literature.

What Campbell saw in Bonn put the literary survey out of his mind. The excellence, dedication to scholarship, and above all tolerance – of Protestant by Catholic, and of Jew by Christian – which he observed at Bonn's university fired him with a greater ambition: to become the founder of an English university which would embody the same qualities to an equal degree. But the main collaborator Campbell found for the enterprise – the lawyer, politician, and educational reformer Henry Brougham – soon eclipsed Campbell's own influence. He had been brought into the project by an open letter from Campbell in *The Times* in February 1825, and immediately became its guiding spirit. Brougham in turn introduced a group of Radicals and Dissenters who had been associated with the creation of the London Mechanics' Institution in late 1823, and it was this that contributed so much to the innovative features of the University of London when it eventually opened in 1828.

The Mechanics' Institution movement began in Scotland, and can be dated back to courses for working men on 'the mechanical properties of solid and fluid bodies' by the Professor of Natural Philosophy at Glasgow's Anderson's Institute, George Birkbeck. Birkbeck was succeeded in 1804 by Andrew Ure, who continued the mechanics' class; and in 1821 the Glaswegian model was imitated by Leonard Horner when he established the Edinburgh School of Arts to teach chemistry, mechanics and mathematics to working men.[1] Notwithstanding the name, this was the first Mechanics' Institution, whose foundation was closely followed by the Glasgow Mechanics' Institution, created by the Anderson Institute's mechanics' class in 1823. News of these new initiatives in popular education soon reached London, where J. C. Robertson and Thomas Hodgkin, with the support of Birkbeck, founded the London Mechanics' Institution. For this they sought the assistance of Francis Place, who introduced them to a number of radicals and reformers, among whom were Brougham, Jeremy Bentham and James Mill. The London Institution was formally inaugurated in December 1823, with Birkbeck as the first President. Its *Rules and Orders* stated that the object of the Institution was 'the instruction of the members in the principles of the Arts they practise, and in the various branches of science and useful knowledge.'[2] Teaching therefore ranged across the arts and sciences in a fashion not to be found in any other institution in England at the time; and it was the nature of this curriculum, and the group of reformers it had brought together, that were to prove decisive in the organization of the University of London.

Campbell had elaborated his scheme for a university in his *New Monthly Magazine* in April 1825,[3] and in the same month he was approached by a group of Dissenters who had been discussing a proposal for a university in central England. Catholic emancipation was a major political problem at this time, following the fall of the Whig Ministry on precisely this issue; and it was the same constellation of culture, education and religion that was later to provide the basis for the foundation of King's College, London as an Anglican response to the University of London.[4] By late April 1825 the Dissenters had joined with Brougham and Campbell into a planning committee which

1 T. Kelly, *A History of Adult Education in Great Britain*, 2nd edn, Liverpool: Liverpool University Press, 1970, pp.119–20.

2 Cited in Kelly, *History of Adult Education*, p.121.

3 T. Campbell, 'Suggestions respecting the plan of an university in London', *New Monthly Magazine*, Vol.13 (April 1825), pp.404–19. A second part followed in July 1825 under the title 'Suggestions respecting the plan of a college in London' (Vol.14, pp.1–11).

4 Supporters of the plan for the second London college were either anti-secular, or anti-Catholic, or both. In fact King's early financial hardships were very much the outcome of a deep split in the Church and political establishment. One of the most influential backers of the scheme, Lord Winchilsea, was a fervent anti-Catholic who took exception to the 'softness' of the Duke of Wellington on Catholic emancipation. This might not have mattered, except that the Duke had presided over the inaugural meeting of backers for the new college. Winchilsea not only withdrew his support, but challenged the Duke to a duel, which was in fact fought in March 1829 – F. J. C. Hearnshaw, *The Centenary History of King's College London 1828–1928*, London: George C. Harrap, 1929, pp.39–53.

regularly met, over the following months, in a number of London's public houses. Brougham's political connections proved important in gaining the support of many prominent Whigs, and by July 1825 a prospectus was printed in *The Times*. A council was elected in December 1825, and the Deed of Settlement which brought the new institution into existence was signed in February 1826.[5] Finance was to be raised by the selling of shares at £100 each – a move which led to predictable jibes about commercial enterprises presuming to take on the nomenclature of Oxford and Cambridge.

London University's initial appeal was to those interests excluded from Oxford and Cambridge. The former would not even admit students from outside the Church of England; the latter's policy was to admit them and then deny them degrees. Catholics, Dissenters, and Jews, in fact, had a near majority on London University's original council, and perhaps its most powerful figure after Brougham was the millionaire financier, Isaac Lyon Goldsmid. But the rationale for the new university went far beyond religious toleration alone. Campbell's original ambition that it should serve 'the youth of the middling rich', the sons of fathers with 'small, comfortable trading fortunes',[6] remained the University's aim long after Campbell, resentful of his relegation to the sidelines by Brougham, had lost interest and resigned from the council. And it was the growth of a new commercial and professional constituency which, more than any other single factor, created a demand for a kind of education which the older universities could not satisfy.

This should not be taken to imply that purely utilitarian and vocational demands were made upon the new university. Men might feel, as Joseph Priestley put it, that 'a different and a better furniture of mind is requisite to be brought into the business of life';[7] but this was not a plea for more practical education for the counting-house; rather it was a recognition that nothing existed between such practical education and the kind of university course of which the finest achievement was Sydney Smith's 'young classic':

5 The first council was composed as follows – Whigs: James Abercromby, Lord Auckland, Alexander Baring, Lord John Russell, Viscount Dudley and Ward, John Whishaw, Sir James Mackintosh, John Smith, Marquis of Lansdowne; Catholics: Duke of Norfolk; Dissenters: O. G. Gregory, Benjamin Shaw, Henry Waymouth, Thomas Wilson; Utilitarians: George Grote, James Mill, William Tooke, Henry Warburton; Evangelicals: Zachary Macaulay; Others: George Birkbeck, Isaac Lyon Goldsmid, Brougham, Joseph Hume – H. H. Bellot, *University College London 1826–1926*, London: University of London Press, 1929, p.29.

6 T. Campbell, letter to *The Times*, 9 February 1825.

7 J. Priestley, *Lectures on History and General Policy: To which is Prefixed, An Essay on a Course of Liberal Education for Civil and Active Life*, Birmingham, 1788.

If a young classic of this kind were to meet the greatest chemist, or the greatest mathematician, or the most profound political economist of his time, in company with the greatest Greek scholar, would the slightest comparison between them ever come across his mind? – Would he ever dream that such men as Adam Smith and Lavoisier were equal in dignity of understanding to, or of the same utility as, Bentley and Heyne? We are inclined to think that the feeling excited would be a good deal like that which was expressed by Dr. George about the praises of the great King of Prussia, who entertained considerable doubts whether the King, with all his victories, knew how to conjugate a Greek verb in $\mu\iota$.[8]

In their rejection of this figure and all he represented, the founders of London University consciously adhered to the Scottish pattern of higher education. The aim was to emulate the intellectual vigour of the liberal education on offer from the ancient Scottish universities; the means were to include such distinctively Scottish methods as an intensive system of lecturing, the non-residence of students, and the dependence of the professors upon fees. Nearly half of the original group of professors had had a Scottish training, and of those actually of Scottish birth the best known to the outside world was the Professor of Political Economy, J. R. McCulloch.

McCulloch was at this time one of the best known economists of his generation. From its foundation in 1817, he had written the economic articles in the *Scotsman*, becoming the principal writer on political economy in the *Edinburgh Review* the following year, and publishing his *Principles of Political Economy* in 1825. If there were any other candidates besides McCulloch for the London chair, their names have not survived. His inaugural lecture on 2 February 1829 consisted almost entirely of an extended definition of the scope and nature of political economy, a formula which can hardly have been very exciting even in 1829, and which was to produce a long line of spectacularly dull inaugurals later in the nineteenth century.

Meanwhile, McCulloch's first students had signed on. Heading the list was the 19-year-old Peruvian Viscount Rocafuerte, in London from Lima to study political economy and Spanish literature. The thirty-three pioneer students included two peers and the son of a peer, and the fourteen recorded ages ranged from 19 to 45, the average being 25 or thereabouts. As for McCulloch himself, he confided early on to an acquaintance that he 'was glad to accept the Chair of Political Economy as a step to something better, and was resolved to cut it the moment a

8 *Edinburgh Review,* Vol. XV (1810), pp.46–7.

superior or even an equivalent situation was in his power.'[9] This attitude was to surface in public before very long. As the number of students in McCulloch's class dropped to sixteen in 1829–30, and then to six in 1830–1, he had a protracted argument with the University Council about the minimum number of pupils needed for him to give his lectures. Both the original financial arrangements made by the University, and its proposals to tighten them when students numbers proved disappointing, played a part in this dispute.

A cardinal principle in the university's policy was that professors should depend entirely upon fees. However, recruiting as it did from a young professoriate of yet-to-be-established reputation, its founders recognized that the 'virtuous circle' of good teaching and good incomes needed an exogenous push to set it in motion. Most of the professors, therefore, were assured of an income of £300 for the first three years of the university's existence. Professors of languages, for some reason, were offered less, while the unfortunate Professor of Botany was subjected to unconstrained market equilibrium from the start. One or two of the professors, by contrast, insisted on and secured additional guaranteed incomes, among them McCulloch himself, at £400 per annum.

The university found itself in financial difficulties from the start. The problem was one of student numbers. Instead of the 2,000 students that had been hoped for, or even the 1,100 needed to break even in the first year, a mere 624 men registered in 1828–9, and only six more the following year. Accordingly, the council considered the early termination of the system of guaranteed salaries, and reversion to payment by results, the chief proponent of this measure being the Warden, Leonard Horner (whose own £1,200 a year was to be exempted from any economy measures). Horner's relationship with the professoriate was exacerbated by his support of the medical students' campaign to remove G. S. Pattison, the Professor of Anatomy. That this gentleman regularly appeared at his lectures in hunting pink was the least of the students' complaints: he was also guilty of 'unusual ignorance of the old notions and total ignorance and disgusting indifference to new anatomical views and researches'.[10] Other professors might have sanctioned the removal of their inefficient colleague if Horner had not publicly and aggressively aligned himself with every successive student complaint against Pattison, regardless of the evidence or lack of it. As it was, they saw the issue as one of professorial independence, while McCulloch, in particular, can hardly have welcomed Horner's comment, apropos of the salaries question,

9 T. Murray, *Autobiographical Notes*, Dumfries 1911, p.87.
10 *London Medical and Surgical Journal* 1 November 1830, p.443.

that new professors in a new college ought to remember that 'their reputation has to be earned'.[11]

Thus, although McCulloch's resignation was put off until 1835, his latter years at the University saw an ailing course limping along against an acrimonious political background. When he did resign, it was two years before an attempt was made to fill his chair, and neither of the two applicants for the post had an established reputation as an economist. One, John Marshall, also applied for the vacant professorship of geography, expressing regret that his ignorance of the language prevented his being a candidate for the chair in Chinese as well! Instead of testimonials he submitted a two-volume compendium of statistical tables, the Introduction to which the appointing committee found 'ungrammatical, confused and obscure; consequently afford[ing] strong presumption that his processes of thinking are illogical'.[12] The other candidate, M. Arnaud, sent in a specimen lecture which, though 'lacking pretensions to originality or profundity', was judged to be 'perspicacious, clear, lively and well fitted to excite attention on a dry subject'.[13] Unfortunately, however, Arnaud's personal modesty was exceeded only by his lack of enthusiasm for the post:

> I sincerely hope, however, that they may obtain the assistance of some person every way more competent to the task than I can pretend to be, and in a situation better suiting him to make the sacrifice required for an unendowed chair of so unpopular a science as Political Economy unfortunately is.[14]

No further attempt was made to advertise the chair, although in 1840 a Reverend Hincks was given leave to apply for it. When he was rejected, he offered to give a course of lectures without the chair, and was turned down for this too.

After this, the college council enjoyed four years of freedom from the importunities of would-be professors of political economy. Their luck ran out in 1844, when they found that they could only dissuade Thomas C. Banfield, a Civil Servant in the Education Department of the Privy Council Office, by promising to advertise the post in the newspapers shortly. Banfield appears to have been an impatient man with little experience of the proprieties of English university administration; within a mere three-and-a-half years of exacting the above promise, he was writing to the council asking if they intended to carry it out. The

---

11 *The Sun*, 22 April 1830.
12 'Report of Senate Committee appointed to advise full Senate on Appointment of Professor of Political Economy', reproduced in Council Minutes, 1837.
13 Ibid.
14 E. Arnaud to C. E. Atkinson (College Secretary), 3 August 1837.

council's answer has not survived: indeed, Banfield's next letter (3 March 1848) seems to indicate that it never existed. In some desperation, Banfield even threw in 'the hazardous experiment about to be tried in France' as proof of the importance of 'a course of political economy from a safe quarter' at University College. The council remained mute and unperturbed.

University College (as the University renamed itself in 1836)[15] did not try very hard to find a successor to McCulloch, and in effect, with regard to political economy, the College was back in the position from which the temporary income guarantees of 1828 had been designed to extricate it. The College's evident complacency regarding this situation is nevertheless surprising. True, the council minutes of 1 August 1835 resolved that 'the recommendation of the Committee of the Senate of the inexpediency of omitting the lectures on political economy in the next session be hereby adopted', but even this hardly suggests a sense of great concern or urgency, and there is no further intimation that anyone was worried about the lack of a political economy course. Yet political economy had been given a prominent place in the University's original prospectus. The questions with which it dealt had become no less urgent in the intervening ten years; indeed, the growing agitations over the Corn Laws and factory conditions, together with the rise of Chartism and its interaction with an increasingly strong and self-confident radical strain in Ricardian political economy, makes one wonder whether the University council acquiesced in the demise of political economy precisely because of the subject's increasingly uncomfortable implications.

Be that as it may, the Chair of Political Economy remained in abeyance for almost twenty years. (This was far from the record: the professorship of geography was vacant from 1836 to 1903.) The teaching ceased with the chair, and was only revived in 1854 when a former student of the College volunteered to give a course of lectures in the spring term. Jacob Waley was one of the College's more distinguished alumni – double first in classics and mathematics, only the fourth Jew to have been called to the Bar, and later the first President of the Anglo-Jewish Association – and he was also the brother of the then famous but now forgotten composer, Simon Waley. Waley announced an evening class to cover 'The Production and Distribution of Wealth, including the Principles of Population and the Theories of Wages, Profits and Rent, Theories of Value and Price – Money, Credit, Commerce and Taxation'. His first examination required students to answer all sixteen questions set, and warned them that 'Where the

15 Consequent upon the creation of the University of London as an examining body for affiliated institutions in 1836.

answer is a matter of opinion, it should be accompanied by a statement of reasons'.

After a term's lecturing, Waley applied for and was rewarded with the vacant professorship. Again, the Report of the Senate Subcommittee appointed to consider his application betrays little enthusiasm for political economy or concern over its long extinction at the College, but it does ask whether the acceptance of the Ricardo Library in 1841 involves 'the obligation of keeping up a living school in the science', and Waley himself is praised as an excellent lecturer whose doctrines 'are soundly built on the foundations of Adam Smith and Ricardo'.[16]

Waley's lecture notes have not survived; but his examination papers were as arduous as his brother's symphonies. In 1856 students were expected to 'Define Political Economy and discuss its claims to be considered a science' merely as an overture to the remaining fifteen questions. The paper of 1858 began on an equally broad note: 'Mention any economical errors which have been widely diffused; and add a brief statement of the grounds on which they were held and the leading arguments by which they were refuted'. In 1862 the examination led students to the brink of Jevons by instancing Whately's remark that men dive for pearls because they fetch a high price (not vice versa), and inviting candidates to 'Compare, in its light, conditions governing the value of pearls with those governing the value of gold'.

However, Waley's growing practice at the Bar left him less and less time for his professorial duties, and in 1866 he resigned the chair. Three candidates applied for the vacancy. One, the Reverend Cosmo Gordon, was immediately excluded on the grounds that, although 'the testimonials put forward by him say much of the merit of his sermons and of his work as a clergyman, [they] make not the slightest allusion to any acquaintance with Economic Science'.[17] The second candidate, Henry Dunning Macleod, was rejected as too unorthodox and erratic to be suitable to teach beginners. The fact that all his testimonials came either from non-economists or from Frenchmen does not seem to have told decisively against him; the clinching argument was that Waley was in the habit of using Macleod's ideas 'as an abundant source whence to obtain fallacies for exercising the critical talents of his class'.

So, with palpable relief, the committee turned to the final candidate, John Elliott Cairnes, Professor of Political Economy at Queen's College, Galway, who had simply submitted a list of his publications and a letter of recommendation from John Stuart Mill. However, the committee was sufficiently impressed with these to take the 'very exceptional' step of

16 'Report of the Committee appointed to consider Mr Waley's application', June 1854, University College Archives.
17 'Report of the Committee on the professorship of political economy', 1866, University College Archives.

appointing Cairnes without requiring that he vacate his Galway chair.

Cairnes's influence on the subject was well established, his reputation as Mill's most distinguished disciple secure. But by now he was an invalid, and this sadly restricted his impact on the department:

> There was something awful – I use the adjective advisedly – about that Political Economy class-room; something at once profoundly sad and loftily inspiring. Strong and well, Cairnes must have been a fine figure of a man, one could see that, even from the wreck of him that was painfully convoyed along the corridor, and slowly lifted into and out of the professorial chair. The pale countenance, set and grim, relaxing rarely into a smile, told its own tale of tortured nerves, and a high spirit waging a hopeless battle with inevitable doom. Every now and then we saw his face distorted by some uncontrollable throe of pain. The next moment he was himself again, taking up quietly the thread of argument and illustration dropped, but still unbroken.[18]

Nevertheless, Cairnes began his tenure by increasing the number of lectures in the course to twenty-five, introducing such new topics as co-operation, land tenure in Ireland, and the theory of foreign exchange. The following year his health became so poor that T. E. Cliffe Leslie, Professor of Jurisprudence and Political Economy at Queen's College, Belfast, was asked to stand in for him. The doctrinal differences between Cairnes and Leslie were wide, and getting wider. (In a few years time Leslie was to start advertising himself as the upright inductive-thinking disciple of John Stuart Mill, with Cairnes as his decadent Ricardian *Doppelgänger*.) But allegiance to particular schools of thought does not seem to have worried the appointments committees at University College, and Leslie, once installed, lost no time in reshaping the course to a more empirical and historical specification. The theories of value, distribution, and money were compressed to one-third of their former length, thereby making room for 'The Political Economy of the Sixteenth Century, of the Seventeenth Century, of the Eighteenth Century, of the Nineteenth Century', the early history of industrial society, 'Military Systems of Great Britain, France and Prussia economically examined', and much else besides. Leslie's examination questions indulged in what now seems to be shameless begging: 'Point out the economic truth in the saying "up corn, down horn": and thence show the mischief to English husbandry of protective duties on corn.'

In 1869 Cairnes took the reins back for another three years, and gave an introductory lecture to the 1870–1 course (later published in the

---

18 B. P. Neuman, 'Gower Street in the "Seventies"', in *The Nineteenth Century and After*, Vol.87 (1920), p.297.

Fortnightly Review) on the reasons for London's lack of interest in political economy. Cairnes's estimate was that the number of students of economics in London was well under one hundred, which, taking the number of economists per thousand population as the criterion, made the 'not very flourishing town of Galway' at least six times more interested in political economy than the capital. Perhaps, Cairnes modestly suggested, the subject was not very well taught in London, in which case it was still necessary to ask why London did not take the trouble to supply itself with better teachers. Cairnes found the root of the matter in the popular identification of political economy with *laissez-faire*. The work of the principles of *laissez-faire*, he argued, was largely done, with the result that political economy's potential audience was divided into a 'languid' component, who felt that its very success in the past had narrowed its present scope to a point where it ceased to be interesting, and an actively hostile one, who saw it as a barrier to any constructive reforms which involved active participation by the state. Cairnes took issue with both groups, arguing for, and claiming the sanction of established political economy for the view that 'the maxim of *laissez-faire* has no scientific basis whatever, but is at best a mere handy rule of practice, useful, perhaps, as a reminder to statesmen on which side the presumption lies in questions of industrial legislation, but totally destitute of all scientific authority'.[19]

Cairnes's dismissal of *laissez-faire* rested on two unrelated arguments: that *laissez-faire* doctrines required a belief in the identity of class interests; and that the laws of orthodox political economy existed to describe, classify, and explain the phenomena of wealth, not to prescribe one economic system in preference to another. If popularizers of political economy alienated the working man by telling him that the subject 'condemned' strikes, 'hesitated' about co-operation, and 'looked askance' at proposals for limiting the hours of labour, it was hardly surprising, Cairnes said, that the working man should take an equally jaundiced view of political economy. The urgent task of 'economic science' was to proclaim and demonstrate its neutrality between different social arrangements – a proclamation which would have sounded more effective if Cairnes had refrained from going on to describe socialism as 'that rank growth of economic ignorance'.[20]

Without doubt, Cairnes's outstanding achievement at University College was his introduction of women into his class in 1871, the first co-educational class in a British university.[21] But by 1872 his health had

19 J. E. Cairnes, 'Political economy and *laissez-faire*', *Fortnightly Review*, 1 July 1871 (Vol. X, NS), p.86.
20 Ibid., p.97.
21 See N. B. Harte, *The Admission of Women to UCL: A Centenary Lecture* (published by the College in 1979), p.15.

declined further, and he had to resign in favour of Leonard Courtney. The latter simply announced that 'The lectures will be devoted to a systematic investigation of the Principles of Political Economy', but made up for this brevity by a set of examination questions so verbose that they must have been almost as long as some of the answers. The questions, however, were agreeably topical: the Paris Commune resulted in an invitation to students to state and assess the force of 'The principal economic objection to Communism'; and when the onset of depression after 1873 brought back the 'lump of labour' fallacy, Courtney was quick to invent the island of Laputa, which had just passed a law compelling each workman to work with his left hand tied behind his back, on the grounds that this would more than double the demand for labour – 'Examine this argument'.

In 1876 the chair was taken over by the most distinguished of all its incumbents, William Stanley Jevons. By this time his *Theory of Political Economy*, the book which had ushered in the 'marginal revolution' in English economics, was five years behind him, but as far as Jevons's own writing was concerned, the marginal revolution stayed largely confined to value theory. Perhaps this explains why, although he immediately increased the number of lectures from twenty-five to forty, Jevons initially taught a syllabus exactly like Waley's of twenty years earlier, except that it included 'The Mathematical Theory of Value'. However, 1877 saw the addition of 'the theory of utility', 'the laws of con-sumption', and 'the coal question', while the examination offered a chance to 'State Mill's four propositions concerning capital, and criticise the first three'. Walras made his appearance in the syllabus the following year, when 'the so-called historical school of Economists' was also on the examination paper. In Jevons's final year the number of lectures was reduced to twenty, and the examination paper cut to a chiselled form which left little scope for fudging or evasion:

1. What are the proper limits, if any, of the science of economics?
2. Investigate the ambiguities of the terms utility and value.
3. Enumerate some of the principal methods of maximizing utility.
4. Criticise the cost-of-production theory of value.
5. Assign precisely the relations between the degree of utility, ratio of exchange, degrees of productiveness, quantities exchanged, costs of production, prices and values of two commodities in the same market.
6. How far do wages conform to the same laws as rent?
7. Explain how the use of metallic money is economized in this country.
8. Write a dialogue between a monometallist and a bimetallist.

When Jevons resigned in 1881, six applicants for the chair pre-sented themselves, of whom two were rejected as lacking any teaching experience, another because he proposed to combine the professorship with his existing post at the Department of Education, and a fourth because none of his testimonials was less than four years old. The choice between the two remaining candidates, F. Y. Edgeworth and H. S. Foxwell, was evidently a difficult one. Edgeworth (later to hold the Drummond Chair at Oxford for thirty-four years) represented the marginal revolution at its most exuberantly mathematical, and his originality and theoretical brilliance were given full weight by the electors in their report. So was his substantial list of publications, against which Foxwell could offer no more than a proposed new edition of *The Wealth of Nations*, and a plea that his teaching commitments had been onerous ever since he had graduated. But a reliable and experienced teacher was obviously a priority, for on this basis Foxwell was the first choice.

Foxwell's connection with the College was to last for forty-nine years, and was to be a solace and an outlet for him as Marshall's influence progressively pushed him into the background at Cambridge. From the start, Foxwell injected into the department the kind of energy and spirit which, for different reasons, Waley, Cairnes, Courtney, and Jevons had been unable or unwilling to sustain. Not content with restoring the main course to forty lectures, Foxwell also introduced two new courses. An evening class of twenty lectures was offered 'not so much for the systematic student of the subject as for those whose interest in it is mainly connected with its practical bearings', although students from the principal course were encouraged to attend this one too. The third term saw twelve lectures on *The Wealth of Nations*; and Marx's name appeared on the examination paper for the first time.

In 1883 the department's one-man status came to an end at last when a fund raised in memory of William Newmarch was transferred to the College. Its stipendiary was to deliver at least six lectures each year on 'Political Economy as illustrated by Statistics', and if the professor himself could not deliver the course in any year, a special Newmarch Lecturer was to be appointed. (Foxwell, in fact, did choose to give the lectures himself up until 1891.) The lectures were examinable, although a discussion of the relative merits of arithmetic and geometric means was the mathematical high point of the first paper Foxwell set. In 1886–7, the Newmarch Lectures were on the history of Socialism and, judging from the examination paper, not at all statistical:

9. The socialistic movement may be said to have partly originated in a reaction against the tone and teaching of the Jevonian school. Yet the most extravagant doctrines of writers like Karl Marx and Henry George are avowedly founded on Ricardo's theories. Briefly explain this and discuss the points of contact between socialism and Ricardianism.

31

By now the lecture programme was expanding rapidly. In the years of 1891–2 twenty lectures on the economics of industry and the theory of value were offered ('This course will cover most of the topics dealt with by Professor Marshall in the first volume of his *Principles of Economics*') twenty on the economics of currency and finance; sixteen on the history of Socialism (with the odd choice of Ruskin and Carlyle to represent Christian Socialism); and finally the six Newmarch Lectures, by Edgeworth, on 'The Use and Abuse of Statistics'. Edgeworth was the first of the special Newmarch Lecturers; thereafter the College was to employ, among others, Higgs, Price, Bowley, Flux, Layton, and (in 1918) Keynes. With such a cast, it is not surprising that the subjects lectured upon were highly variable, but so were Foxwell's 'mainstream' lectures: the Physiocrats, for example, put in an appearance for the 1900–1 session alone.

The foundation of the London School of Economics in 1895 had no obvious immediate impact either on teaching or on student numbers at University College; the former continued an expansion scarcely justified by the latter. Thus for 1902–3 the College offered a general economics course of fifty-five lectures, fifteen lectures on economic history, the Newmarch Lectures ('Methods of Statistics' by G. Udny Yule), three lectures by Clara Collet on 'Economic Questions Requiring Medical Answers', and, for the first time, a series of 'Jevons Memorial Lectures' delivered by Pigou. The programme as a whole was timely; it narrowly anticipated the subsumption in 1905 of the College's examinations into the new University of London Intermediate Examination in Economics. But with the latter comprising one paper in economic history, three in general economics, and one each in public finance, statistical methods, and commercial methods (all compulsory), students at University College were now being set a test for which even their much expanded lecture programme was barely adequate. The College introduced a further course on 'The Mathematical Theory of Economics' the following year, but a new decline in student numbers began soon afterwards, and in the final pre-war session of 1913–14 the College had only four economics students.

This relative decline of University College, even by mid-nineteenth century standards, was not only a direct result of the founding of the London School of Economics as a new and adaptable institution dedicated to the new social sciences; it also followed from the reorganization of the University of London as a teaching, rather than an examining, body. When the London Faculty of Economics was established in 1900, it was almost entirely composed of members of the London School of Economics, providing an institutional mechanism for the pre-eminence of the new School. Within the new federal structure of the University of London, whereby common examinations were eat by constituent colleges but the senate and committees, themselves responsible for examinations, were composed of college staff, specialist institutions would necessarily determine the syllabus to be followed by all colleges. Growth would moderate this problem, but the near simultaneous foundation of the London School of Economics in 1895 followed by the University of London Act in 1898 lent the School a major advantage in dictating the development of the social sciences in Britain.

The University had initially been chartered in 1836 as an examining body only, partly as a result of the government's failure to persuade the council of King's College to merge with the Gower Street institution.[22] The senate of this new body was appointed by the government, and included three liberal lords (Brougham, Macaulay and Monteagle), four liberal Bishops, Dr Arnold of Rugby and George Grote.[23] Detailed syllabi for examinations in arts, law and medicine were issued in 1838 – to be examined for matriculation and finals only.[24] Candidates for the BA, the first examination for which was held in May 1839, had to be students of affiliated colleges and satisfy the examiners in four main groups of subjects, the fourth of which was logic and moral philosophy.[25]

Major changes were made in 1858 to the University, in part due to growing pressure on examination space (there were 288 candidates for matriculation in 1858), but also as a result of developing academic specialization. As a direct response to the latter, a Faculty of Science was established together with its B.Sc. degree; the former problem was resolved by removing the condition that candidates had to present a certificate of study at an affiliated institution. Henceforth any student could study for, and sit, London University degrees; and these examinations could also be taken in provincial centres, Owens College, Manchester and Queen's College Liverpool being designated the first of such centres in 1859. A two-part BA was also introduced with a Part I examination requiring passes in Latin and Roman history; English language, literature and history; mathematics; and either French or German. The Part II examination required passes in classics, Grecian history; natural philosophy; animal physiology; and logic and mental and moral philosophy.[26] Hence anyone sitting for a London BA was

22 A parallel charter altered the name of the latter to London University College.

23 Hearnshaw, *The Centenary History of King's College*, pp.132–5.

24 The matriculation examination was common to all faculties and had three sections: mathematics; chemistry and natural history; and classics, English history and geography.

25 Seventeen candidates passed the 1839 examination – N. Harte, *The University of London 1836–1986*. London: Athlone Press, 1986, pp.92–3.

26 Harte, *The University of London*, p.105. Political economy was included in this last subject.

expected to be familiar with some elementary political economy, regardless of the standard of teaching in the subject available. These changes in the organization of the University of London provided the population of the English provinces with an accessible route to a university degree, for which the extension movement and the new civic colleges formed the local point of support.

Neverthless, the function of the University was still that of an institution concerned solely with examinations, rather than teaching, and this gave rise to some criticism. The foundation of the Victoria University in 1880 lent these criticisms new force, since the staff of University College and King's College realized that the federal nature of the northern institution gave its constituent colleges the kind of autonomy that they themselves lacked. An 'Association for Promoting a Teaching University of London' was formed in 1884, and reform of the old structure was pushed through by Haldane, in alliance with Sidney Webb.

King's College was in fact rescued by the new University. Faced with mounting debts, an appeal was launched in 1902 for £500,000 simply to pay these off. Something less than £30,000 was forthcoming, and it became starkly clear that the College would only survive if an increased inflow of public funds could be secured. This required the abolition of religious tests, however, still enshrined in the College statutes at the beginning of this century. The statutes were duly rewritten in 1903, after which student numbers rapidly increased, and public funds flowed in.[27]

King's College, London had opened in October 1831, three years after its conception at a meeting chaired by the Duke of Wellington and attended by no less than three archbishops, seven bishops, and 'the principal nobility'.[28] The ecclesiastical interest stemmed from Gower Street's exclusion of all religious teaching from the curriculum, which produced this typical reaction from the Lord Mayor's Chaplain, the Revd T. W. Lancaster, who complained that to exclude religion from education was to exclude 'the only thing, for the sake of which education, as a national measure, can justly be considered needful'.[29] The prime founder of the College – King's College's Henry Brougham – was the Revd Dr George D'Oyly, who believed that the Church of England 'presents Christianity in its most pure and perfect form'.[30]

27 Hearnshaw, *The Centenary History of King's College*, pp.409–13.
28 N. B. Harte and J. North, *The World of University College, London, 1828–1978*, London: University College London, 1978, p.45.
29 T. W. Lancaster, *The Alliance of Education and Civil Government with Strictures on the University of London*, London 1828, p.34.
30 Quoted by Harte and North in *The World of University College*, p.45.

King's College provided a focus for all the disparate strands of opposition to London University except one: it could not afford to support the view that the University was subverting civil order and spoiling individual lives by lifting industrious youths out of their proper environments, because it was aiming to do the same thing itself!

King's College, unlike University College, had not initially intended to establish a chair in political economy. But when it was found that the Drummond Professor at Oxford, Nassau Senior, was eager to come and lecture at King's, he was immediately made a professor. Senior was paid as Francis Horner had wanted McCulloch to be paid – by results, collecting three-quarters of the fees of any students he might attract.

Senior had got as far as preparing a course of lectures when the government appointed him a tithe commissioner. The lectures remained undelivered, and Senior resigned in March 1832, to be replaced the following year by the Revd Richard Jones. Jones's approach was more inductive than Ricardian, as he stressed in his formal application for the chair:

> In the present state of political economy, the thing most to be desired appears to me to be a better *method* of enquiry – the getting rid of all hypotheses founded on hasty opinions – the substituting for them what knowledge we now have fairly deduced from the facts – and the accumulating of more – with the view of gradually establishing inductively (perhaps slowly) a body of principles, which may at last entitle us, or those who succeed us, to call the subject a science.[31]

Few students at King's were to have the benefit of these sentiments, however. Jones gave only two courses of lectures, 'The Wages of Labour' in 1833–4 and 'The Progress of Opinions on Political Economy in England' in 1834–5, before he was appointed to the professorship at Haileybury, and King's ceased to interest him. Nominally, however, he retained the King's chair; his slumbers in it being interrupted after nineteen years when the College council actually demanded that he started giving lectures again. Jones's reply was properly dignified:

> I am almost sorry to say that consistently with my various avocations, I feel that I cannot properly undertake such a continuous and lengthened [sic] course of lectures as you appear to have in view and you will, of course, deal with my professorship as you may find most convenient. I have what, I hope, is a temporary affection of the eye which prevents my writing to you in my own hand.[32]

31 Jones to College Secretary, 1833.
32 Jones to Cunningham (Secretary of King's College), 28 February 1854.

The vacant chair was promptly advertised. Four applications were received, but none of the candidates was considered good enough, and economics teaching languished for another five years, until the foundation of the Tooke Professorship of Economic Science and Statistics in 1850. The chair carried a salary of £50 in addition to three-quarters of all student fees, and required its incumbent to give not less than twenty lectures per year, at least half of which had to be held in the evenings. Five candidates applied, including Henry Dunning Macleod, but the electors (John P. Boileau, William Newmarch, and William A. Guy) unanimously recommended the appointment of the Revd James E. Thorold Rogers, then a private coach at Oxford, subject to the approval of the College Principal, Dr Jelf. A letter from Jelf was then read out to the College council, stating that 'he had known Mr Rogers for some time, that he had a great respect for his abilities, attainments, and character; and that, although his manner was a little offhand, he knew of nothing to disqualify him for the office and much to prove his fitness for the Post'.[33]

No comprehensive record remains of student numbers on the various courses at King's in the nineteenth century, but it is clear that Rogers had trouble in securing adequate attendance from the start. In January 1862 he wrote to the Secretary from Oxford, telling him that he had turned up at King's the previous night for his first lecture but no one had entered for the course. Matters improved somewhat later in the year when King's, with the agreement of the India Office, launched a daytime class for candidates for the Indian Civil Service. Rogers himself played a major role here, assuring the Secretary that he would 'not only be willing but very anxious to do all in his power'[34] to promote the new course, and later pressing the India Office for financial as well as verbal support for the programme. Meanwhile, the evening class settled down with 'A Course of Lectures on the Elements, Causes, Conditions, and Phenomena of National Wealth'. Rogers began by defining wealth as 'consisting of objects possessing value in exchange' – the labour theory of value seems to have been given a fairly minor role – went on to a somewhat cursory consideration of the functions of money and the analysis of international values, and ended with an extensive look at the pros and cons of different forms of taxation. Soon after this, however, the Indian course began to experience attendance problems; Rogers' complaint of February 1865 that 'I have been four or five times at half past three for my lecture to the Indian candidates, but I learn that the term has not yet begun for

33 Council Minutes, King's College.
34 Rogers to Cunningham, May 1862 (no date).

them'[35] suggests that communication and common sense were in very short supply.

So, too, was discipline. By December 1866 Rogers was complaining that with no register of attendance and no way of compelling students to answer the questions he had set, his 'insufficient authority' over the class had become a serious problem. He received a somewhat cold reminder that 'all the Professors of the College have in themselves powers of discipline which can be enforced by appeal to the Principal and if necessary to the Council'. Rogers's own casual attitude to his classes cannot have helped; he thought nothing of altering the day of a particular lecture if he had to be in London for some other reason, and he quickly adopted the practice of appointing a substitute lecturer for the Indian Civil Service course if the numbers enrolled made his own attendance unremunerative. This arrangement worked smoothly until 1868, when Rogers, with only two students on his books, turned the course over to a Mr Cutler. At the last minute, however, the numbers trebled to six, and Rogers naturally claimed the course back again. Pained at receiving an 'exceedingly unmannerly' letter from Mr Cutler, Rogers canvassed his students at the next lecture and was pleased to be able to report that 'the majority of them would not have attended a Cutler class'. Since they had stated this at a time when Cutler was the designated lecturer, this seems a little odd; however, it is pleasant to be able to report that the ill-bred Cutler was not heard of again.

The syllabus of 1869 shows Rogers, like Cliffe Leslie at University College, pushing his course in a more historical – and historicist – direction. Hallam's *Middle Ages* joins Mill's and Ricardo's general treatises on the reading list; the economy of ancient civilization, the economic interpretation of history, and the nature of Communism are among the lecture topics. By 1872 Rogers was focusing the syllabus specifically on 'The Distribution of Wealth' and promising to show why distribution rather than production was 'the first consideration of the economist'. The ninth lecture of the series, however, demonstrated 'the fundamental fallacy' of (apparently all) 'schemes for the reconstruction of Society', though Rogers did devote some time to 'their apparent defence'.

The problems of attendance and discipline appear to have receded in the 1870s. No less than nineteen students enrolled for the evening class in 1874–5; while in 1877 Rogers told the Principal that 'the attendance in my lectures is from 12 to 20 persons. Once or twice I have had more, never, I think, less than the above numbers'. Asked how the numbers might be raised, Rogers was discouraging: 'Political Economy will never be a very popular subject with such persons as attend our

35 Ibid., February 1866 (no date).

evening classes; for many people have a superficial knowledge of it, while the solution of its more difficult problems needs a great deal of acuteness and patience'.

As Rogers approached his final years at King's, his syllabuses became increasingly unpredictable: 1879–80 was based on 'some disputed points in Mr J. S. Mill's *Principles of Political Economy*'; 1880–1 included a section on 'The Economical History of the British Army'; and 1883–4 offered a straightforward 'economical and industrial history of the English people', which was replaced the following year by 'The Aims, the Machinery and the Prospects of Socialism to be treated historically and on economical principles'. The College Calendar for 1882–3 leaves a blank under the political economy section; the only clue we have on the choice of subject comes in an assurance to the Secretary that Rogers' parliamentary remarks about silage and the 'great stir' on the subject 'will produce some audience of an exceptional kind'. Exceptional is probably the right word.

Thorold Rogers resigned the Tooke Chair of Economics and Statistics in July 1890, three months before his death. The original Chair of Political Economy had been revived and bestowed on Edgeworth in 1888, but on Rogers' retirement Edgeworth took over the better endowed Tooke Chair, which he held for only eight months before accepting Rogers' Drummond Professorship at Oxford. A number of candidates applied for the vacant chair, one of whom, Robert J. Griffiths, assured the electors that 'it would be a source of great pleasure to me to show students of Economic Science how a complete study of the Stock List will teach them more about Economic Science than the mere study of Mill and Ricardo'. There was never any doubt about the front runner, however. Cunningham was the subject of glowing testimonials from both Foxwell and Rogers himself, as well as a rather more ambiguous one from Marshall:

> because my own work has lain chiefly in the study and analysis of the economic conditions of our own time, I cannot speak with much authority of that work relating to earlier times by which Dr Cunningham has earned a high reputation in the whole Western World. I know enough however to be sure that it is excellent of its kind . . . and not without strong signs of an aptitude for economic analysis.[36]

In replacing Edgeworth with Cunningham, King's was replacing the most radical exponent of the new mathematical economics with its fiercest critic. Cunningham used his inaugural lecture to warn economists that such authority in practical matters as they still possessed

36 Marshall to the Council of King's College, London, 13 April 1891.

could only be further diminished if they insisted on travelling down the blind alley (as he saw it) of neo-classical analysis. Much of the general public, he said, was still ready to be given substantial guidance by political economy – perhaps more guidance than it could currently give. The economist's task – and Cunningham's own task at King's – was, first, to reduce any exaggerated ideas of what economics could do, and, second, to enhance its *genuine* practical authority:

> If there is one thing from which political economy has suffered more than another it is from the fact that the public have formed an undue estimate of what it could really do and have then been disappointed because it has failed to come up to their expectations. I have thought that in beginning my work as Professor, nothing can be more important than that I should not come under false pretences.[37]

He then went on to consider the related question of the desirable moral influence, if any, of political economy, beginning with a passage which, taken in isolation, sounds like a strong plea for the reunification of economics with ethics:

> The economic calculus . . . only tells what tends to happen; it only explains how bargains are adjusted. Whether these bargains are wise or foolish, whether they are tending on the whole to the good of human beings or natural power, are matters on which individual economists may offer excellent opinions, but these are things on which the science in its most recent form has nothing to say as science.[38]

He concluded by saying that political economy 'certainly cannot set forth positive rules of duty. All it can do, as a practical doctrine, is to prescribe means to a given end . . . It cannot lay down any criterion as to the end which ought to be pursued.'[39]

Thus Cunningham's criticism of 'the science in its most recent form' cannot be taken to mean that he thought economists should make ethical judgements. It can only be interpreted as a criticism of what he saw as their inadequate powers of guidance even when social ends were given. He also believed that, while some of the exponents of marginal utility theory might caution against the dogmatic application of so partial a view of human motivation, its authoritativeness was bound to be exaggerated by others and taken for granted by much of the intelligent public. The neo-classical economist must either neglect his

37 Cunningham, 'The relativity of Economics Doctrines', reprinted in *Economic Journal*, Vol.1 (1892), pp.1–16.
38 Ibid., pp.11–12.
39 Ibid., p.15.

advisory function, thereby allowing its misuse by others, or else misuse it himself.

It is clear that Cunningham saw his professorship at King's as a platform from which to oppose Marshall's influence upon, and plans for the emerging economics profession. (He had openly stated that this was his main reason for wanting the Drummond Professorship at Oxford, for which he had applied, unsuccessfully, in 1888.) His inaugural lecture, although it did not mention Marshall by name, was clearly intended as a rebuttal of Marshall's own inaugural at Cambridge in 1885, and of the opening historical chapters of *Principles of Economics*. Cunningham dropped Marshall's *Principles* from the reading list as soon as possible, replacing it in 1894 with the first volume of Nicholson's *magnum opus*, which had just been published. (It should be remembered that at this stage Marshall's work was also advertised merely as the first volume in a series.) Otherwise Cunningham's professorship seems to have been uneventful. On his resignation in 1897, he was replaced by the 32-year-old Director of the London School of Economics, W. A. S. Hewins.

With Hewins and his two successors, C. S. Loch (elected 1904) and E. J. Urwick (1908), the political economy course at King's associated itself once and for all with social problems. Doubtless the interpretation changed when the holistic and protectionist Hewins gave way to Loch, Secretary of the individualistic Charity Organisation Society, but unemployment, vagrancy, housing, Charles Booth and his book, underpayment and sweating, and public health policy remained of primary concern. Attendance, however, still languished, and with the foundation of the LSE economics at King's inevitably looked even more marginal than ever. Walter Smith, the new College Secretary, summed up the official attitude well enough when he informed Loch (14 October 1904) that 'Political Economy has never been taken seriously as part of the Arts course, but students are at liberty to do so if they like'.

It is hard to imagine many students accepting this grudging invitation: more noteworthy is the failure of successive professors at King's – and, with the partial exception of Foxwell, at University College too – to make any effort even to expand the economics syllabus, let alone to move towards a fully-fledged economics department. It may be that London, unlike the provinces, was incapable of attracting missionaries and enthusiasts. The 'vicious circle' argument of low student demand and lack of resources also provides some explanation, but, like all arguments of its kind, it cannot explain why the vicious circle came about in the first place. Why is it that University College and King's did not pre-empt the London School of Economics? Why did it not even occur to Foxwell that University College might do so? For once a largely individualistic explanation seems appropriate. University and King's Colleges were undoubtedly successful in attracting able economists to fill their chairs, but they were unlucky with regard to the enthusiasm and conscientiousness with which the attendant professorial functions were discharged.

2

OXFORD ECONOMICS IN THE LATER NINETEENTH CENTURY

Alon Kadish

The development of the study of economics at Oxford during – roughly – the last third of the nineteenth century, was largely determined by its association with the School of Modern History.[1] The 1850 statutes had established that while an honours degree in arts could only be obtained by reading *Literae Humaniores* (Greats), students could also take courses from different Schools. These new Schools – Mathematics and Physics, Natural Science, and Law and Modern History – although not yet fully-fledged Honours Schools, were generally regarded as a way of rounding off an Oxford education with additional evidence of scholarly attainment. This later led to the custom amongst Oxford's more ambitious arts students of reading for more than one Honours School, the one remaining Greats, the prestige of which survived later reforms unchallenged.

The historical side of the curriculum of the Law and Modern History School allowed students to choose between two periods: the Conquest to the accession of Henry VIII, or Henry VIII to the reign of Queen Anne. Students reading for an honours degree were expected to study both periods and also to continue their survey of English history up to 1789. They could also decide whether they read Adam Smith's *Wealth of Nations* (McCulloch's edition) in addition to the reading required for either period, or as a substitute for one of the books on the additional list. And from 1864 students were allowed to study Adam Smith (or 'some other approved work on political economy') and the history of British India instead of either period of English history. Finally, those reading for an honours degree who did not sit for both English and Roman law could replace one of these with either international law 'or some approved work on political economy'.[2]

In 1871 the School of Law and Modern History was divided into two separate Schools, which were designated as Honours Schools in 1872.[3]

1 The School of Law and Modern History had been founded in 1853.
2 The *Oxford University Calendar 1853*, p.126; ibid. *1861* p.158; ibid. *1864*, p.124.
3 *Oxford University Gazette (OUG)*, 2 June 1871, and 28 May 1872.

Students of the new School of Modern History were expected to demonstrate 'a knowledge of Political Economy, of Constitutional Law, and of Political and Descriptive Geography.' In Greats, political economy was one of the subjects included under the heading of political philosophy. The subject was also taught for the pass degree, and students were required to read portions of Adam Smith, J. S. Mill's *Principles of Political Economy*, and, later, F. A. Walker. Although the pass degree did not expect much in the way of academic excellence (there were some exceptions to this, such as Arnold Toynbee and Edwin Cannan), it did create a steady demand for tutors and coaches in political economy.

W. J. Ashley, who read modern history in the early 1880s, regarded the inclusion in the curriculum of a paper combining economic theory and economic history as one of its best features. Admittedly, it was common knowledge that the questions on economic theory could 'be answered out of Jevons's *Primer*, got up the night before! Still the principle was recognized that something was wanted to check or modify a merely narrational frame of mind.'[4] Political economy, regarded at Oxford as including theory and history, thereby became associated with the study of political and constitutional history. Like philosophy in Greats,[5] economic theory and political philosophy were taught as responses to specific historical conditions rather than as exercises in abstract speculation on ideal conditions. Consequently, the teaching of economics often became a simple extension of the responsibilities of the history tutor.

The regulations of 1871 constituted a compromise between three approaches to the study of history:

1 the traditional view, championed by E. A. Freeman, whereby the history of Western civilization formed an uninterrupted continuum, beginning in ancient Greece, the totality of which must be understood before studying any particular period in depth;
2 the study of special periods, which tended to divide history into a series of partially overlapping 'ages', each with its own peculiar characteristics, and using chronicles as primary sources;
3 special subjects, requiring specialization and the study of primary sources of a more particular and technical nature.

These three approaches were not mutually exclusive, since all serious students were expected to progress from general surveys to specialization in specific periods and subjects, but they did pose a problem of

4 W. J. Ashley, 'The place of economic history in university studies', *Economic History Review*, Vol.1 (1927), p.7.
5 'Review of E. A. Freeman, *Methods of Historical Study*', *Oxford Magazine*, 27 October 1886.

priorities. The balance between the three was largely determined by the current understanding of the aims of the School. The most common view, influenced by Greats, was that a university training in the arts was a preparation for life; it was widely assumed that the majority of history students were 'not embryo historians, but men who are going into practical life!', and the School should accept as its main function their training for future careers:

> A minister, lawyer, banker, manager of a factory, or Justice of the Peace, or master in a secondary school, or journalist, would draw inestimable advantage from having passed through the curriculum at Oxford, in spite of all its limitations. Many of those who had to deal with the organization of the Modern History School were convinced that it was serving its purpose sufficiently well by training the average good citizen from the governing classes in the past annals and present problems of the British Empire.[6]

An overall view of the course of Western and, in particular, English history was considered essential for this, since history was believed to hold the key to an understanding of the present and planning for the future. In the words of Richard Lodge, who obtained a first in history in 1877, history 'furnished the only means by which a man can fairly understand the present, or can form a reasonable and prudent forecast of the future.'[7]

A minority within the School, represented by C. H. Firth, Regius Professor of Modern History from 1904, wished to see the standards of scholarship raised. Firth wanted the School to emphasize 'careful instruction in the value and handling of original authorities',[8] and thereby emulate the work done by the German and French schools of history. The 1871 statutes confirmed the need for some specialization, and candidates aiming for a first- or second-class degree were expected to offer a special period or subject 'carefully studied with reference to original sources' (statute 5). And in order to encourage budding historians to develop an area of special interest at an early stage, history students were allowed to offer special subjects which had not been suggested by the Board (statute 7). The less ambitious were excused a special subject altogether.[9]

A. L. Smith of Balliol, who was probably more representative of the

---

6 C. Oman, *On the Writing of History*, London: Methuen & Co. 1939, pp.247–8. See also ibid., p.230; and D. J. Medley, *The Educational Value of the Study of History*, Glasgow: J. Maclehouse & Sons, 1899, p.10.

7 R. Lodge, *The Study of History in a Scottish University*, Glasgow: J. Maclehouse & Sons, 1894.

8 C. H. F[irth], 'Foreign history schools', *Oxford Magazine*, 13 April 1884.

9 Ashley, 'The place of economic history', p.7.

majority of the history tutors than Firth, summarized the defects of the 1871 statutes as:

(1) the excessive mass of books to be read, (2) the encouragement of memory rather than thoughtfulness, (3) the undue extent of the Foreign Periods and their disconnection from the contemporary English history, (4) the practical neglect of [theoretical] Political Economy . . . [as well as] the disproportionate length of the different special subjects, the liability of these subjects to become worked out, and the tendency to ignore social and literary history.[10]

The statutes were amended in 1884[11] in order to deal with some of these complaints; but little was done to ensure that all students studied primary sources. The History School remained a finishing school for England's future leaders and only incidentally developed as a school of historians by creating an extra-curricular course of specialization.

In addition to the didactic value of a general view of the course of history, the first generation of self-proclaimed scientific historians[12] perceived history as being governed by identifiable laws. The more traditional view assumed that these laws were essentially static, somewhat like the laws of physics. The younger historians, influenced by positivism and the supposed application of Darwinism to human history, viewed history as an evolutionary process following laws similar to those of biological evolution. But both traditionalists and evolutionists agreed that the laws of history could only be formulated by means of induction. The wider the scope, the better the chances of deriving from history sufficiently comprehensive inductive laws. These laws were to take the form of patterns of collective human action. According to this view, history could not be reduced to a narration of the deeds of great men, nor did it take the form of Buckle's materialistic determinism. Instead, it consisted of acts by bodies of men in which free will had to be taken into account as an active and important factor.[13] This view of history as a guide to current action and the search for inductive laws of social activity provide the rationale for James E. Thorold Rogers' claim that the economist's duty was to establish the laws regulating human economic activity. Economists should

10 A. L. S[mith], 'The new history school', *Oxford Magazine*, 10 February 1886.
11 *OUG*, 5 February 1884.
12 A. Kadish, 'Scholarly exclusiveness and the foundation of the English Historical Review', *Historical Research*, Vol.61 (1987), pp.183–98.
13 See E. A. Freeman, 'On the study of history', *Fortnightly Review*, Vol.35 (OS), 1881; [J. Morley], 'Mr Froude and the science of history', *Fortnightly Review*, August 1867; and H. A. L. Fisher, 'Modern historians and their methods', *Fortnightly Review*, December 1894.

take the concrete and intricate facts of human society and examine the tendency of all which he notes, separately and collectively . . . When the economist has made a careful analysis of all the facts which he can get at in his concrete case, and has gone back as far as possible . . . he may draw his inferences.[14]

Yet, despite their claims, neither the scientific historians nor Rogers seriously attempted to formulate a comprehensive body of inductive laws of history. Their occasional generalizations were usually intended as statements of immediate relevance. In this respect, Rogers enjoyed the relative advantage of having at his disposal the corpus of theory concerning economic activity in an ideal state, which, while speculative, was in principle attainable. In the course of his work, Rogers had experienced considerable misgivings about the attempts made by economists to explain historical reality by means of deductive theory. But he adopted the ideal of free economic intercourse between individuals and nations as a moral and practical touchstone in the evaluation of historical events. Rogers assumed an inherent harmony between free market economics and morality: deviation from one necessarily entailed deviation from the other; 'clean thing cannot come out of uncleanliness'.[15] On the whole, he was content to use the prevalent classical theory whenever convenient;[16] and when he came across what he perceived to be an injustice, he assumed that there had been a subversion of the laws of free economics. It was only during the early 1870s that an attempt to reveal the differences in economic interests between tenant farmers and landowners was to lead him to denounce the Ricardian theory of rent and Ricardian economics in general.

Born in 1823,[17] James Edwin Thorold Rogers was the eleventh son of George Vining Rogers of West Meon, Hampshire. Rogers studied first at Southampton and then at King's College, London. On 9 March 1843 he matriculated at Magdalen Hall, Oxford, where he obtained a first in Greats in 1846. Following his ordination in 1849, Rogers was technically entitled to a college fellowship, but halls rarely, if ever, appointed former students as fellows, whereas the colleges were naturally keener

14 J. E. T. Rogers, *The Relations of Economic Science to Social and Political Action*, London: Sonnenschein & Co., 1888, p.36.

15 J. E. T. Rogers, *The Law of Settlement. A Cause of Crime and an Hindrance to the Christian Ministry*, Oxford: G. and T. Shrimpton, and London: Smith and Elder, 1861, p.9.

16 For an a priori use of theory for the purpose of historical analysis, see Rogers' calculation of the size of England's pre-Black Death population in J. E. T. Rogers, 'England before and after the Black Death', *Fortnightly Review*, 1 December 1865, p.191.

17 See W. A. S. Hewins's article in the *Dictionary of National Biography (DNB)*.

to look after their own.[10] Instead Rogers became a private coach, and in the meantime pursued his clerical career. He was appointed Curate of St Paul's, Oxford, and in 1856 added the curacy of Headington to his responsibilities. Rogers was ordained in December 1856, but by the mid-1860s his growing radicalism and political ambitions made him anxious to resign from Holy Orders.

A successful private coach enjoyed a handsome income which easily surpassed the stipend of most college fellows.[19] Rogers, who had been very successful,[20] used his experience as a coach to illustrate a general principle: coaches embodied the virtues of free competition, relying entirely on their reputations as teachers; college tutors, on the other hand, suffered from the consequences of their monopoly:

> the least efficient of the seniors cling to the lectures, which they have read for so many years, the rest of the lectureships are in the hands of younger masters, who are eager to get away from a work which is destitute of all ordinary human motives.[21]

College lecturers and tutors were isolated from the wholesome rigours of free competition.[22]

Initially Rogers had regarded himself as a classicist. It was not until the late 1850s that he became interested in economic issues. Rogers' curacies brought him into direct contact with rural poverty for the first time. In fact, he soon discovered that this poverty seriously handicapped his work as a clergyman. In a sermon, in 1861, he stated:

> Most people who have parochial duties are aware how difficult it is to awaken any religious sense in the labouring poor . . . There is nothing so certain in the current history of English life as the brutal condition of the working folk . . . Hopeless, sensual, godless, they are prevented from the excesses of savagery by the coercion of physical restraint, or by the awkward openness of a purposeless fear.[23]

The clergyman's unique position of relative objectivity and direct contact with local conditions brought with it, Rogers believed, a responsibility to enquire into the causes of rural poverty and to lead the struggle for their removal. In 1857 he wrote to Richard Cobden:

18 J. E. T. Rogers, *Education in Oxford: Its Method, its Aids, and its Rewards*, London: Smith, Elder and Co., 1861, p.204.
19 See, for example, S. M. Burrows (ed.), *Autobiography of Montagu Burrows*, London:Macmillan & Co., 1908, 1861, p.204.
20 See Rogers to Gladstone, 22 July 1861, BM Add. MS 44396, f. 247: 'having had some 900 private pupils since I have lived in Oxford.'
21 Rogers, *Education in Oxford*, p.120.
22 Ibid., p.147.
23 Rogers, *The Law of Settlement*, p.10.

We are the greatest producers in the world and yet our cost of living is the highest. Yet we have the right to expect the very contrary.

I shall try to collect facts on this subject and if I am able give a lecture on it. Has not a person a right to speak . . . for the poor, without being called a demagogue.[24]

Richard Cobden's father had at one time been a tenant of Rogers' father, and the latter's second son had married Cobden's eldest sister. Thus it was that Rogers came to know Cobden, who was to be a major influence on the development of Rogers' views on economics, and who was one of the few, if not the only person whose approval seems to have really mattered to him.[25] Cobden may well have encouraged Rogers to study the origins of rural poverty, and their discussions on economic problems in general and the question of land in particular helped him to formulate a general theory along lines reminiscent of the Manchester School, the main tenet of which was described by Rogers as the principle whereby 'freedom was the natural condition of the individual, and . . . restraint must always be justified in order to be defended.'[26]

Much of Rogers' early analysis of rural conditions was in essence Ricardian. The landowners were parasites, thriving on an ever-increasing demand for the product of the natural resource which they happened to monopolize, not out of industry, but through legislative robbery. 'It should never be forgotten', Rogers wrote in 1864, 'that the right to strict settlement is an aftergrowth of class legislation and chicanery.'[27] Land monopoly was singled out by Rogers as the main cause of England's social problems: by controlling the population of estates and closed villages, the landowners flooded the towns and open villages with surplus labour; by increasing rents, which required little from them in terms of investment in farming improvement, the landowners were depriving English agriculture of the capital investment to improve rural conditions.

Initially Rogers made no reference to possible differences of interest between landlords and tenant farmers, or the viability of increasing agricultural output by high farming. But he did choose to modify slightly the orthodox definitions of rent as a price-determined surplus due to diminishing returns. He seems to have preferred what might be

24 Rogers to Cobden, 20 January 1857, BM Add. MS 43669, f.74.
25 E.g. see Rogers to Cobden, BM Add. MS 43671, f.142.
26 J. E. T. Rogers, *Cobden and Modern Political Opinion*, London: Macmillan & Co., 1873, p.x.
27 Letter to the *Morning Star*, 'Land and its owners', 1 February 1864. See also an earlier letter in the same newspaper, 11 January 1864.

regarded as the accountant's view of rent, i.e., a price-determined surplus, while questioning the exclusiveness of diminishing returns as its causal explanation.[28] Rent, he argued, could be raised by factors other than diminishing returns, for example, an artificial reduction of wages. At the International Statistical Congress in 1860, William Newmarch suggested a general project for the 'collection of comprehensive and accurate statistics of Prices and Wages'[29] from the beginning of the fifteenth century to the present day. To examine the period which ended in 1790, Newmarch proposed that scholars should concentrate on two main factors: prices of leading kinds of grain; and wages of common agricultural labour. Upon his return to Oxford, Rogers searched the Bodleian for material. Having found little data on the fourteenth century but a great deal on the sixteenth, he decided to start work on 'the change of values which took place in the sixteenth century.'[30] Beginning with printed sources – the account books of post-Reformation wealthy households – Rogers soon began to explore college muniment rooms and uncovered material that allowed him to take his inquiries as far back as the thirteenth century.

Rogers found that the Reformation had ended a period of relative rural prosperity which had begun with the shortage of labour caused by the Black Death and the breakdown of feudalism. Compulsory labour service had been abandoned, wages rose, and, with the help of the land-and-stock lease system, a new class of yeomen evolved.[31] Virtually all agricultural workers owned some means of production, usually a small plot and some livestock, and since these labourers were also to some extent producers, wages were high. This, Rogers believed, was a general law: 'Wherever peasant proprietorship is the rule of tenancies, the wages of labour are comparatively high, because hired labourers are scarce.'[32] Supplied with material comforts, 'Men began to reason about their rights, and to question the principles of society'.[33]

28 J. E. T. Rogers, 'On a continuous price of wheat for 105 years, from 1380 to 1484', *Journal of the Statistical Society*, Vol. 27, March 1864, p.76.

29 W. Newmarch, 'On methods of investigation as regards statistics of prices, and of wages in the principal trades', *Journal of the Statistical Society*, Vol. 23, December 1860, p.479.

30 J. E. T. Rogers, *A History of Agriculture and Prices in England: Vol. 2, 1259–1400*, Oxford: Clarendon Press, 1866, p.xi; and 'Facts and observations on wages and prices in England during the thirty-nine years 1582–1620', *Journal of the Royal Statistical Society*, Vol. 24, December 1861, pp.535–85.

31 J. E. T. Rogers, 'England before and after the Black Death', and 'On the social and local distribution of wealth in England during the first half of the fourteenth century', *Macmillan's Magazine*, Vol.13, January 1866.

32 Rogers, 'On the Social and Local Distribution of Wealth', pp.249–59.

33 J. E. T. Rogers, speech to Manchester Reform Club, 12 August 1868.

The implications were obvious: the creation of a peasant proprietorship would break the vicious cycle created and perpetuated by the land-owners' monopoly on land, as well as terminate their economic and political hold on rural society. However, it was also clear that the landowners would not relinquish their privileges without a fight.

During the latter half of Henry VIII's reign, rural economic conditions took a turn for the worse. One of the reasons for this, the import of precious metals from the Americas, was external, but the rest were directly attributable to the Crown's policies, which included the dissolution of the monasteries and the adoption of mercantilism, bringing with it a class of profit-oriented landowners intent on maximizing the social and economic profits from their investment in land. Compared to wages and prices, there had been a disproportionate rise in rent since the fifteenth century, even in districts which had not undergone a process of agricultural improvement. Rogers believed that this was the result of the Law of Settlement, which had served to decrease wages, and of strict settlements, which had preserved the landowners' monopoly on land. Since the Law of Settlement had been abolished with the 1834 Poor Law Act, Rogers concentrated on ownership as the key to rural change.[34]

In 1862 Rogers was elected to the Drummond Chair of Political Economy, in addition to his 1859 appointment to the Tooke Chair of Economic Science and Statistics at King's College, London. Rogers had already begun to publish his initial findings on wages and prices, and he therefore came to the chair with the beginnings of a reputation for economic scholarship. His experience as a coach may also have counted in his favour, as it did with Montagu Burrows, the first Chichele Professor of Modern History.

While still a coach, Rogers had complained that 'professorial teaching is not effective in Oxford, and ... attendance on the lectures of professors is rarely serious, and never studious.'[35] The availability of textbooks and the monopoly of college instruction combined to keep students away from professors' courses: here, as elsewhere, monopoly resulted in stagnation and decay. Poor attendance figures discouraged professors from doing more than was absolutely necessary according to the statutes. In view of the paucity of special instruction in history, Rogers believed that determined action by the professors could create an attractive alternative to college lectures, thereby renewing demand for their courses and, in turn, encouraging the development of a dynamic professoriate. An additional personal incentive to try to

34 Letter to the *Daily News*, 'The hindrances to sanitary reform', signed 26 August 1871.
35 Rogers, *Education in Oxford*, p.59.

change the system from within was provided by a parliamentary act which allowed the University to alter the regulations of the Drummond Chair and opened the way to changes in the statutes defining the professor's responsibilities. From the outset, Rogers chose to define his own duties:

> For two years I gave about eighty lectures a year, taking no fee, and constantly instructing members of the University as private pupils, also taking no fee for this labour. I spoke from time to time to the members of the University [Hebdomedal] Council, with whom lies the initiative of local legislation, as to the amount of my labours, and in 1865 my stipend was raised [from £100] to £300 a year. This change was embodied in an academic statute, passed with all the formalities of our most solemn acts of legislation. I was consulted on the draft of the statute, and the second clause, defining the duties of the Professor was my composition.[36]

In Michaelmas Term 1867 a statute was passed allowing re-election to the Drummond Chair after the statutory five years, and Rogers came to regard the chair as permanently his. A lobby opposed to his re-election at first succeeded in having the statute rejected in Congregation, but a protest led to a new vote, and the statute was passed, leaving the opposition to concentrate on foiling the re-election by supporting an alternative candidate – Bonamy Price.[37]

Following the elections, one of the main organizers of the opposition stated that his main objection to Rogers was that he used his university position to lend authority to his political statements.[38] However, at the time few objected to those academics, like Montagu Burrows, Rogers' colleague in the History School,[39] who took an active part in politics. University professors and college dons gave their support to both parties,[40] as well as to a variety of public causes. Indeed, one could hardly expect otherwise of an institution that sent two members to Parliament. Rogers was not opposed because he had opinions: the opinions themselves created the opposition. In the course of the campaign, Rogers was implicated as a supporter of the Reform League,

36 Letter to the *Morning Star*, 'The election of the political economy chair at Oxford', signed 15 February 1868.
37 For a detailed account of the 1868 election, see N. B. De Marchi, 'On the early dangers of being too political an economist: Thorold Rogers and the 1868 election to the Drummond Professorship', *Oxford Economic Papers*, Vol.28 (1976).
38 H. Hall, 'The late election', 13 February 1868, Bodleian Library, c. 84 (418).
39 S. Burrows, *Autobiography*, pp.232–4.
40 See, for example, C. Harvie, *The Lights of Liberalism: University Liberals and the Challenge of Democracy 1860–86*, London: Allen Lane, 1976.

church disestablishment, the ballot, the repeal of rate-paying qualifications for the franchise, and the redistribution of seats. Rogers and his friends protested against the conspiratorial methods adopted by his opponents, but they could hardly dismiss the substance of their allegations.

In his defence, Rogers argued that he had adhered to the normal standards of conduct expected of a university professor:

> In academical questions, I have never suffered my judgement to be biassed by political feeling. I do not, therefore, make any defence of my political views ... The means which I used to enforce my views were: public speaking and open writing; means hitherto considered honourable. I have not as yet condescended, nor can I ever condescend, as long as I have power and opportunity, to openly avow my opinions on matters of public duty and expediency.[41]

Rogers firmly believed that it was his duty as a citizen and a scholar to use his knowledge, backed by his academic authority, in the interests of progress. The true economist was the guardian of society's best interests.[42] He had little time for scholars who extended the claim of scientific objectivity to social and political impassivity. It never occurred to him, then or later, that his academic position should entail political neutrality.

The strongest argument in support of Rogers' re-election was his teaching record, including the fact that he had increased his teaching load *before* asking for an increase in salary. His supporters argued that this did not set a precedent for future holders of the chair, and therefore there was no guarantee that his example would be emulated. However, Bonamy Price promised to live in Oxford, if elected, and to apply himself fully to the task of teaching,[43] thereby accepting Rogers' initiative as the norm.

Bonamy Price was born in Guernsey in 1807.[44] At the age of 14 he became a private pupil of the Revd Charles Bradley of High Wycombe, from whence he proceeded to Worcester College, Oxford, where he matriculated on 14 June 1825. Price distinguished himself in 1829 by obtaining a double first in Greats and mathematics. While an undergraduate he studied with Dr Arnold, and when the latter became

---

41 J. E. T. Rogers, 'The election to the chair of political economy', Bodleian Library, c. 84 (418).
42 See his presidential address to Section F of the British Association for the Advancement of Science, *Journal of the Statistical Society*, Vol.29 (1866).
43 Price to the Provost of Worcester College, 17 December 1867, Bodleian Library, c. 84 (401).
44 See W. A. S. Hewins's article in the *DNB*.

headmaster of Rugby he offered Price the mathematical mastership.[45] Price accepted Arnold's offer in 1830, and in 1832 he switched from mathematics to classics. In 1838 he was put in charge of a division of the upper fifth form known as 'the Twenty', a select band of talented pupils who competed against each other for places in the sixth form. For twelve years, therefore, the best Rugby boys, including G. J. Goschen, A. P. Stanley, George G. Bradley, Richard Temple, and W. S. Seton-Karr, were taught by Price before entering the headmaster's form. Price was described by Arnold's successor, A. C. Tait, as 'one of the most successful teachers in England',[46] and if he had been ordained then he, rather than Tait, may well have been Arnold's successor. Instead he resigned in 1850 to become a London business man.

Price thought of himself as something of a scholar, although it was J. R. Mozley's distinct impression that the one thing he 'emphatically was not, was a student, a learned man.'[47] In 1851 he applied for the Greek Chair at Edinburgh, and in 1862 for the Drummond Chair at Oxford. Politically he appears to have been something of a Whig, although his distaste for the excitement and passions engendered by the Reform agitation of the 1860s led younger Liberals to regard him as a Conservative. However, Price insisted that *he* had remained a true Liberal while the rest of the Party had shifted towards radicalism.

In the late 1840s Price had been one of the early supporters of the Royal Commission of Inquiry into the Universities of Oxford and Cambridge. Unlike Rogers, he had little regard for private coaches, but he, too, deplored the advent of the college system at the expense of professorial teaching. An Oxford student was given a general education; an appointment, shortly after graduation, to a college lectureship or a fellowship left him only half-formed as a scholar;[48] nor did his college work train him for any other profession. The University had become no more than a glorified public school, whose ablest and most promising men departed to develop and establish their reputations elsewhere, in more congenial environments.[49]

By the time of his election to the Drummond Chair in 1868, Price's solution to this took the form of an active professoriate, who represented

45 *The Times*, 9 January 1888; *Saturday Review*, Vol.14, January 1888.
46 'Additional testimonials in favour of Mr Bonamy Price, late of Rugby School (1851)', Bodleian Library, 211. e. 262 (3).
47 J. R. Mozley, 'Professor Bonamy Price', *Temple Bar*, Vol.83, No.333, August 1888, p.496.
48 B. Price, *Suggestions for the Extension of Professorial Teaching in the University of Oxford*, London: Whittacker & Co., and Rugby: Crossley and Allington, 1850. See also B. Price, *Oxford Reform*, Oxford and London: James Palker and Co., 1875.
49 B. Price, 'Oxford', *Fraser's Magazine*, Vol.78, November 1868, p.551.

the most advanced stage of scientific scholarship, and a class of 'sub-ordinate instructors', who were entrusted with the elementary 'catechetical instruction' of students. The subordinate instructors would be

> animated by the spirit, and guided by the science of their chiefs, labouring in a sustained process of self-improvement in the respective branches of study on which they are engaged, stimulated to exertion by rewards both of reputation and income that shall swell with their efficiency, and shall be contained within herself . . . The sub-professor will take the place of the present tutor . . . He will not be the nominee of a small society, nor chosen because he belongs to it. He will not teach in many subjects; he will teach in one, and will himself be also a student in that one . . . [H]e will think of Oxford as offering a vocation for life, he will be willing to improve his knowledge, and acquire both the possession and the reputation of learning, because they would bring him influence, position, and income within the University.[50]

Eventually the successful sub-professors would become the University's professors. Should they achieve promotion, their 'office will be twofold: to maintain that progress in knowledge which has won for them their post, and to guide and animate the sub-professors.'[51] The professor would set the standards for both research and examinations; he would not have to give compulsory lectures and, with the additional incentive of a high salary, he would, Price predicted, come to regard the University as his natural home.

Price also advocated the creation of autonomous Honours Schools, which would allow those students who had passed Moderations to specialize a little. A first in Greats would always retain its pre-eminence, but there were also 'vast fields of knowledge, besides the classical, which the circumstances of modern civilization render necessary for the well being of the people.'[52] Price, then, appears to have anticipated the establishment of the new Honours Schools in 1871; but the changes that they brought about fell short of the transformation he had envisaged.

During his years in London (1850–68) Price developed something of a passion for questions of currency and banking, and he soon found himself in disagreement with prevailing city views on monetary policy. With a tendency towards over-confidence in his analytical capacity and an inclination to adopt positions which were 'more definite . . . than facts would justify',[53] Price set out to vindicate his opinions by use of

50 Ibid., p.561.
51 Ibid., p.563.
52 Ibid., p.566.
53 *The Spectator*, 14 January 1888.

scientific analysis. Practical experience, the final authority of the business man, did not necessarily, in Price's opinion, guarantee sound reasoning. Furthermore, it often justified the adoption of spurious theories which, in turn, were endowed with the 'pompous authority of experience':

> The difference which separates the man of science from the man of Practice does not consist in the presence of general views and ideas on the one side, and their absence on the other. Both have views and ideas. The distinction lies in the method by which those views have been reached, in the breadth and completeness of the investigation pursued, in the vigorous questioning of facts, and the careful digestion of the instruction they contain: in the co-ordination and logical cohesion of the truths established.[54]

Price's economics were not part of a comprehensive *Weltanschauung* as they were with Rogers. For the latter, all issues were reducible to a few general principles, which could usually be expressed in economic terms. His personal commitment to these principles was both total and inflexible. For Price, on the other hand, economics was an important but limited facet of reality. Rogers regarded economic and moral laws as two different expressions of the same truth; Price saw the possibility of economics and morals conflicting. The conclusions of economic enquiry, therefore, were 'not final, not supreme. They may be over-ridden, modified, or rejected at the dictation of yet a more universal science, by the order of still wider and higher knowledge.' Hence the need to separate economics from politics: 'The function of the economist is solely to report on the matters within his cognizance to the statesman; but it is the statesman, and the statesman alone, whose prerogative it is to judge their application.'[55] Scientific impartiality would ensure general respect for the scientist's work. By allowing political bias to intrude upon academic work, 'the true dignity of the science is defaced'.[56]

Price only developed such an independent position on a few economic questions, but he held these views with the utmost confidence. He argued that money was merely a commodity,[57] and that, given an adequate supply of precious metal, its quantity was determined by demand, in other words, the amount of coin required for cash trans-actions.[58] An over-supply of coin (assuming stability of value) was impossible, since the amount of money in practical use was regulated by

54 B. Price, *Inaugural Lecture*, London: Macmillan, 1868, pp.3–4.
55 Ibid., p.14.
56 Ibid., p.18.
57 B. Price, *Currency and Banking*, London: H. S. King & Co., 1870, p.13.
58 Ibid., p.24.

the public 'and not the law, nor issuing bankers, nor any extraneous force or authority.'[59] Admittedly, 'a great cheapness of gold would create a very serious inconvenience',[60] but only by making it necessary to use more coins than before for the same transaction; the economy itself would hardly be affected. Consequently, Price thought that the policy of retaining large reserves, which was supported by the City and defended by Bagehot, was ridiculous.[61] It was a universal law that gold 'cannot be placed in the reserve of the Bank of England or of any other bank, except at the cost of diminishing the other wealth of the country';[62] by withdrawing coin from circulation, the economy was severely handicapped.

In view of the popularity of what Price regarded as erroneous and dangerous views, educating bankers, policy makers, and the public at large in the science of political economy (i.e. monetary theory) became a special priority.[63] Price described his motives for applying for the Drummond Chair as having originated in

> a long-cherished strong desire to carry out among the young men of Oxford practical teaching in a very important department of political economy. I have long occupied myself especially with a portion of the science which is in a most unsettled and unsatisfactory state all over Europe, although it enters deeply into the financial life, public and private, of every nation; and I have arrived at a complete certainty in my own mind that it can be brought to a clear and simple state. And because I feel this and am eager to communicate this knowledge to the students of Oxford, and through them to the country at large, I seek the professorship as a means of teaching orally, and with the advantage that such a position confers, doctrines which I have hitherto been able to promulgate only in the papers and periodicals.[64]

As an alternative to Rogers, Bonamy Price seemed a sound enough choice: his outspoken opposition to liberal radicalism made him politically safe; he was Broad Church when Broad Church was becoming respectable; he had served on two Royal Commissions; and his credentials were adequate. But while Price was fully confident of his own fitness for the chair, he was hardly of the stature to either change or come to terms with the institutional constraints imposed on the professoriate. Furthermore, he lacked the scholarly reputation of

59 Ibid., p.69.
60 Ibid., pp.25, 27.
61 Ibid., p.153.
62 Ibid., pp.122–3.
63 Ibid., pp.148–9.
64 Price to the Provost of Worcester College.

Rogers, who, even when shunned, commanded respect within the University. Unlike Rogers, he was not seized by a compulsion to discover the historical and economic reasons for current conditions, nor did he share Rogers' sympathy for the lower classes.

Whereas Price's work on currency could be seen as an attempt to develop a systematic monetary theory based on a few simple and clear principles, his position on most other economic questions was merely eclectic, if not eccentric. Setting himself up as a critic of Ricardo and J. S. Mill, 'He protested against the worship of Mill' – he declared that Mill 'singularly abounded in false theory' and in 'unfounded subtleties'; he disallowed him the title of a great man.[65] Like Rogers, he was unable to offer a comparable theoretical alternative; unlike Rogers, he lacked the historical scholarship to argue the merits of a non-theoretical approach. Instead, Price attacked the scientific pretence of economics, which, he maintained, had originated with Ricardo.[66] Orthodox theory was essentially hypothetical and, therefore, impractical; abstract ideas, in economics as elsewhere, were the malady of the age, the pretence of universal validity dangerously confusing current issues. True, i.e. practical, political economy was based on common sense, and ought to be expressed in simple intelligible terms.[67] In reality, rational economic action was based on experience and took the form of widely shared truisms, which it was the task of the political economist to explain and promulgate.

In the heat of this argument, Price virtually rescinded his previous criticism of the City's over-reliance on experience and the neglect of scientific reasoning. He now questioned not only the scientific status of economic theory, but the value of its method as well, especially the use of calculus and the development of a technical terminology. In fact, all Price did was to reduce political economy to an art by avoiding questions of causality, 'making, so to speak, a report on the appropriate methods of obtaining a single limited object',[68] i.e. wealth, a definition Price himself often found too narrow.

As a teacher, Price did his best to adapt his courses to the curricula of the History School and Greats, giving frequent lectures on Adam Smith's *Wealth of Nations*[69] and Mill's *Principles of Political Economy*.[70] Occasional courses included, in the 1870s, currency and banking, and

---

65 Mozley, 'Professor Bonamy Price', p.495.
66 B. Price, 'What is rent?', *Contemporary Review*, Vol.36, December 1879, p.631.
67 B. Price, *Chapters on Practical Political Economy*, London: C. Kegan Paul & Co., 1878, pp.2–3.
68 Ibid., pp.21, 121.
69 *OUG*, 13 December 1870; 20 January and 21 March 1881; 11 June and 11 October 1872; 16 June 1874; 26 April 1878; 1 June and 15 October 1880.
70 *OUG*, 28 January 1870; 10 October 1873; 23 January 1874; 14 October 1881.

free and fair trade,[71] and, in the 1880s, socialism, land nationalization, and bimetallism,[72] all of which were subjects of popular debate likely to appear as questions in finals. In 1879–80 he even lectured on the questions which had been set in the recent examinations for Pass Group B.[73] On the whole, then, there was a reasonable correlation between the subjects of Price's lectures and the questions on economic theory and its policy applications (but not economic history) in finals.[74] In addition, Price stated in the *Gazette* that he was ready to receive at home any of his students who wished to discuss economic questions in detail. Yet his influence as a teacher was minimal: his manner was considered more suitable for schoolboys than for university students;[75] his views were too eccentric; he did not have a system or any striking insights to offer. And, finally, Price suffered from the general isolation of Oxford professors, strengthened in the History School by the development of the combined college lectures.

The system of combined college lectures, whereby college lecturers' courses were open to each other's pupils, had begun in 1868 with a nucleus of history tutors from Oriel, Merton, and Corpus.[76] By 1868 six colleges were involved, and by 1877 all the Oxford colleges, with the exception of Hertford and Worcester, and non-collegiate students.[77] The system was immensely popular with both students and dons. For students it offered a wide choice of lectures, tailor-made for finals, given by lecturers many of whom were, or had been examiners, with the result that

> while professors like Stubbs and Burrows still drew round their professorial chairs only small companies of the select, these young tutors had sprung into the position of deputy professors [without necessarily accepting the professors' authority], and filled college halls with crowds of hearers from all the associated colleges.'[78]

71 *OUG*, 19 March 1872; 17 April 1874; 9 April 1875; 13 April 1877.
72 *OUG*, 12 October 1883; 18 January 1884; 16 January 1885; 15 January 1886.
73 *OUG*, 24 January and 10 October 1879; 16 January 1880.
74 E.g. In Trinity Term 1878 he lectured on exchange and free trade in connection with Adam Smith; the political economy paper in the history finals that term included the question: 'Is protection under any circumstances advantageous?'. In Michaelmas Term the same year he lectured on capital labour; the history finals included questions on strikes and co-operatives. See *Examination Papers 1878–79, Second Public Modern History*, Bodleian Library, 2626 e. 66.
75 *Oxford Magazine*, 18 January 1888.
76 L. Creighton, *Life and Letters of Mandell Creighton*, Vol.I, London: Longmans, Green & Co., 1904, pp.60–1.
77 Revd A. H. Johnson, 'Faculty of arts, honour school of modern history', prepared for the Education Exhibition of 1900.
78 E. A. Knox, *Reminiscences of an Octogenarian 1847–1934*, London: Hutchinson & Co., 1935, p.88.

At the same time, it allowed a better division of labour amongst college lecturers, enabling them to specialize, and provided work for those non-tutorial fellows who were prepared to take on the surplus students, a practice which became increasingly common with the rapid growth of the History School.

Nominally the History School was administered by a Board of Studies (reconstituted in 1877 as a Faculty Board), whose members included: the Regius Professor of Modern History; the Chichele Professor of Modern History; the Regius Professor of Ecclesiastical History; the Chichele Professor of International Law and Diplomacy; the Drummond Professor of Political Economy; and the Rawlinson Professor of Anglo-Saxon. The Board soon acquired the reputation of 'a refuge for the destitute, into which all the anomalous Professors, who had no other refuge, were indiscriminately shovelled.'[79] Power rested with the non-professorial members of the board – current examiners, all previous examiners for the last three years, and up to three members co-opted by the board and elected for two or more years.[80] Most examiners were, or had been intercollegiate lecturers, but some were appointed from outside the University and therefore did not attend those Board meetings that did not have examinations on the agenda. Thus, the most cohesive group within the Board was the college lecturers and teachers, with the result that some professorial members absented themselves from the meetings. Following his re-election to the Drummond Chair in 1888, Rogers admitted:

> I have, indeed, taken little interest in the proceedings of the Faculty, for I speedily discovered that there was a board within the board, a lecturers' association which prepared business, which brought it forward, cut and dried, and secured its acceptance. In the nature of things such a combination is an organization, the rest of the Board is a mob.[81]

This organization – the Tutors' Association, which regulated the division of labour amongst the college lecturers – was managed by an informal clique known as the 'History Ring' or the 'Gang', and consisted of A. H. Johnson, A. L. Smith, Richard Lodge, and C. R. L. Fletcher.[82] Those who supported the intercollegiate system saw in it 'the chief reason for the revived confidence in Oxford teaching . . . The

79 *Oxford Magazine*, 20 February 1889.
80 *OUG*, 2 June 1871. Until 1883 there had been three examiners per year, four from 1884 to 1891, and five from 1892.
81 J. E. T. Rogers, 'The four Oxford history lecturers', *Contemporary Review*, Vol.57, March 1890, p.455.
82 M. Lodge, *Sir Richard Lodge. A Biography*, London and Edinburgh: William Blackwood & Sons, 1949, p.32.

combination of lecturers economises labour, renders possible some measure of specialisation in study, gives a spur to ambition, and provides a training for men who may themselves be Readers and Professors in the future.'[83] Professors were invited to co-ordinate their courses with those of the Association, so long as they did not try to impose their authority. The schedule of lectures was worked out at termly dinners and passed on to the Board for its official approval. Those professors who did not try to fit their courses into the Association's schedule risked isolation. Either way the professor had little say in running the School and limited contact with the students, who, in an examination-oriented system, preferred the practical instruction provided by college lecturers.

Co-operation between professors and lecturers was not impossible, as William Stubbs demonstrated during his tenure as Regius Professor of Modern History (1866–84), i.e. the period during which the intercollegiate system came into being. In his inaugural lecture, Stubbs expressed his hope of 'being instrumental and able to assist in the founding of an Historical School in England which shall join with the other workers of Europe in a common task', starting with a systematic and comprehensive collection and arrangement of primary sources.[84] Yet Stubbs did not break with the traditional primary aim of an Oxford education, which was not the training of professional scholars. The aim of historical teaching, he stated in his last public lecture in 1884, was 'the training of judgment to be exercised in the moral, social and political work of life.'[85]

By his own admission, Stubbs was the last person to try to force a change or impose his authority on the History School: 'I have', he confessed upon leaving Oxford, 'more dread of making enemies than is at all consistent with a properly constituted moral courage . . . I have abstained from controversy, religious, political or historical . . . I hope that I have never intrigued, or bullied . . . if there was temptation to do so, I claim to have resisted it.'[86] He may well have found his small audiences disappointing, but he had no intention of taking on the intercollegiate system, choosing instead to defend the division of labour it imposed on him.[87]

Stubbs was by no means isolated at Oxford, however. He was universally acknowledged as Oxford's, if not England's, foremost historian. His

83 'Professor Freeman on Oxford', *Oxford Magazine*, 4 May 1887.
84 W. Stubbs, *An Address Delivered by Way of Inaugural Lecture*, Oxford: James Barker and Co., 1867, p.19.
85 W. Stubbs, *An Address Delivered by Way of a Last Statutory Public Lecture*, printed at Oxford 1884, p.2.
86 Ibid., p.15.
87 W. Stubbs, 'Two lectures on the present state and prospects of historical study delivered 17 and 20 May 1876' (printed, but not published), pp.8–9.

Constitutional History of England, the first volume of which was published in 1873, and his *Select Charters* instantly gained the status of the main textbooks of history teaching at Oxford (the former was adopted as a textbook in 1876, the latter became the subject of courses from 1878). In his writing and teaching Stubbs emphasized the empirical dimension of historical work. The historian's main task was the discovery, analysis, and arrangement of facts: 'I desire', he stated, 'to use my office as a teacher of facts, and the right habit of using them.'[88] Like many of his contemporaries, Stubbs possessed a philosophy of sorts, but it was his message of empiricism rather than his own digressions which was remembered and adopted by students of history as their guiding principle: empirical truth, regardless of the historian's personal bias, was attainable. Beyond a general agreement on methodology, Stubbs did not deem it necessary to impose his scientific authority on his Oxford colleagues: '[A]lthough we may be earnest and glad to work together,' Stubbs asserted in 1876, 'we may never be in danger of thinking all alike, on those topics at least upon which constitutional opinion and controversial criticism must be content to permit differences of view',[89] i.e. in the interpretation of facts rather than in their statement.

Stubbs's academic stature and his policy of non-intervention in the intercollegiate system helped to establish his authority at the point at which the work of the college lecturer ended – in supervising advanced studies. In 1876 Jowett, sensibly overlooking Stubbs's High-Church sympathies, arranged for the latter to be appointed Chaplain of Balliol, on the understanding that he should also tutor four Balliol undergraduates.[90] Thereby providing a temporary solution to the absence of a Balliol history tutor (a position eventually filled by A. L. Smith). The existence of the Brackenbury Scholarship and Balliol's generally high reputation meant that it soon became a veritable nursery for historians. So, through his presence at Balliol, Stubbs was able to reach beyond the small audiences of his lectures and directly influence a generation of future Oxford historians.

Stubbs's accessibility to students and the growing interest in research combined to extend his contact with students beyond Balliol. In 1881, Samuel Brearly, an American undergraduate at Balliol, founded a history society, later known as the Historical Seminar or the Modern History Society.[91] Brearly succeeded in persuading Stubbs to accept the society's presidency, a position which he in fact assumed with considerable alacrity.

88 Stubbs, *Inaugural Lecture,* p.29.
89 Stubbs, 'Two Lectures', p.10.
90 R. Lodge, 'Thomas Frederick Tout. A retrospect of twin academic careers', *Cornhill Magazine,* January 1930, pp.119–20.
91 *Oxford Magazine,* 3 December 1890.

Stubbs's successor, E. A. Freeman, adopted a more belligerent posture in his dealings with the intercollegiate system, denouncing the tutors' termly dinner as the 'crammers' cram'.[92] Nor did he enjoy Stubbs's indisputable scholarly prestige. Having spent his life outside academia, he found himself at the age of 61 out of step with most younger Oxford historians. His unflagging advocacy of the principle of continuity led him to lament the exclusion of ancient history from the School's curriculum, which increasingly emphasized the importance of special periods and special subjects.[93] Yet, although not as genially accessible as Stubbs, Freeman succeeded in attracting sufficient numbers of advanced students to form a private seminar,[94] while the History Seminar was taken over by young graduates and dons.

Whatever the level of co-operation between professors and tutors in history, it was far in advance of the state of affairs in political economy. Price's virtually non-existent academic reputation, his membership during the early 1880s of the Duke of Richmond's Commission on Agriculture and Lord Iddesleigh's Commission on the Depression of Trade, his failing health (from February 1886), and his general dislike of the intercollegiate system, only increased his isolation. He left no positive mark on the development of economics at Oxford. If anything, his repeated re-elections to the chair, up until his death in 1888, impeded any possible advancement of economic studies through his failure to provide either leadership or scholarly inspiration. Rogers' re-election in 1888 did nothing to improve matters.

Price's election in 1868 freed Rogers to throw himself into the first general election since the 1867 reforms. As a clergyman, Rogers could not stand for Parliament, but the passage of the Clericals Disabilities Act in 1870 allowed him to retire from his clerical profession and take up politics in earnest. In 1872 he held discussions with members of the Oldham Liberal Party,[95] and in 1873 he was adopted as a candidate for Scarborough, a two-seat constituency, where he campaigned unsuccessfully in 1874 against one Conservative and two right-wing Liberals.[96] In December 1878, Rogers was chosen as the Liberal candidate for

---

92 J. A. R. Marriott, *Memories of Four Score Years*, London and Glasgow: Blackie & Son, 1946, p.60.

93 See W. Boyd Dawkins, 'In memoriam E. A. Freeman', *Oxford Magazine*, 23 March 1892.

94 H. H. Henson, *Retrospect of an Unimportant Life, 1863–1920*, Oxford: Oxford University Press, 1942, pp.7, 127; and W. H. Hutton, 'Preface' to E. A. Freeman's *Sketches of Travel in Normandy and Maine*, London: Macmillan & Co., 1897, p.xiii.

95 J. Newton to Rogers, 20, 25, and 28 May 1872, Bodleian Library, Rogers' Correspondence, fos. 518–20.

96 Harvie, *The Lights of Liberalism*, pp.184–5.

Southwark,[97] where one of the two seats was held by a Conservative. In the general election of 1880 he was finally elected to Parliament.

In addition to Rogers' political career, he also ran courses at King's College, London, and in 1872 he accepted an invitation from W. G. Wren to lecture to pupils preparing for the Indian Civil Service examinations at his coaching establishment in London.[98] He had recently run into some technical difficulties in collecting material for the third and subsequent volumes of his *History of Agriculture and Prices*[99] (the second volume had been published in 1866, while the third did not come out until 1882), and as a consequence Rogers was left with little time and no inclination to involve himself in the work of the History School or the intercollegiate system, to which his college – Worcester – did not belong.

Following the 1885 redistribution of seats, Rogers was returned for Bermondsey with a majority of a mere eighty-three. In the 1885 Parliament he chose to support Gladstone's Home Rule policy, with the result that in the 1886 election he lost his seat. His defeat did not dampen his appetite for politics. Rogers remained on the lookout for a new constituency.[100] 'To the last', the *Yorkshire Post* wrote in his obituary, 'he yearned for political distinction and he did not conceal his dissatisfaction that his party had not done more to advance his wishes in this respect',[101] presumably by offering him a safe seat.

Not until Trinity Term 1887 was a course by Rogers included in the intercollegiate lecture list.[102] Shortly afterwards, Bonamy Price's indifferent health forced him to leave Oxford, and L. R. Phelps of Oriel deputized for him in Hilary Term 1888. Price died in January 1888, and on 16 March Rogers was re-elected to the Drummond Chair.[103] Due to a change in the statutes, the choice was made by a Board of Electors, consisting of the Chancellor of the University (Lord Salisbury); the current Chancellor of the Exchequer (Goschen); the Regius Professor of Modern History (E. A. Freeman); the Whyte Professor of Moral Philosophy (W. Wallace); and a representative of All Souls (John A.

---

97 Southwark Liberal Association to Rogers, 9 December 1878, Rogers' Correspondence, fo. 642.
98 Wren to Rogers, 13, 17, and 20 September 1872, Rogers' Correspondence, fos. 721–3.
99 See J. E. T. Rogers, *A History of Agriculture and Prices in England. Vol.III 1401–1582*, Oxford: Clarendon Press, 1882, pp.x–xi.
100 See F. Schnadhorst to Rogers, 1 July 1890, Rogers' Correspondence, fo. 602; and *Leeds Mercury*, 14 October 1890.
101 *Yorkshire Post* (Leeds), 14 October 1890.
102 *OUG*, 25 April 1887.
103 A. Kadish, *The Oxford Economists in the Late Nineteenth Century*, Oxford: Oxford University Press, 1982, pp.175–80.

Doyle). With Goschen absent, the Board was equally divided between Rogers and Phelps, and it was Goschen, Price's old pupil, who, when he arrived, 'at once declared, without waiting to hear the views of his colleagues, that there was only one man in England who could fill the office, and that was Professor Rogers'.[104]

The new statutes required that the professor should 'lecture and give instruction on the principles of Political Economy'. Initially Rogers repeated his college lectures on the economic interpretation of English history, which included lectures on such topical themes as land nationalization, rent regulation, copyrights and patents, and state control of railways. The course continued throughout Michaelmas Term 1888, with Rogers discussing the development of credit agencies, transit, the history of chartered trade companies, etc.[105] For Michaelmas Term 1888 he also advertised a course entitled 'Adversaria to Mr Mill's Principles of Political Economy', later changed to 'The Place of Mr Mill in the History of Political Economy and the Influences under which he Was Brought', followed by a course on 'Definition of Terms Used in Political Economy', and, for Michaelmas Term 1890, 'History of the Use and Definitions of Leading Terms in Political Economy'.[106] Rogers concentrated on two general themes: the importance of the economic/ historical perspective for understanding current problems; and the historical reasons behind previous attempts to deviate from a policy of *laissez-faire*, thereby arguing the relativism of all economic theories other than *laissez-faire*.

Rogers had by then completely denounced orthodox theory as false and dangerous, largely an outcome of his reconsideration of the question of rent. Until the early 1870s, Rogers remained essentially a Ricardian,[107] but by 1879 he began to attach greater importance to agricultural improvements as a rent-raising agency. Whereas previously he had believed that the historical increase in rent had been due to a combination of increased demand and artificially low wages, Rogers now argued that the main reason for past and current rises in rent was increased productivity. Ricardo's theory of rent had only been valid whilst the Corn Laws had been in force.[108] Since 1846 rent had risen as

104 *Daily Chronicle*, 14 October 1890.
105 *OUG*, 20 April and 12 June 1888. The lectures were posthumously published as *Industrial and Commercial History of England*, London: T. Fisher Unwin, 1892.
106 *OUG*, 20 April and 20 October 1888; 18 June and 11 October 1889; 17 June 1890.
107 See J. E. Cairnes to Rogers, 20 December 1869, Rogers' Correspondence, Add. 8; and 'Lord Salisbury and the burdens on real property', *Daily News*, 5 April 1871.
108 J. E. T. Rogers, 'English agriculture', *Contemporary Review*, Vol.35 (May 1879), p.308.

a result of 'the diffusion of agricultural skill – *i.e.* . . . the increased power of the farmer to produce equal quantities of produce at less cost, or greater quantities at equal cost', aided by the competition for farms. High rents robbed the farmer of the fruits of his labour and tied down capital necessary for improved farming.

The change in Rogers' position on rent may have been influenced by his findings, but most of his objections to Ricardo's theory had already been raised during the 1830s and 1840s by Wakefield, Torrens, T. C. Banfield, and others. All Rogers did was to support their arguments with historical evidence. But whatever the origins of his reassessment, it appears to have been related to his growing interest in undermining the position of the landed classes by converting the tenant farmers to liberalism.[109]

Rogers' new position on rent was accompanied by a more strident and general denunciation of Ricardo and abstract economics. In 1873 he still held that 'almost all the effects bearing upon the material progress of the country and its general prosperity and opulence, have been due to the teaching of political economists.'[110] During the 1880 general election campaign Rogers stated:

> With those who believe that Political Economy, taken apart from facts, is always a barren, and very often a dangerous theory, nothing which throws light on the process by which farmers' rents have been developed, will be without its value in the economical interpretation of social problems.[111]

And, in his lectures on the economic interpretation of history, delivered at Worcester College Hall in 1887–8, Rogers, somewhat misleadingly, alleged a lifelong opposition to economic orthodoxy: 'Many years ago I began to suspect that much of the political economy which was currently in authority was a collection of logomachies which had but little relation to the facts of social life.'[112] His historical work had supposedly led him

> to discover that much which popular economists believe to be natural is highly artificial; that which they call laws are too often

109 For the relevant political background, see H. J. Hanham, *Elections and Party Management. Politics in the Time of Disraeli and Gladstone*, Hassocks: Wheat-sheaf, 1978, pp.29–32; and J. R. Fisher, 'The farmers' alliance: an agricultural protest movement of the 1880s', *Agricultural History Review*, Vol.26 (1978), pp.15–25.

110 'The representation of Scarborough: an address by Professor Thorold Rogers', 29 April 1873.

111 J. E. T. Rogers, 'The history of rent in England', *Contemporary Review*, Vol.37 (April 1880), p.673.

112 J. E. T. Rogers, *The Economic Interpretation of History*, London: T. Fisher Unwin, 1918, p.vi.

hasty, inconsiderate, and inaccurate inductions; and that much which they consider to be demonstrably irrefutable is demonstrably false . . . It must, I think, be admitted that political economy is in a bad way.[113]

So, whereas the substance of his criticism of economic orthodoxy was hardly revolutionary, Rogers rejected all theory *en bloc*, while preserving his faith in *laissez-faire*. He had no theory to replace the one he so roundly rejected, nor could he propose an alternative system of economic laws of the type envisaged by the Positivists. While a later generation of economic historians were to become increasingly empirical, suspicious of all attempts to reduce history to a number of clear-cut principles or to seek its meaning, they were also to claim greater objectivity and detachment than Rogers exercised. Rogers in 1888 was a disappointed and bitter man. His habit of saying unpleasant things in an unpleasant way, his extremism, his anti-Semitism and general xenophobia, his rancour – the result of a perceived lack of appreciation for his academic[114] and political work – and his somewhat doleful appearance,[115] appear to have made him unapproachable to younger Oxford students. They were advised to avoid his lectures, 'except for amusement, when they had an hour to spare. His hearers dwindled latterly to as few as half a dozen.'[116]

Throughout, Rogers remained at loggerheads with Oxford's college tutors and lecturers, resulting in a public exchange of insults and recriminations.[117] With the sole exception of Henry de Beltgens Gibbins (1865–1907), who wrote some of the first school textbooks on English economic history, none of Oxford's historians or economists admitted to having been greatly influenced by Rogers. Yet the economics taught by college tutors appears to have effortlessly incorporated Rogers' empirical work. Like the History School in general, political economy tended towards the empirical and the topical, and the history finals' political economy paper included such questions as: 'Point out at what periods of our history the circumstances of the agricultural labourer in England have been either greatly depressed or greatly improved, and explain the causes which were at work in

113 Ibid., pp.vi–vii.
114 Rogers, *A History of Agriculture and Prices*, Vol.III, p.x.
115 See Spy's cartoon in *Vanity Fair*, 29 March 1884.
116 'Reminiscences of Thorold Rogers', *Pall Mall Gazette*, 1890.
117 *Oxford Magazine*, 6 February 1889; J. E. T. Rogers, 'Oxford professors and Oxford tutors', *Contemporary Review*, Vol.56 (December 1889); ibid., Vol.57 (February 1890); J. E. T. Rogers, 'The Four Oxford History Lecturers', *Contemporary Review*, Vol.57 (March 1890); A. H. Johnson, 'A reply to Professor Rogers', *Oxford Magazine*, 12 March 1890. See also J. E. T. Rogers, 'Parliament and higher education', *Fraser's Magazine*, Vol.24 (July 1881).

producing the changes' (Trinity Term, 1878; see also Trinity Term, 1885). Or, 'Is a greater distribution of land in England desirable? What obstacles lie in the realisation of such a scheme?' (Trinity Term, 1878).[118] But interest in land ownership and rural conditions did not begin or end with Rogers' work, nor was it the sole, or even the main, subject of debate outside Oxford to find its way into the history curriculum. Other subjects included free trade and protection, trade unions, co-operatives, England and her colonies, the poor laws, various monetary questions (the Bank of England, paper currency, etc.), socialism, Ireland, etc. When history students were asked: 'In what way does the study of history afford material for training in practical politics?' (Trinity Term, 1885), they were expected to consider political economy as an integral part of history.

Initially, teaching political economy was a simple extension of the history tutor's duties which did not require specialization. Throughout the 1870s economics was taught by history dons who did not pretend, either then or in retrospect, to possess any special knowledge of the subject.[119] Nor did the structure of the history curriculum justify specialization, since no college was likely to appoint a tutor solely responsible for teaching economics. Due to the widening scope of history, economic history was not strictly departmentalized, and questions on economic and social history were likely to appear on virtually all history papers – English and foreign, medieval and modern.[120] However, during the late 1870s two counter-trends became discernible which served to encourage some specialization in economics, albeit largely within the History School rather than as an independent discipline. The mid-century reforms, the popularity of the History School, and the advent of the intercollegiate system, all combined with the growing importance assigned to specialized research in the study of history to produce scholars whose commitment to research was greater than to teaching: 'They wished more leisure for the pursuit of their own studies and researches, less concentration on preparing their pupils for

118 Other questions which may have been influenced by Rogers' work include: 'Explain Ricardo's theory of rent. Is it affected by the change in the causes which since his day govern the prices of agricultural produce in England?' (Trinity Term, 1885). And, 'How far is it true to say that Ricardo's theory is a correct analysis of rent but does not account for its origin?' (Trinity Term, 1887).

119 E.g. Jayne (Jesus), Johnson (All Souls), Knox (Merton), Gladstone (Keble).

120 E.g. English History I, Trinity Term 1878: '3. Examine the distribution of property in England after the Conquest, showing the position of the greater Norman families, and tracing its effects on subsequent history. 4. Compare the state of society in England and Normandy at the time of the Conquest'. Political Economy, Trinity Term, 1879: '7. Sketch the history of the villein from the Norman Conquest to the beginning of the reign of Edward III'.

the Schools, a pursuit of knowledge for its own sake and less for ulterior ends, however valuable.'[121] With the incorporation of economic history into main-line political and constitutional history, for example, in the study of economic policies or economic and social legislation, some history scholars, notably W. J. Ashley, chose to concentrate on economic history, or, at least, to admit its importance. At the same time, throughout the late 1870s and early 1880s economic and social problems coming to the fore required urgent application and viable solutions. Neither teachers nor students could seriously maintain that history prepared them for practical life unless it considered the origins of current social and economic problems and investigated possible remedies. Out of a sense of civic duty, then, or even personal ambition, a student or teacher might concentrate on economics in a policy-oriented manner, without spending too much time on theory.

These trends are discernible in the work of Arnold Toynbee, who inspired a generation of students as well as many of his fellow dons. Arnold Toynbee (1852–83)[122] came up to Oxford in January 1873 with little experience of formal schooling. His father, Joseph Toynbee, a well-known London aural surgeon and philanthropist, died when Arnold was fourteen. Consequent (possibly exaggerated) economic straits interrupted Arnold's education, and rather than going to public school as originally intended, he spent two uninspiring years at a military preparatory school, followed by occasional classes at King's College, London, and long periods of solitary reading in rented lodgings in a number of remote villages. Having inherited some money from his father, Arnold entered Pembroke College, Oxford at the relatively advanced age of twenty-one. The absence of systematic education was evident in his lack of training in the art of essay writing, cramming, and public debating, as well as in the absence of those social skills acquired when brought up within a group. He was mainly self-taught, and possessed a variety of half-baked and haphazard views, but yet was perfectly confident of his ability to master any subject he chose to make his own.

Toynbee soon despaired of Greats, his choice of School, and of Pembroke, his college. With some difficulty, he eventually managed to transfer to Balliol, where he rapidly found his feet both socially and intellectually. At this time he was preoccupied with the religious dilemma of the reconciliation of Christian dogma and faith, and, with the help of R. L. Nettleship and T. H. Green, he discovered Broad-Church Anglicanism, where dogma was treated as relatively unimportant

---

121 J. W. Mackail, *James Leigh Strachan-Davidson. Master of Balliol*, Oxford: Clarenden Press, 1925, p.56.

122 Unless otherwise stated, the passages on Toynbee are based on A. Kadish, *Apostle Arnold. The Life and Death of Arnold Toynbee 1852–1883*, Durham N. C.: Duke University Press, 1986.

compared to faith and the realization of the Christian ideal of a moral life by means of service and duty. In a manner not unlike the treatment of economic and political theory in Schools, dogma was regarded as the way in which each generation sought to express its concept of faith. The essence of religion, therefore, was not the formal expression of faith, but its manifestation in an individual's way of life. With his dilemma resolved, Toynbee set out, with Green's guidance,[123] to find the best means of realizing his sense of duty, the practical manifestation of his Christian faith.

While sitting for the Brackenbury Scholarship, it became clear to Toynbee that he was physically incapable of withstanding the strain of prolonged examinations (at the age of 13 or 14 he had suffered a severe concussion, which resulted in recurring migraines). He soon abandoned plans to take an honours degree and settled instead for a pass, which he obtained in 1878. In spite of his technically unimpressive academic record, Toynbee's character and ability had attracted sufficient notice for him to be offered a Balliol tutorship in charge of the probationers of the Indian Civil Service. In 1881 he was made Senior Bursar, and at the time of his death in 1883 he was about to be elected a fellow.

Inspired by Green and his philosophy, young Oxford liberals of the 1870s often attempted to work out, individually and collectively, the means of ensuring the perpetuation of progress beyond the scope of modified *laissez-faire* or the classical liberalism of J. S. Mill.. Having produced a theoretical justification for some state intervention, Green had stopped short of developing a programme for state action. But by personal example and by recruiting undergraduates of Toynbee's generation to take part in some local political and civic activities, he had set the course by which the realization of one's sense of duty might be sought. At the same time, his reluctance to lay down a clear-cut programme emphasized the need for a careful study of social and economic problems as the basis of any specific remedial schemes. Undergraduate Oxford at this time was becoming increasingly politicized: various political clubs were founded,[124] and smaller groups, often centred around charismatic young dons such as A. Sidgwick, A. H. D. Acland, and, later, S. Ball, carried out studies of current problems in a pronounced practically oriented manner. With some of his contemporaries, including A. Milner, P. L. Gell, D. G. Ritchie, and F. C. Montague, Toynbee started a similar group, intending eventually to influence the policies of the Liberal Party.

123 For an appreciation of Green's influence, see F. G. Brabont, 'The intellectual life', in J. Wells, *Oxford and Oxford Life*, London: Methuen & Co., 1892, p.79.

124 See Kadish, *Oxford Economists*, pp.15–19.

As an undergraduate, Toynbee came briefly under Ruskin's influence, and, although he remained sceptical of Ruskin's more extreme notions and his total condemnation of industrial society, Toynbee did accept the principle of the inalienability of economics from ethics. For his pass, Toynbee had read Adam Smith and Mill's *Principles*, agreeing with the latter's assertion that whereas the laws of production, which took on 'the character of physical truths', had been given their final theoretical formulation,[125] distribution was determined by 'the laws and customs of society' and, therefore, was changeable. A study of distribution, then, could and should take into account moral factors. With his interest in the moral ends of progress, and his growing awareness of the importance of material amelioration as a prerequisite to any future improvement in the moral outlook of the working classes, Toynbee undertook a study of the organization of consumption.

At first Toynbee assumed that modern political economy was based on qualified *laissez-faire*; classical theory could be dismissed whenever convenient on the grounds that it was either irrelevant or its premises were morally unacceptable. Once Toynbee discovered that modern theory was somewhat different, he began to experiment with alternative methodologies for dealing with current issues. In 1881–2, he delivered his first and only intercollegiate course on the economic history of England 1760–1846,[126] posthumously published as the 'Industrial Revolution Lectures'. Although far from being a complete study, the course proposed a shift from economic theory to economic history as a way of dealing with contemporary problems.

Toynbee was not a product of the History School, and his approach was not typical of Oxford historians. By 1881–2 he had abandoned an earlier tendency to presuppose a simple correspondence between economic theory and historical fact, and his work had become increasingly empirical, based on both new primary sources and printed chronicles (Young, Defoe, Eden, Cobbett, etc.). But, unlike the majority of Oxford-trained historians, he did not instinctively turn to the Middle Ages or to the seventeenth-century revolutions; instead he began his narrative in the second half of the eighteenth century.[127] Toynbee also appears to have been more impressed by the Positivists' suggestion of

---

125 Book III, chs.1, 31, and 'Preliminary remarks'. The statement was posed as a question in the history finals for Trinity Term 1888, indicating the change in Mill's status as a final authority: "The laws of the *production* of wealth are based on unalterable natural facts; the *course of distribution* is modified by the changing ordinances of society'. Criticise.'
126 *OUG*, 14 June, and 14 October 1881.
127 It was not until 1886 that the finals included 1714–1815 as a special period. English History I and II went as far back as the Conquest and earlier.

an alternative approach to economic problems[128] than most of his Oxford contemporaries. He assumed the existence of progressive laws of social and economic evolution, and accepted the equal importance of all simultaneous modes of human progress. He therefore argued that in order to understand current economic and social problems, one had to look first at economic and social history as relatively autonomous fields of investigation, neither divorced from nor subservient to political and constitutional history. And, since each evolutionary stage was essentially unique, there was no need to go any further back than the beginning of industrialization when studying industrial society.

In keeping with the approach common at Oxford, Toynbee adopted a relativist view of the development of economic thought. In his course he combined economic history and economic theory – the two subjects in the political economy paper in finals. Theory was regarded primarily as a product and a reflection of particular economic and social conditions, and could therefore serve as a supplementary primary source similar to political thought. And, although Toynbee at first admitted that theory also offered an analytical tool for factors which the historian might otherwise overlook, during the course of his lectures he repeatedly qualified the utility of theory in historical analysis, and stressed the need for reliance on empirical research.

In his industrial revolution lectures, Toynbee provided an attractive variation on the Whig interpretation of English political history,[129] which, in response to the challenge of the French and subsequent European revolutions, had described the course of English history since 1688 as one of continuous, non-violent, and progressive change, whose aims – greater equality and freedom – were as revolutionary as those of the European revolutions, but without their violence, destruction of property, and terror. Toynbee extended this view of English history to social and economic history. Democracy had not been halted by industrialization; contrary to the Marxist interpretation, industrialization and democratic reform went hand in hand. Despite its initial attendant misery, industrialization had created the means whereby the working classes might attain greater equality in the distribution of wealth as well as political power: previously unknown opportunities for self-help were created; trade unions, co-operatives, and friendly societies had been made possible; the factory system and urbanization facilitated

128 Especially Cliffe Leslie's articles and Henry Crompton's *Industrial Conciliation*, London: Henry S. King & Co., 1876.
129 Whig is used here in the same sense as in H. A. L. Fisher's 1928 Raleigh Lecture to the British Academy – historians whose political identification with the Whigs is noticeable in their interpretation of history rather than any teleological view of history.

71

working-class organization; collective pressure had brought about the factory laws and the extension of the franchise; real wages were rising; and there were encouraging signs of better understanding between workers and employers, such as in the operation of Boards of Conciliation. Neither the economic nor the political system were static; both the classical economists and the revolutionary socialists were wrong – the industrial revolution was in essence another stage in the ever-evolving English revolution.

Toynbee did little to explain the dynamics of industrialization, but he did help to direct historians' attention to its social and economic background and to its consequences. By dealing separately with agriculture and industry he demonstrated the multiple nature of economic change and the different patterns of rural and urban social development. Despite his posthumous reputation, Toynbee was not a pessimist. He did condemn the misery caused by the early phases of industrialization, but his view of history was progressive. Collective and conscious action by the working classes would ensure their just share in the division of wealth and power without resorting to the extreme measures advocated by revolutionary socialists or Henry George and his followers.

Toynbee turned to economic history in order to justify his view of society. He lacked the stamina and compulsive single-mindedness of the professional scholar, able to transcend an ideological point of departure to produce a work of durable scholarly merit. He was constantly distracted by seemingly urgent issues demanding immediate attention: rural poverty, working-class housing, Henry George, and the demands of the Irish Land League, all seemed to conspire to tear him away from the main theme of his course. Although the published version of the industrial revolution lectures was soon adopted in universities and schools as a standard work, it was not until the beginning of the twentieth century that historians took up the study of industrialization and its social consequences. Yet Toynbee had a profound influence on contemporary Oxford, stimulating interest in social and economic problems either through direct contact, or by means of the Toynbee legend and the Toynbee memorials. Young Oxford men undertook the study of economics out of a sense of duty towards society, hoping to assist the course of progress; Oxford was 'full of economic theorists interested in the solution of the problems of the day'.[130]

For a short while, the merits of economic theory were defended by Marshall, who was appointed to the Balliol tutorship vacated by

130 *Oxford Magazine*, 27 February 1889.

Toynbee,[131] and J. N. Keynes, who taught at Oxford for a term[132] following Marshall's appointment to the Cambridge chair. Historians were expected to master some economic theory, but a general acquaintance with Mill's and Walker's work, usually from a critical point of view,[133] was considered sufficient. In 1887, W. J. Ashley wrote:

> the so-called 'principles' of Political Economy are at any rate not universally true for all times and places, and, in consequence, contribute scarcely at all to the understanding of the economic life of the past. For this it is necessary to study economic institutions in the light of the ideas of the time and to examine those ideas, not in relation to modern conditions which did not then exist, but in relation to the conditions amid which they arose.[134]

W. J. Ashley was the first Oxford-trained historian to become an academic economic historian. The son of a journeyman hatter,[135] Ashley came up from St. Olave's, Southwark, having won the Brackenbury Scholarship, for which he had been coached by Tout. At Balliol he was tutored by A. L. Smith and J. F. Bright, and obtained a first in history in 1881. He became interested in medieval history as a member of the Historical Seminar during Stubbs's presidency. As was customary for ambitious history students, he visited Germany in 1880 and attended Reinhold Pauli's lectures on English medieval history at Göttingen, returning to Germany in 1883 and 1884. At first Ashley had planned to follow his first in history by reading Greats, supporting himself by coaching history students, but he was eventually forced to abandon these plans, and in February 1885 (after four previous failures) he was elected to a fellowship at Lincoln, followed by an appointment to a lectureship at Corpus.

As a young graduate, Ashley had attended Toynbee's industrial revolution lectures and 'caught fire from Toynbee's rapt enthusiasm'.[136] Under Toynbee's influence, Ashley became interested in social

131 J. K. Whitaker, 'Alfred Marshall: The years 1871 to 1885', *History of Political Economy*, Vol.4 (1972) pp.1–61; A. Kadish, 'Marshall on necessaries and travel: a note on a letter by Marshall to the *Pall Mall Gazette*', *History of Economic Thought Newsletter*, No.26 (Spring 1981), pp.15–18.

132 *OUG*, 20 April 1885.

133 A typical question on Mill in the 1880s was: 'State and criticise Mill's theory of profits' (Trinity Term 1886).

134 W. J. Ashley, 'Modern history', in A. M. Stedman (ed.), *Oxford: Its Life and Schools*, London: G. Bell & Sons, 1887, p.303.

135 A. Ashley, *William James Ashley. A Life*, London: P. S. King & Son, 1932; Kadish, *Oxford Economists*, pp.1–4; J. F. Rees, *DNB*, 1922–30.

136 W. J. A[shley], 'The Master of Balliol', *The Nation* (New York), 12 October 1893.

reform,[137] and, subsequently, in economic history. Toynbee advised him to use the history of economic theory as a means of combining history and economics: 'Take some one subject e.g. wages, and, beginning with Adam Smith, read in chronological order what each noteworthy English economist has said upon the subject, and see if you can make out the way in which various doctrines have arisen and been modified.'[138] And although Ashley was not quite ready to abandon medieval history, he was to reflect years later that 'it does occur to me that perhaps a good way of introducing abstract economic thinking to historical students is by an outline course on the historic movement of economic doctrine.' Economic doctrines, he added, 'form significant chapters in the movement of European thought. They cast light on, and receive light from, contemporary events; they stimulate an attitude of questioning; they should send the student back to "pure history with a fresh zest".'[139]

As an historian, Ashley was something of a Positivist. He criticized Freeman[140] and constitutional historians in general for their narrowness – their tendency 'to think of "constitutional development" and to forget the condition of the people'.[141] But he also insisted on the importance of an overall view of history, the only way in which the general course of human evolution could be revealed.[142] Despite this criticism of constitutional historians, however, Ashley himself was an institutionalist.[143]

He had little interest in individual actions and relations, or in attempts to discover the laws governing them. What we must attempt to discover, he wrote in the preface to the first part of his major work, *An Introduction to English Economic History and Theory*, 'are the laws of social development – that is to say, generalizations as to the stages through which the economic life of society has actually moved.'[144]

As an intercollegiate lecturer, Ashley taught a wide variety of subjects,

137 Ashley to Brentano, 25 March 1913, quoted in H. W. McCready, 'Sir William Ashley: some unpublished letters', *Journal of Economic History*, Vol.15 (1955), pp.34–43.

138 Ashley's 'Review of F. C. Montague, *Arnold Toynbee*', in *Political Science Quarterly*, Vol.4 (1889), pp.531–4.

139 Ashley, 'The place of economic history', p.7.

140 Ashley's 'Review of W. R. W. Stephen, *The Life and Letters of E. A. Freeman*, in *The Nation*, 18 July 1895.

141 W. J. Ashley, 'Feudalism', in H. O. Wakeman and A. Hassall (eds), *Essays Introductory to the Study of English Constitutional History*, 2nd edn London: Longmon's & Co., 1891, p.111.

142 Ashley's 'Review of E. Bontny, *Le Développement de la Constitution et la Société Politique en Angleterre*', in *English Historical Review*, Vol.3 (July 1888), pp.570–1.

143 A. Ashley, *Ashley*, p.33.

144 W. J. Ashley, *An Introduction to English Economic History and Theory*, Part I, London: Rimingtons, 1888, p.xii.

including constitutional history, comparative politics, economic history, history of economic theory, and Mill's *Principles*.[145] He appears to have approved of the history curriculum and adopted some of its features at the University of Toronto when he was appointed Professor of Political Economy and Constitutional History there in 1888.[146] But he found the burdens of the tutorial system unbearable: they kept him from doing any independent work, and did not allow him to supervise the more promising students beyond the study of the standard *Select Charters*.[147] Like Firth he felt that Oxford offered a sound enough basis, but the system's rigidity failed to encourage research amongst teachers, let alone the more able students.

Ashley had some first-hand experience of trying to encourage and sustain research through the Historical Seminar and its economic counterpart, the Oxford Economic Society, which he helped to found. The Economic Society was intended to provide a forum similar to the Historical Seminar, where work done by graduates and young dons was presented in the form of papers and discussed in detail. Neither Rogers nor Price took any interest in the Society, which, like the Historical Seminar after Stubbs's resignation, was run by young dons.

Oman appears to have represented the majority of the History School when he dismissed the need for technical training such as palaeography or diplomacy. He believed that 'zeal, insatiable curiosity, a ready mind to shape hypotheses, a sound judgement to test them, above all a dogged determination to work at all times and in all places, are the real requisites of the historian rather than any array of technical training.'[148] The same could be said of those who, in the 1880s, were attracted to the study of economics. Regardless of whether they had had any basic schooling in theory or in history, they were expected to plunge into research virtually on their own. The younger members of the Oxford Economic Society – M. E. Sadler, E. Cannan, L. L. Price (who had attended Marshall's lectures), H. Ll. Smith (one of J. N. Keynes's Oxford students), and W. A. S. Hewins – could count on sympathy and encouragement from the slightly older teachers of economics and economic history, but not from the Drummond Professor. Indeed, the Society eventually disintegrated in 1890 after an attempt to recruit F. Y. Edgeworth, Rogers's successor in the Drummond Chair, as its president.[149]

145 *OUG*, 16 January and 23 April 1888; 17 January and 18 October 1887; 25 January, 3 May and 18 October 1886; 19 October 1885.
146 See Ashley to Seligman, 23 November 1888, in Seligman papers.
147 [W. J. Ashley], 'The study of history at Oxford', *The Nation*, 11 April 1895.
148 C. Oman, *Inaugural lecture on the study of history*, 7 February 1906, Oxford: Clarendon Press, 1906, p.24.
149 Kadish, *Oxford Economists*, p.203.

F. Y. Edgeworth, who had obtained a first in Greats in 1865, had had little contact, if any, with Oxford economists before his election to the Drummond Chair following Rogers's death in 1890. Professionally he was much closer to Marshall, who had arranged his appointment as secretary of the new British Economic Association, and the editor of its journal, the *Economic Journal*. Not surprisingly, the *Oxford Magazine* found it regrettable that the electors to the Drummond Chair did not choose a 'candidate better known to Oxford . . . and more closely associated . . . with the recent study and teaching of the subject in the University.'[150] Even Marshall, who liked Edgeworth and approved of his work, regarded him as an exceptionally extreme exponent of theoretical economics.[151] His reputation for abstract theory and the use of mathematics led the *Oxford Magazine* to express the hope that 'the reminiscences of the School of Literae Humaniores . . . and consideration of human weakness, will lead him to treat the subject in Oxford in a wider spirit than that of the Calculus.'[152] Not only was his work of little application to current problems as seen and studied at Oxford, but Edgeworth also consciously avoided taking sides in most current debates, thereby prompting the speculation that: 'A Professor may have *this* reason also for being unwilling to impart his own opinion on burning questions to his pupils – he may not have one.'[153]

Edgeworth did not try to evade his statutory duties. He taught courses on general theory (Mill 'in connection with recent additions to the Science'),[154] an advanced course on some of the more difficult questions raised in the general course, courses on special topics such as bimetallism, commerce, trade unions, and wages,[155] and he offered informal instruction 'to advise students about their reading and to correct their exercises'.[156] He introduced a course on statistics,[157] and had arranged for a number of external experts to lecture on their subjects, including Acworth on railway rates, Giffen on the use of statistics, and Flux on the economic effects of internal migration.[158] But he did little to try to change the status of economic studies, either within the existing School, or in agitating for the diploma in economics

150 *Oxford Magazine*, 25 February 1891.
151 Marshall to J. N. Keynes, 20 January 1902, Keynes 1 (125), Marshall Library, Cambridge.
152 *Oxford Magazine*, 25 February 1891.
153 Ibid., 28 October 1891.
154 *OUG*, 17 April 1891; 20 January 1893; 12 January 1894.
155 Ibid., 23 April and 12 October 1894; 26 April 1895.
156 Ibid., 17 April 1891.
157 Ibid., 22 April 1892; 24 April 1896.
158 Ibid., 2 February 1897; 8 November 1898; 19 January 1900.

which was eventually secured in 1903.[159] He took little interest in the working of the History Board, of which he was an ex-officio member, and appears to have accepted the continued rule of the intercollegiate lecturers. Although accessible and friendly, his high theory lectures attracted few listeners.

Throughout the 1890s, then, the status of economics remained unchanged. It was taught by tutors who were competent,[160] but who had no particular training in economics. W. A. S. Hewins, a protégé of Firth's who lectured in the early 1890s, failed to convince his college (Pembroke) that they should have a tutor in economic history[161] and economics, or the Board of Studies of the need to foster greater specialization amongst college tutors and lecturers, and he left Oxford in 1895 to take up the directorship of the new London School of Economics. Ashley left in 1888, when he was appointed to a chair in Toronto; E. Cannan lived in Oxford, but taught at the LSE; and L. L. Price remained at Oxford as Bursar and non-tutorial fellow of Oriel. (When the Committee for the Diploma was set up in 1903, Cannan and Price were nominated by the Vice-Chancellor.) The general interest in economic and social questions did not flag, however: the Oxford branch of the Christian Social Union published the *Economic Review* in 1891, the first economics quarterly in England;[162] the Social Science Club, organized by S. Ball of St. John's, where guest speakers discussed subjects of current interest, remained active throughout; and the popular university settlements encouraged Oxford men to study aspects of the life of the urban working classes at close quarters. But the study of economics did not advance beyond the status of an auxiliary discipline, in which specialization was only acceptable at a postgraduate level.

For a more detailed account of the subject see A. Kadish, *Historians, Economists and Economic History,* London: Routledge, 1989.

159 See N. Chester, *Economics, Politics and Social Studies in Oxford 1900–85,* London: Macmillan, 1986, ch.1.
160 Including H. A. L. Fisher, J. A. R. Marriott, G. H. Wakeling, and H. W. Blunt.
161 W. A. S. Hewins, *The Apologia of an Imperialist. Forty Years of Empire Policy,* London: Constable & Co., 1929, pp.23–4. Hewins believed that his lectures were boycotted for fear that dons would be forced to teach more subjects than they had time for. However, the course in English economic history, first delivered in 1893, was repeated in 1894 and 1895.
162 Kadish, *Oxford Economists,* pp.183–90.

3

THE TEACHING OF POLITICAL ECONOMY IN THE EXTENSION MOVEMENT

Cambridge, London and Oxford

Alon Kadish

The story of the academic institutionalization of economics in England should not be confused with the more general issue of the development and dissemination of economic thought. Long before English universities came round to recognizing the claims of economics as an academic discipline, economic doctrines of one sort or another, and at various levels of theoretical sophistication, had become an integral part of popular perceptions of current reality. So-called 'popular economics' may partly have originated with the writings and activities of the early socialists and the Owenites.[1] But by around the middle of the century, more liberal concepts of the economic dimensions of social activity appear to have prevailed throughout society.

University economists were not unmindful of the importance of popular notions of economics, as may be evinced from the early history of the University Extension movement.[2] In May 1873 a special university syndicate recommended that Cambridge should adopt for a trial period a scheme for extension lectures drawn up by the syndicate's secretary, James Stuart, a fellow of Trinity College. The Cambridge University Syndicate for Local Lectures was founded as a consequence, with Stuart and Vincent Henry Stanton (1846–1924) as its first secretaries. The syndicate's work commenced with lectures delivered by three Trinity

---

1 For recent studies of early popular socialist and Owenite economics, see N. Thompson, *The People's Science: The Popular Political Economy of Exploitation and Crisis 1816–34*, Cambridge: Cambridge University Press, 1984; and G. Claeys, *Machinery, Money and the Millennium: From Moral Economy to Socialism, 1815–1860*, Oxford: Polity Press, 1987.

2 For a general history of the extension movement, see J. F. C. Harrison, *Learning and Living 1790–1960* London:Routledge & Kegan Paul, 1961, ch. 6. For the history of the Cambridge extension, see E. Welch, *The Peripatetic University: Cambridge Local Lectures, 1873–1973*, Cambridge: Cambridge University Press, 1973.

fellows during the autumn of 1873 in Nottingham, Derby, and Leicester.[3] These included a course on political economy that Stanton delivered in all three towns, followed the next autumn by a course in the same locations by the Revd William Moore Ede (1849–1935).

The eventual establishment of a regular Cambridge syndicate was largely due to Stuart's success in attracting sufficient demand for extension courses. From thirty-one courses in Lent (January to April) 1875,[4] demand increased to fifty-six courses in Michaelmas (October to December) later the same year.[5] The syndicate's first report, covering the period Michaelmas 1875 to Lent 1876, gave the number of students examined at the end of each term as 744 and 980 respectively, of which 113 and 177 had studied political economy and logic.[6] Courses in political economy were delivered during Michaelmas 1875 in twenty-two centres (fifteen in Lent) by six lecturers. On the whole, the examiners expressed satisfaction with the students' work, although in one instance it was found that

> there is little evidence of much use having been made of the extensive and careful references to books appended to the syllabuses of the lecturer; on the contrary the very elaborateness of the syllabus has sometimes tempted candidates to content themselves with merely reproducing the words of these. There is manifest generally an exaggerated deference to the statements of the lecturer, and this, although it testifies to his efficiency, is on the whole a questionable gain . . . With those portions of the subject touched upon more lightly in the lectures the candidates shew no really useful acquaintance.[7]

The examiner's conclusion was that courses should be more narrowly defined and that local centres should ensure that introductory courses precede more advanced ones, so as to develop a more systematic approach to the analysis of economic problems.

Any indications of the adoption of such an approach to economics became the standard measure of success of extension courses. Lecturers and examiners sought to impress upon extension students the importance of developing an analytic view of economics, which in their view could be achieved only by means of some form of systematic training. This would ideally lead to independent thinking, which might take the form of student study groups, intent upon sorting out for themselves

3 A list of courses arranged according to locality may be found in the Cambridge Extension Archive, University of Cambridge Library, BEMS 26/1.
4 BEMS 22/1/58–9.
5 BEMS 22/1/62–3.
6 *Cambridge University Reporter* (*CUR*), 20 June 1876.
7 Ibid. The examiners in political economy were Stanton, Cunningham, and James Ward.

economic goals and means, free from the pernicious effects of popular prejudice and demagogy. Instead it would seem that most, although not all, students preferred their economics to be simple and even dogmatic, not unlike the works of Harriet Martineau or Jane Marcet. Modern criticism of orthodox dogma, J. A. Hobson argued,

> has broken down the public confidence which rested on the idea of a rigid definite system of economic dogmas, and the hard-headed practical citizen has not yet summoned up his intellectual courage to face the difficulties of the newer economic teaching ... [T]his reluctance ... is explained by the natural craving of practical people for that premature exactitude which was fostered by the writings of the classical economists.[8]

On the other hand, most economics lecturers regarded as counter-productive the teaching of dogma without method, and without the necessary qualifications and conditions relevant to any attempt to apply theory to reality. Such efforts to simplify the teaching of economics would only serve to promote an illusory view of its nature, and help to perpetuate popular misconceptions.

As for the suggested schedules for the systematic study of economics, these were rarely, if ever, affected by actual extension teaching experience. In a report submitted to the newly founded syndicate in 1875, for example, E. Moore Ede suggested that the teaching of extension economics should, in effect, follow the Cambridge curriculum, whereby economics was taught within the history and the moral sciences triposes. Ede accordingly suggested a three-year programme:

> First term, a course on Logic to teach the students the first principles of reasoning, and to instruct them as to the nature of a proof. This would be especially beneficial to working men. Second term, a course on Constitutional History. This would complete one session.

> The first term of the 2nd session, a course on Political Economy, to be followed by another set of lectures on the same subject.

> The 3rd session might begin with a course on Social History, taking the same periods as has been treated constitutionally. Here the knowledge acquired in the study of Political Economy would be applied to the History of the English People. The last term might be spent in studying Political Philosophy, or in a comparison between the history of some other nation and our own.[9]

8 J. A. Hobson, 'The teaching of economics', *The University Extension Journal*, March 1896.
9 Revd W. Moore Ede, *Report Presented to the Syndicate for Conducting Lectures in Populous Places*, Cambridge 1875.

A later scheme submitted by W. Cunningham reflected his own approach to the study of economics as opposed to Marshall's efforts to establish the subject's autonomy. Cunningham wanted a systematic course of studies to include 'a complete survey of the Social History of his own country, the Theory of Political Economy, in itself and in application to familiar facts, the History of Political Economy and its dependence on the Theory of the State, all treated in connection with one another as parts of a whole'.[10] Hence, whereas Ede's scheme was intended to offer the extension student a programme approximating the teaching of economics at Cambridge, Cunningham wished the extension to adopt a materially different approach, an approach he would have liked to see Cambridge institute as well. Cunningham also offered a six-term, three-year programme, in which in the first year, the Michaelmas term was spent studying English economic history from the Domesday survey to the disturbances consequent upon the suppression of the monasteries; and the Lent term covered English economic history from the accession of Elizabeth to the repeal of the Corn Laws. The subjects covered would demonstrate 'how our existing industrial system came into being. The reign of Elizabeth is the most convenient point to take for the beginning of modern society, though there is no hard and fast line between medieval and modern life.' Then, in the second year, the Michaelmas term would deal with the modern theory of political economy – value, money, price, credit, rent, etc.; and the Lent term would cover the application of the theory of political economy – rents, profits, wages, taxation, etc. These second-year courses were 'to state the theories which explain the working of industrial conditions, the origin of which has been previously described; and to show how the theory may be applied to passing practical questions'. In the Michaelmas term of their final year, students would concentrate on the history of the doctrines of political economy; the mercantile theory; and the Physiocrats, Adam Smith, and Ricardo. And in the Lent term they would look at the history of the doctrines of political economy; the early French socialists, Owen, Lassalle, and Karl Marx (and, a later addition, 'the international, Katheder Socialisten').[11] Cunningham believed that politics determined economic conditions,

10 R. G. Moulton, *The University Extension Movement*, London: Bemrose & Sons, 1886, Appendix 3; and BEMS 21/1/136.
11 In a 'Review of the English translation of L. Cossa, *Guide to the Study of Political Economy* (1880)', in the *Cambridge Review*, 8 December 1880, Cunningham criticized Cossa's omission of Marx and Lassalle. Although, he argued, they had not 'contributed to what is generally considered sound Political Economy, they have enunciated doctrines which have won a wide circle of adherents, and thus formed a school that should not be utterly ignored'.

which in turn were reflected in economic theory.[12] Hence the third-year courses were meant to 'show the changes in the doctrines of Political Economy which have been brought about partly by changes in industry or commerce and partly by changed views of the nature and function of the state'.

However, despite schemes such as Cunningham's, the choice of courses was entirely up to the local extension committees. Lecturers could offer any subject they wished, subject to the syndicate's approval. But the relatively low demand for systematic studies in economics rendered such schemes impractical. On the other hand, the extension's freedom from Cambridge's rigid examination system [13] allowed it greater flexibility in its list of course subjects, which often proved wider-ranging and more innovative than that provided by the university. Consequently, the extension movement was regarded at the time as something of a vanguard. In retrospect, some of its innovations, such as the appointment of women lecturers, proved to be predictive of things to come.[14]

The contents of the courses and the list of lecturers reflected the changes in economics from the 1870s onwards. In the absence at the time of a specialized course of studies in economics at Cambridge, none of the early Cambridge extension lecturers had undergone any special academic training beyond that provided in the history and the moral sciences triposes. And none, except for H. S. Foxwell and Cunningham, was to make a name for himself as an economist. Some, such as Warren Maude Moorsom,[15] taught straightforward economic orthodoxy. In his lectures at the Crewe Mechanics' Institute, Moorsom outlined the standard orthodox view of the anticipated working-class progress:

> 'Justice', 'self-control', 'self-government' . . . these are the principles of action which will lead the labourer to a better kind of life;

12 In teaching economics to Cambridge students reading history, Cunningham concentrated on economic history, while introducing 'explanations of the meaning of value, coinage, credit, etc., incidentally as the subject arose in concrete terms in actual history'. Audrey Cunningham, *William Cunningham: Teacher and Priest*, London: SPCK, 1950, p.64.

13 See Moulton, *University Extension*, p.10.

14 The first woman to be appointed a Cambridge extension lecturer was E. A. McArthur in 1893.

15 W. M. Moorsom (b. 1840), the son of Captain (later Vice-Admiral) C. R. Moorsom (1792–1861), chairman of the London and North-Western Railway from 1860 to 1861, had read mathematics at Trinity College, Cambridge, where he had been a close friend of Stuart's. At the time of his extension lectures at Crewe, he had been the manager of the LNWR rail-mill. See A. Kadish, 'University extension and the working classes: the case of the Northumberland miners', in *Historical Research*, Vol. 60, no.142 (June 1987), pp.195–7.

the practice should be, intelligent forethought ... and wide and accurate observation of the condition of the labour market, in this and other countries, and prompt action thereupon, readiness to move from a place where living is difficult to those where it is easier, and a similar readiness and capacity to relinquish one trade when it is paying badly and take up another which is doing better; a higher and ever-rising standard of living, so that starvation wages and fever-hatching dens, and the attractions of drunkenness and other sensualities may be rejected with contempt; in short, independence gained by the labourers' own frugality and readiness to supply just that kind of labour which is wanted at any given time. Let the labourer keep a portion of the wealth that passes through his hands, and if he has the wealth and opportunities which fall to most men, he will before long have his head sufficiently above water to bargain with his employer as an equal – just as able to withdraw his labour from the falling market as the employer is to withdraw his capital. [*Loud applause*] [16]

Others, such as Ede, added moral qualifications. For instance, he condemned trade-union attempts to control the number of workers in any given trade as likely, if adopted by a sufficient number of unions, to 'cause a great influx into the unskilled classes of labourers, and lower wages in these classes would be the consequence'.[17] Ede also expressed disapproval at the imposition of an artificial limit on the individual worker's output – an act of 'unenlightened self-interest' which might undermine the country's commercial competitiveness – and of the regulation of supply. Although he did accept that

it was true that in the case of generally produced commodities the unions aimed [by means of regulation] at effecting stability of the market. By doing this they had to suffer the loss consequent on their not being able to take advantage of times of great activity for goods they produced; but what the unions said was that they were willing to submit to the loss of extra work and other benefits for the sake of stability and regularity of prices and wages.

However, on the whole Ede perceived the unions as morally progressive for placing 'class-interest in the place of self-interest of the individual'. There admittedly existed the danger resulting from the 'self-seeking of class against class'. But all things considered, it 'was to the moral effect of trades unions that he looked for the greatest amount of good – as providing a solution of the question of self-education of the masses.

16 'Workmen's unions and employers' associations', in the *Crewe Chronicle*, 25 March 1876.
17 The *Keighly News*, 28 March 1874.

Our local self-government had very much declined . . . and substitute came to take its place to teach the people the art of self-government.'

Generally speaking, the Cambridge extension did not aim its work at any single class. 'In all our towns and rural districts', R. D. Roberts, assistant secretary from 1881 to 1885 and secretary of the syndicate from 1894 to 1902, wrote in 1891, 'there are men and women living obscure lives, eager for knowledge, using their leisure in reading and following up, with very meager facilities, the study of some subject in which they are interested', and it was for them that, in his view, the extension existed.[18] In particular, Roberts identified women, who 'have been among the warmest supporters [of the extension] . . . and . . . constituted at least half the audiences';[19] and 'business and professional men, sometimes well over middle age'[20] who, contrary to initial expectations, seemed to outnumber young school-leavers and white-collar workers. Roberts also mentioned schools, especially girls' schools, who turned to the extension for instruction in subjects other than those required for local examinations.[21] And finally there were the working classes. Not, Moulton noted in 1886, 'that the movement is intended more for them than for others, but . . . it is the first instance in which a University system has distinctly set itself to meet the wants of the Working Classes'.[22]

What these wants were depended on one's social perceptions. Roberts associated working-class adult education with leisure activity. The 'improvement which has taken place during the last fifty years in the material condition of the *industrial classes* and the increased leisure thus secured', he observed, 'have given rise to wide-spread desire for ampler intellectual opportunity'.[23] Others, including many of the economics lecturers, hoped that their teachings would be adopted by the working classes as the means towards self-betterment, both material and cultural. They sought acceptance as impartial observers who, in the case of economics, could be trusted to produce a faithful picture of the workings of the economic aspect of human affairs. During the 1870s, a common theme in extension economics was the harmony of interests which, in truth, was inherent in inter-class relations. 'He was sure', Stuart told a Bradford audience, following an extension course by Cunningham, that if the same statements as those made by Cunningham had been put to them by 'persons connected either with the

18 R. D. Roberts, *Eighteen Years of University Extension*, Cambridge: Cambridge University Press, 1891, p.4.
19 Ibid., p.8.
20 Ibid., p.13.
21 Moulton, *University Extension*, p.15.
22 Ibid., p.17.
23 Roberts, *Eighteen Years*, p.8.

employers or with the employed, [they] would have been received with suspicion. [*hear, hear*] What was most desired was that both parties – employers and employed – should be able to draw in the principles from a source in which both had confidence.'[24] So far, he added, 'as he was himself concerned, his endeavour ... had been chiefly with a strong desire to see the working classes benefit'. A similar sentiment was expressed by Ede in inaugurating a course in Derby in 1874 (the course which introduced Hobson to economics): the aims of the socialists generally were good, but the hasty means which they proposed were unsound, and destructive of some of the primary principles on which society and political economy are based. He thought that to realize their aims they should proceed rationally, and without violent reversion, improve the present condition of things.[25]

Throughout the first decades of the Cambridge extension, the modified Millian economics of most of its lecturers appears to have met with little, if any, criticism from their working-class students. Indeed, Ede's aforementioned cautious praise of trade unions had been considered dangerously radical by the Keighly conservative newspaper:

> We admit that trades unions have done good, and that without combination the working men would have suffered grinding which through the unions they have escaped. But Mr Ede misses the chief objection against them. He thinks class interest, a more elevating motive than self-interest ... Water cannot rise higher than its source; and unionism cannot rise higher than the level of the inferior workman to whose size the superior workman and his chances for self-elevation are ruthlessly sacrificed ... [T]rades unionism levels down the individual while undertaking ... to regulate wages and work so that the class may wrench a good share of the profits from the employer.[26]

Consequently, the extension's failure to attract a steady working-class following was in no way associated with the content of its courses. The relatively large demand for courses in political economy in the 1875–6 season proved a fluke. During the 1876–7 season, out of a total of 75 courses, only 5 (of which 3 were for one term only) were in political economy. The student numbers for Michaelmas 1876 and Lent 1877 were 68 and 72 out of a total of 634 and 441,[27] with numbers of political economy courses and students further dropping over the next few years. This was partly the result of a general, if less drastic, decline in the demand for extension courses following the initial spate of

24 *Bradford Observer*, 28 March 1874.
25 *Derbyshire Advertiser and North Staffordshire Journal*, 16 October 1874.
26 The *Keighly Herald*, 28 March 1874.
27 *CUR*, 12 June 1877.

enthusiasm. The reasons given at the time included: too many courses at too few centres, so that when a relatively small number of centres ceased to operate the extension experienced a disproportionate drop in demand; and the emergence, mainly in the Midlands and the north, of university colleges which tended to take over local adult education,[28] with the result that when demand did eventually revive after 1882 it was mainly in the south. Yet even after 1882, demand for courses in political economy remained sluggish.

The relative lack of popularity of political economy was not necessarily a reflection on its teachers. They had all studied economics in association with other subjects, be it moral sciences – as in the case of Carveth Read (1848–1931),[29] E. Moore Ede,[30] Cunningham, Foxwell, and Arthur Temple Lyttelton (1852–1903)[31]; history – Charles James Cooper (1849–1932)[32] and John Mainwaring Brown (1854–88)[33]; or mathematics – W. M. Moorsom and John Elliotson Symes (1847–1921).[34] Hence they saw no reason to confine their lecturing to political economy. Cunningham, for instance, resided as an extension lecturer

28 These included Yorkshire College, Leeds (1874); Mason Science College, Birmingham (1875); University College, Bristol (1876); Firth College, Sheffield (1879); and the University Colleges in Nottingham (1880), Liverpool (1881), Cardiff (1883), and Bangor (1884).

29 Graduated in 1871 with a first. From 1878 Read lectured at Wren's coaching establishment in London, and in 1903 he was appointed Grote Professor of Philosophy at the University of London. See *The Times*, 9 December 1931.

30 Graduated in 1871 with a first. Ede was ordained in 1872. He filled a variety of church and academic positions, culminating in the Deanery of Worcester from 1908 to 1934. See *The Times*, 3 June 1935.

31 Graduated in 1873 with a first. Son of the fourth Baron Lyttelton, he served as a curate at St Mary's, Reading from 1876 until his appointment as a tutor at Keble College, Oxford in 1879, where he was a member of the Lux Mundi group. In 1882 he became the first master of Selwyn College, Cambridge, and in 1878 Suffragan Bishop of Southampton.

32 Cooper read both moral sciences (1873), and law and history (1874). In 1877 he was called to the Bar. He practised on the western circuit until deafness led him to leave the Bar and take orders.

33 Graduated in 1876 with a first. Brown was called to the Bar in 1876, and in 1882 was appointed Professor of English Language and Literature and History and Political Economy at the University of Otago, New Zealand. He was lost in a mountain expedition in 1888.

34 Graduated in 1871; president of the Union in 1870; ordained as a deacon in 1873 and as a priest in 1875. Symes's extension work led to his appointment in 1881 as Professor of English Language and Literature at University College, Nottingham, where he was one of its first four professors. He served from 1890 until 1912 as the college's principal. See A. W. Coats, 'John Elliotson Symes, Henry George and Academic Freedom in Nottingham during the 1880s', in *Renaissance and Modern Studies*, Vol. 7 (1963), pp.110–38; and Peter d'A. Jones, *The Christian Socialist Revival 1877–1914*, Princeton N. J.: Princeton University Press, 1968, pp.105–7.

in Liverpool from 1874 to 1878 (when he returned to Cambridge as the syndicate's assistant secretary), where he lectured (either in Liverpool or in Everton) for every term from Michaelmas 1874 to Lent 1878. But it was only during his first terms in either place that he taught political economy, his other courses including logic and history. Similarly, Ede, who taught in Sheffield for every term from Lent 1875 to Lent 1878, lectured on political economy during his first three terms, later adding courses on logic and English history. A lecturer's popularity, then, was not entirely dependent on the popularity of any single subject.

Most of the extension's early lecturers, who had been personally recruited by Stuart or Stanton, did not as a rule regard extension work as their ultimate vocation, and soon turned to other things. An early and often-voiced complaint was that the extension failed to retain the services of experienced lecturers as the result of its inability to offer them some form of job security, such as a college fellowship or a university appointment with extension teaching responsibilities.[35] At the same time, it is doubtful whether many of the early lecturers would have chosen to pursue a full-time extension lecturing career.

While requests for courses in political economy were never to reach the figures of 1875–6, there did develop a steady demand for courses in economic and social history, which, whenever preceded by an introductory course in economics, was regarded by the extension as approaching a systematic course of studies. But by the late 1870s, many centres found it difficult to maintain continuous lecturing on any subject. In the syndicate's report for 1879 it was stated that 'A considerable number of towns have had lectures for a time and then have dropped out of the list, in almost all cases from want of local pecuniary support, and not from any want of educational success. In other cases the lectures have been continued in a more or less desultory manner.'[36] It was feared that, rather than catering to those unable to study at the universities and yet eager to obtain some higher education in a manner which approximated university studies in both standard and method, the extension would become merely another educational agent offering occasional lectures. Matters were exacerbated by the policy adopted by some local educational institutions who might otherwise have provided the extension with a firmer base. Such was the case with the Crewe Mechanics' Institute, one of the bodies whose appeals helped to persuade the Cambridge Senate to set up the syndicate for local lectures.[37] Local interest in extension lectures had been largely sustained

35 See e.g. R. D. Roberts, 'Report of visits to centres between Easter 1882 and Easter 1883', 3 March 1883: BEMS 22/1; and Roberts, *Eighteen Years*, p.105.
36 *CUR*, 4 June 1879.
37 Roberts, *Eighteen Years*, p.91.

by Moorsom's efforts, and when he left, it soon dissipated.[38] Furthermore, the institute's stated policy was to spend as little as possible on lectures, or, as the council put it, to do its 'utmost to get free lectures for the members of the institution and to benefit them in every way'.[39] Moorsom's lectures on political economy (1875–6) were offered free of charge after the council had moved against inviting Cunningham to come from Liverpool to lecture for the standard fee, on the grounds that there was not 'sufficient interest taken in the subject to justify them in spending the necessary amount of money upon the lectures'.[40] The fact that Moorsom succeeded in attracting an audience of 150 appears to have had little impact on the council's policy.

The failure of local centres to sustain demand for extension courses was commonly attributed to the lack of sufficient local financial support. In a similar manner, the paucity of working-class attendance was blamed on the high price of tickets. Harold Cox (1859–1936), who lectured on political economy in York and in Hull from Michaelmas 1882 to Lent 1883, found that at York even subsidized tickets of 5s. per term proved to be too dear for local working men. When the price of tickets was further reduced and a free introductory lecture was given, the number of artisans in the audience rose, and an average attendance of 125 students was maintained throughout. But at Hull, Cox discovered that in addition to the prohibitive price of tickets, local labour customs undermined working-class attendance. Fridays apparently were convenient not only for lecturing; Friday

> was also the great day for overtime. The men were so anxious to get their Saturday half-holiday that when there was extra work to be done, they made an effort to clear it off on Friday night. The system too of working in shifts or relays in order to keep the machinery running very much hampers the men in any effort to obtain permanent evening instruction, because a man has to take the night and day shift in alternate weeks, and would therefore miss one lecture out of two.[41]

By way of a solution, Stuart suggested in 1885 that a fund of £2,500 should be established to help subsidize courses.[42] On the other hand,

---

38 Moorsom had been a teacher and an examiner at the institute from 1864, and from 1866 a member of its council: W. H. Chaloner, *The Social and Economic Development of Crewe 1780–1923*, Manchester: Manchester University Press, 1950, p.244.

39 *Crewe Guardian*, 10 February 1872. See also Crewe Municipal Library, Mechanics' Institute Council Minutes, 18 March 1872, on avoiding payment of examination fees.

40 *Crewe Guardian*, 20 March 1875.

41 Roberts, 'Report of visits'.

42 Introduction to Moulton, *University Extension*, p.iv; see also p.21.

the Cambridge extension expressed reluctance to ask for state aid.[43]

Finally, in socially heterogeneous communities, class relations could have an adverse effect on working-class attendance. The presence of middle-class representatives, often women, on local extension committees was usually essential for their success. Middle-class committee members had both the leisure and the contacts to guarantee in advance a sufficient sum to cover a course's expenses and ensure against the centre's financial failure. They naturally tended to dominate the local committees, thereby frequently alienating potential working-class students resentful of any hint of condescension. In some instances, local working men assumed that fees were deliberately kept high and that the subjects chosen were intended to keep them away.[44] On the other hand, the absence of middle-class members in some local committees – in the Northumberland mining villages, for example – meant that fluctuations in local economic conditions had an immediate effect on extension work, as was the case following the drop in the price of coal in the mid-1880s and the unsuccessful miners' strike in 1887.

The university-like trappings of the extension courses – the final examinations, the certificates awarded to successful students, the class lists, the prizes – proved attractive to only part of the extension's students, schoolteachers, for example. Others, including the Northumberland miners, appear to have been more interested in education for its own sake rather than for the opportunities for self-advancement it might offer, and were therefore quite willing to forego examinations, certificates, and the like as a means of reducing expenses. In some villages, miners chose to pursue self-education using contacts made through the extension but without officially engaging extension lecturers, with the result that the Cambridge syndicate lost touch with the local educational activity it had inspired, erroneously assuming that it had failed. This independence of mind was also the impression of an extension lecturer who wrote in 1902:

> I have never found that the business man and working-people of the North expected one to come to them with a complete doctrine

---

43 See the *Cambridge Review*, 16 October 1890, and a Review of M. E. Sadler and H. J. Mackinder, *University Extension* (1890)', ibid., 6 November 1890: '[T]here is a difference in their [Sadler and Mackinder's] conception of the duties and scope of extension lecturing between the two universities [Oxford and Cambridge] which is not uninstructive. For instance, here at Cambridge whether from certain independence of spirit, or from distrust of government interference . . . there is considerable disinclination towards state aid.'

44 See Kadish, 'University extension and the working classes', pp.189–90.

perfect in every part; nor yet did they claim to dictate to one on questions of which they knew nothing. The position is the simplest in the world. One has had opportunities for studying questions in which they are keenly interested, but which they have not had time to study themselves. They generally know their own ignorance, and expect from one a clear and pointed statement of such information as one may be able to offer. On the other hand they expect to be credited with a certain amount of intelligence, and to be left to do the best that they can for themselves with the material which one may have been able to provide for them.[45]

In other words, the syndicate could not always monitor the results of its own work, especially where students did not find it necessary to confine their education to the extension's formal courses.

In any event, the failure of the extension to attract a regular working-class following was perceived differently by its lecturers. Some were content with its success amongst the middle classes; others, like Arthur Pillans Laurie (1861–1949) who lectured for the Cambridge extension in the 1890s, expressed disgust with its abandonment of what he regarded as its original ideals: 'The University Extension Movement soon ceased to have much contact with the working classes, and degenerated into a provision of occupation for the idle hours of the well-to-do young ladies of provincial towns. Good looks; charming manners; and a capacity for any amount of flirtation became necessary qualifications for a successful lecturer.'[46]

In 1876 the London Society for the Extension of University Teaching was founded,[47] and on 13 March 1876 the society's council of twenty-two members was elected with G. J. Goschen as its first president. In the course of its work, the London Society had to co-ordinate its activities with the numerous other educational institutions already engaged in similar activity, some of which were eager to engage extension lecturers, whereas others might be able to offer a convenient venue for the society's work. Accordingly, the council included ten representatives of local educational bodies, as well as the organizing secretary of the Women's Education Union, the chairman of the London School Board,

45 'Five years of university extension. I. The field', *Cambridge Review*, 6 February 1902.
46 A. P. Laurie, *Pictures and Politics: A Book of Reminiscences*, London: International Publishing Co., 1934, pp.67–8.
47 The London Society was registered under the Companies' Act (1867) on 12 January 1876: John Burrows, *University Adult Education in London: A Century of Achievement*, London: University of London, Senate House, 1976, p.2; and E. Welch, 'The London Society for the Extension of University Teaching, 1875–1902', in *Guildhall Studies in London History 1977–79*, Vol.III, pp.56–7.

and the registrar of the University of London.[48] Another characteristic of the society's work was the absence of a sufficient local pool of lecturers and examiners. This problem was partly solved by recruiting lecturers from other extension bodies desirous of teaching within the London metropolitan area, where the society eventually succeeded in establishing a monopoly on extension work. Co-ordination with Oxford and Cambridge was placed in the hands of the joint board, established after some delay in 1878, and whose members included H. S. Foxwell, who resigned in 1894 in protest against the appointment as a lecturer of Helen Denby, the future Mrs Bernard Bosanquet, and James E. Thorold Rogers.[49]

The society consisted of an unlimited number of subscribers who paid 2 guineas a year, and life-members, who paid 50 guineas.[50] Most of the money was used in the form of subsidies. Whereas at Cambridge, G. F. Browne, who had succeeded Stuart as secretary (1876–91), insisted that the work of the local centres should be entirely self-supporting or else aided by private subscriptions,[51] the London Society supplemented the receipts from tickets, thereby encouraging wider attendance from the lower classes. The society identified three classes of potential students and proposed to charge each a different rate: (a) persons of leisure of both sexes – £1. 1s. 0d. for a full course of twelve lectures; (b) clerks and young women employed during the day – 7s. 6d.; (c) workmen, especially artisans 5s.[52] A lecturer's fee for a full course of twelve lectures was £30, and the society was prepared to cover up to two-thirds (and sometimes during the first years, more) of any local centre's expenses, thereby allowing it to set its price for tickets.[53] Thus, during the society's first term – Michaelmas 1876 – three out of its seven courses were delivered at the London Institute at a cost of £90 in

48 The local educational bodies included Bedford College, Birkbeck Institute, City of London College, College for Men and Women, King's College, London Institute, Queen's College, Royal Institute, Working Men's College, and University College.

49 See John Burrows, 'The teaching of economics in the early days of the University Extension Movement in London 1876–1902', in *History of Economic Thought Newsletter*, No.20 (Spring 1978)

50 Welch, 'The London Society', p.57.

51 E.g. the cost of the extension work in the Northumberland mining villages in 1884–5, which had come close to £400, was covered by £80 collected in tickets and the rest by private subscription, including £150 from Cambridge: Kadish, 'University extension and the working classes', p.203.

52 Burrows, *University Adult Education in London*, p.5.

53 University of London Archives, Senate House, EMI, *Report of the Council* (1882), pp.9–12. In addition to subscriptions, financial help was received from the Gilchrist Educational Trust, the City's Common Council, the Clothworkers' Company, and – from 1894 – the LCC's Technical Education Board, and in 1879 the society launched a public appeal.

lecturers' fees and £15. 16s. in printing expenses, whereas receipts from the tickets amounted to only £23. 9s. Matters were different in Wimbledon, where H. H. Asquith taught an afternoon course on political economy (he also taught one of the courses at the London Institute on the same subject) to thirty-five middle-class students. The lecturer's fees were covered by the sale of tickets at 1 guinea each, leaving the committee with a surplus of £6. 16s. As the society's work progressed, the relative amount spent on subsidies tended to diminish from 52.8 per cent in 1876 to 13.7 per cent in 1881, rising slightly to 15 per cent in 1882.[54] Following the Technical Education Act (1889) and the Local Taxation Act (1890), the West Ham council and the LCC's Technical Education Board (TAB) undertook to support local technical education, which, in the view of Sidney Webb, chairman of the TAB, included 'anything under the sun except ancient Greek and theology',[55] thereby ensuring the society's ability to maintain its subsidies.

Young university graduates undertook extension lecturing for a variety of reasons. H. H. Asquith, who in Michaelmas 1876 taught the society's first courses in political economy, did so for pecuniary reasons: 'During my early years at the Bar,' he wrote in his memoirs,

> when briefs were few and the fees were small, I found it necessary to look about for supplementary resources. I had a growing family; and though my wife had a few hundreds a year of her own, and I myself for a time the income of my [Balliol] Fellowship [which expired in 1881], and though our domestic arrangements were of the simplest kind, there was an annual deficit to make good.[56]

Having read Greats, Asquith had a smattering of political economy, although not enough to master recent high theory employing mathematics, a deficiency of which he was made conscious by his discussions with Henry Cunynghame, another early economics lecturer for the society.

Cunynghame, the son of General Sir A. Cunynghame, had abandoned a career in the Royal Engineers to come to Cambridge, and graduated with a first in moral sciences. Like Asquith, he proceeded to read for the Bar, and for apparently similar reasons began to lecture for the London Society in Lent 1877. The younger Asquith considered him 'a first rate mathematician, an expert and ingenious economist of the school of Alfred Marshall',[57] and was instrumental in securing

54 Ibid.
55 Beatrice Webb, *Our Partnership*, London: Longmans, Green & Co., 1948, p.80.
56 H. H. Asquith, *Memories and Reflections 1852–1927*, Vol.I, London: Cassell & Co., 1928, p.66.
57 Ibid., p.58.

Cunynghame's appointment in 1894 to an assistant undersecretary-ship at the Home Office, where he was to remain for some twenty years.

Another early society lecturer, James Bonar, appears to have taken up extension lecturing largely for ideological reasons. Prior to his coming up to Balliol as a Snell exhibitioner in 1873, Bonar had obtained an MA at Glasgow with a first in classics and in mental philosophy, and had spent some time in Leipzig and in Tübingen. Bonar left Oxford with a first in Greats in 1877, and with four other friends moved into a disused beer-shop in Leman Street in the East End, where they set up a household known locally as 'The Friary'.[58] A close friend of Arnold Toynbee's, Bonar had already done some work assisting the Revd S. Barnett during his vacations from Oxford.[59] He began lecturing on political economy for the London Society in Michaelmas 1877, con-fining his work to Tower Hamlets and Shoreditch. All his lectures were held in the evening, and at times the fees were as low as 3s. a ticket, lower than the official minimum set by the society.

During the early years of the London Society, courses in political economy were in fairly regular demand both in East End/working-class and suburban/middle-class centres. Attendance and examination results were seen as encouraging. Commenting on the results of courses by Cunynghame in Putney and Asquith in Wimbledon, one examiner declared that the 'average level of the answers is considerably higher than that of [Oxford] undergraduates . . . Moreover several of the papers are distinctly better than those of the candidates for the [prize] Fellowships.'[60] However, by the early 1880s demand for political economy in suburban centres had dropped. The subject, the council stated in its 1882 annual report, 'once the most popular in the Society's list, has only been taken up at one Centre during the year, viz. Whitechapel, where Mr. Milner has for two consecutive terms gener-ously volunteered his services'.[61]

Bonar had at the same time succeeded in creating a regular study group in economics in Whitechapel.[62] He had taught political economy in Tower Hamlets every term since Michaelmas 1877. Following his course for Lent 1879, a few members of his class continued to meet

---

58 Mrs H. Barnett, *Canon Barnett: His Life, Work, and Friends*, Vol.I, London: John Murray, 1928, p.308.
59 Ibid., pp.194–5.
60 EMI, *Report of the Council* (1878).
61 On Milner's East End courses, see A. Kadish, *Apostle Arnold: The Life and Death of Arnold Toynbee 1852–1883*, Duke University Press, Durham N. C. 1986, pp.213–14.
62 Barnett, *Canon Barnett*, Vol.I, p.358. Other study groups were formed by R. E. Mitchison for the study of philosophy, and by A. P. Laurie.

once a week during the summer in order to discuss the lectures.[63] On 29 April 1879 eight of them met in the Cocoa Tree tavern on Commercial Road and founded the Adam Smith Club (later relocated at Toynbee Hall), devoted to the study and illustration of the works of Adam Smith, and the *Wealth of Nations* in particular. Bonar was appointed president and Toynbee vice-president. Some five-and-a-half years later, Bonar, who was by then serving as a junior examiner in the Civil Service Commission, spoke of twenty-one members (although attendance at the club's meetings in 1884 averaged only seven) who were about to begin work on Adam Smith's *Moral Sentiments*.[64] According to its regulations, the club was to meet at least three times during the extension lecturing terms (October to May) and fortnightly during the summer. Its members defined themselves as 'a community of spiritual aim' whose 'special intellectual purpose' was 'the discovery of the truth about the causes of poverty and wealth'. Bonar got the club to follow the Oxford practice of beginning the study of economics with Adam Smith and then proceeding beyond the *Wealth of Nations* 'to the point where our teacher [Adam Smith] would have himself arrived, if he had lived to our times. The habit of reasoning in the ways he follows, but from premises unknown to him, is his best lesson to us. ... In these times Political Economy is developing with society and with the changes in public opinion.'[65] In keeping with the extension's ambition to spread not just knowledge but the habit of systematic studies, Bonar stated: 'There is room in London, even among those alone who are called by the not very happy name of "self-educated men", for hundreds of the [Adam Smith Club-] kind. Let him among us who feels called to be a founder go forth from us to create them!' As in the case of the Northumberland miners, if such forms of self-education did develop they were not monitored by the society, whose reports make no reference to them. Finally, while the club's rules strictly forbade party politics, and although the members agreed on few practical solutions other than the desirability of productive co-operatives, they were all in their 'other capacities' firm Liberals.

Alfred Milner (1846–1929), another of Toynbee's close friends and Bonar's contemporary at Balliol, had, like Asquith, won a prize fellowship (at New College in 1877) and had been admitted to the Bar in

---

63 'The Adam Smith Club, Tower Hamlets: an address by the President, 28 October 1884', London 1884.

64 It should be noted that the size of Bonar's extension classes diminished from 26 in Michaelmas 1877 to 10 in Lent 1879. When in Michaelmas the price of tickets was reduced from 5s. to 3s., the number of students rose to 22.

65 Jones, *The Christian Socialist Revival*, pp.106–7.

1881. But, as with Bonar, his extension work was embarked upon for reasons other than financial, as his waiver of fees indicates. During the early 1880s, the rising popularity of Henry George amongst England's working classes in general and the trade-union movement in particular, led middle-class intellectuals whose politics tended towards the reformism of the Radical Liberals to try to revive the allegiance of the working classes to the liberal concept of progress, lest they commit themselves to the false and dangerous doctrines of radical socialism. The fear that the working classes might abandon gradual reform and class-co-operation in favour of a doctrine based on the belief in the inevitability of class strife lay behind much of the early work of Toynbee and his friends, and influenced the subject and content of extension courses in political economy.

Of the Cambridge extension's economics lecturers, only Symes and Cox ventured beyond mainstream theory. Symes had been an early supporter of Bradlaugh's Land Reform League and a founder-member of the Land Reform Union, but he did not go beyond land-value taxation, and his economics textbook, published in 1884, was criticized by S. Headlam as conservative. His eventual position on socialism - socialism for the young and old, individualism for the mature[66] – was fairly standard fare for the new liberalism of the 1880s. Harold Cox (1859–1936) had been considered during the period of his extension lecturing (1882–3) to be dangerously close to socialism. He had been greatly influenced by Edward Carpenter, and had even worked for a while as an agricultural labourer. But after teaching four extension courses, he was appointed Professor of Mathematics at Aligarh, from whence he returned 'a staunch adherent of the orthodox school of economics'.[67] The rest of the Cambridge extension's lecturers of the 1880s and 1890s[68] stuck to the standard version of modified Millian economics with some Marshall thrown in, although they did adopt a more apologetic tone when discussing the application of economic laws. H. S. Mundahl,[69] the most active economics lecturer during the 1890s, explained the limits of applicability thus:

66 Coats, 'John Elliotson Symes'.
67 *The Times*, 2 May 1936.
68 They included William Ritchie Sorley (1885–1935), who as a Toynbee Trust lecturer taught for one term (Michaelmas 1887) in Middlesborough and Darlington; Henry Smethurst Mundahl (1865–1938); and Alfred Milnes (1849–1921), an Oxford man who taught an extension course on behalf of Cambridge in Leicester in Michaelmas 1894.
69 After reading mathematics at Cambridge, Mundahl was called to the Bar in 1891. He practised on the north-eastern circuit, and was appointed an extension lecturer on 16 November 1893. He lectured in the north-east from 1894 to 1896.

We realize today that what are called the laws of Political Economy are not rigid and unalterable propositions, but are dependent to a very large extent upon conditions of time and circumstances.[70]

We must consider the subject not merely from the standpoint of the 'economic man', but from that of man as he actually is with his moral and religious views, and as we hope he may become.[71]

Economic laws are flexible statements of probabilities relative to particular times and circumstances.[72]

How far is *laissez-faire* an actual working rule today? How far desirable that it should so continue. Considerable inroads have been made by legislation, while the presumption is in favour of freedom, laissez-faire, though a good working rule is not a scientific doctrine.[73]

A similarly cautious note is evident in the syllabus of a political economy course prepared for the London Society by Lawrence P. Jacks (1860–1955), the future principal of Manchester College, London, and at the time assistant to the Revd Stopford Brooke at the Unitarian Bedford Chapel, Bloomsbury, who lectured for the society during Michaelmas 1887 and Lent 1888:

Each science deals with a certain *aspect* of things; thus Mathematics deals with things under their aspect of quantity, Physics under that of motion, and so on. Political Economy deals with things under their aspect of *wealth* . . . [A]ll science gives *laws*, and Political Economy gives the laws of wealth . . . Its laws do not *prescribe* any course of action; but are *general statements of facts and tendencies*. . . though dealing with the pursuit of wealth, it does not *prescribe* that pursuit.[74]

Jacks also pointed out that the study of the *science* of political economy must precede the discussion of the *art* of political economy, hence the reason for the abstract and value-free nature of most introductory courses. However, the advent of new unionism and the perceived

70 H. S. Mundahl, *Syllabus of a Course of Twelve Lectures on Political Economy*, Cambridge: Extension, 1894, p.3.
71 Ibid., p.5.
72 Ibid.
73 H. S. Mundahl, *Syllabus of a Course of Lectures on the Ideals of Life Being a Discussion of the Economic and Social Views of Carlyle, Kingsley and Matthew Arnold*, Cambridge: Extension, 1897, p.12. See also Alfred Milnes, *Syllabus of a Course of Twelve Lectures on the Making and Sharing of Wealth*, Cambridge: Extension, 1894.
74 Lawrence P. Jacks, *Political Economy: Syllabus of a Course of Lectures*, London: Extension, 1887.

growing militancy of the working classes necessitated, in the view of some lecturers, a discussion of practical aspects of labour-related problems before students possessed a firm grasp of elementary theory, for fear that they might otherwise prove too impatient.

The growing sense of urgency concerning the disintegration of the working class–Liberal alliance characteristic of Toynbee's circle was especially in evidence during the 1880s in the Oxford extension. The Oxford Standing Committee of the Delegates of the Local Examinations was founded on 15 June 1878 for the purpose of organizing extension work.[75] Rather than repeat the method employed by the Cambridge extension, A. H. D. Acland (1847–1926), the Oxford Committee's secretary, tried – with Toynbee's help – to reach working-class audiences by a more direct route.[76] In 1878 Acland joined the Oxford Co-operative Society, intending to persuade the co-operative movement to invest its educational fund in extension-like adult education. His main concern in addressing the working classes was a matter of content rather than form, and he was quite prepared to abandon the university-like features insisted upon at Cambridge if by so doing he might make the lectures he was offering more attractive. Acland also maintained that the 'more general topics of social and economical interest which touch the lives of all who want to live useful and capable lives as any ordinary citizen' were more important for adult education than scientific or technical subjects.[77] There was little point, then, in extension courses striving to approximate a university term's work, and Acland was prepared to offer co-operative societies three-lecture courses on appropriate subjects, hoping to stimulate regular demand for extension courses. Furthermore, the co-operative societies were expected to act as local extension centres, employing their educational funds for the purpose, and thereby overcoming one of the main handicaps of working-class centres.

Acland and Toynbee's vision of the education of the citizen was presented to the 1882 co-operative annual conference, held at Acland's instigation in Oxford. At the time, co-operation – and especially co-operative production – still featured as one of the main tenets of the liberal vision of the future of the working classes. Rather than

75 Minutes of the committee are in the Oxford Extension Archives, currently deposited with the University Archives. On the Oxford extension movement, see A. Kadish, 'Oxford economists and the young extension movement', in T. Rowley (ed.), *The Oxford Region*, Oxford: Oxford University, Department of External Studies, 1980; and A. Kadish, *The Oxford Economists in the Late Nineteenth Century*, Oxford: Oxford University Press, 1982.
76 Kadish, *Apostle Arnold*, ch.7.
77 A. H. D. Acland, 'The education of co-operators and citizens', in *The Co-operative Wholesale Society Ltd. Annual [and] Diary 1885*, Manchester: Co-operative Printing Society, 1885, p.423.

appropriating the means of production by force, workers could, using productive co-operation, transform the existing system into an industrial democracy legally and peaceably, and who was better suited to show the way than the distributive co-operators who had at their disposal the profits of, and the credit afforded to, the co-operative societies? Acland and Toynbee shared a vision whereby a more equitable distribution of wealth, accomplished largely by means of collective self-help coupled with middle-class selfless guidance, would lead to the emergence of a truly democratic society in which the ideal of social harmony would be realized through conscious inter-class co-operation. The lukewarm reception with which their plan was received indicated the gap between their ideals and the more materialistic outlook of most co-operators. Nevertheless, Acland persisted in his efforts, including giving lectures to co-operative societies on 'The Systematic Education of Co-operators in their Work as Co-operators and Citizens' and 'The Education of Citizens'.[78]

Despite official endorsement of the scheme by the co-operative movement's leaders, local response was uneven. In his first lecture tour (December 1882-January 1883), Acland succeeded in drawing only a small audience in Manchester, whereas at Hebden Bridge it was reported that 'several young men have signified their intention of joining the classes [for self-study under the auspices of the local co-operative society] should they be formed'.[79] Undaunted, Acland recruited a number of young graduates to join him in his lecturing, including Michael Ernest Sadler (1861–1943), who had been a member of an informal study group which had met at Acland's home to discuss social questions.[80] Acland appears to have designated Sadler as the next secretary of the Oxford extension,[81] and, having decided early in 1885 to stand for Parliament, Acland succeeded in arranging Sadler's appointment on 30 April 1885.

Sadler, who had graduated from Oxford with a first in Greats in 1884, brought the Oxford extension closer to the tried organizational approach of Cambridge and London, but without abandoning Acland's ideals. Intent upon attracting as many students as possible, Sadler instituted courses which lasted for only six lectures, the idea being that

78 The *Co-operative News* , 28 October and 2 December 1882.
79 Ibid., 20 January, 14 April, 21 April, 28 April, and 5 May 1883.
80 Kadish, *Oxford Economists*, pp.16–17. See *Committee for University Extension*, minutes of meeting, 22 October 1885. In 1885, together with Acland, Sadler delivered a course of 12 lectures on 'Labour Questions' in Ancoats, attended by an average of 270 working men. Sadler was invited back to give 4 lectures with Mackinder on a 'scientific or economical subject'.
81 Michael Sadler, *Michael Ernest Sadler: A Memoir by his Son*, London: Constable, 1949, p.51.

this would allow local centres to commence their work with relatively cheap courses intended to whet local appetite for full-length courses. This was contrary to the principle adopted by Cambridge and London, namely that extension work was to resemble as nearly as possible a university term's work, with courses no shorter than ten lectures and nine classes. Matters were exacerbated when Oxford awarded certificates to the students of the six-lecture courses, thereby undermining the efforts of the other extension bodies to have their certificates recognized officially (e.g. by the Board of Education). It was not until 1890 that Sadler agreed to conform by awarding certificates only to students who had completed a full twelve-lecture course or two short ones.

Sadler brought with him to the Oxford extension most of Oxford's young economists, his fellow-members of the Oxford Economic Society, a study group set up to discuss its members' work on lines similar to the history seminar. 'The greater part of the lecturing staff', Sadler wrote in his annual report for 1886–7,

> will always be composed of young Graduates who are glad to have a University Extension engagement for a year or two after taking their degrees, partly because of the practical experience in teaching which they gain from it, and partly because it gives them in each year twenty-eight weeks of unbroken vacation in which they can continue their studies more uninterruptedly than would be possible in almost any other remunerative occupation.[82]

For many there was an added attraction, expressed by the Revd William Hudson Shaw, one of the extension's most popular lecturers and a protégé of Acland's, in a conference of representatives of local committees in 1887: 'I know that there are some of us who, on the invitation of the Delegates, have undertaken this work because we conceived that it might in some degree assist the working-men of England.'[83] At the same conference, Roberts argued that 'In the early stages the work is chiefly of a missionary kind, but we have now reached the point in which something must be done towards further systematization of the work.'[84] '[I]f it is not a missionary movement,' Hudson Shaw replied, 'there are a good many of us who do not want to have anything to do with it'.[85]

Initially the teaching of economics by the Oxford extension was

82 *Oxford University Extension: Annual Report for the Year 1886–7*, Oxford: Delegacy for Extra-Mural Studies, 1887.
83 *Oxford University Extension Lectures: Report of a Conference of Representatives of the Local Committees, Oxford April 20–21st. 1887*, Oxford 1887, p.74.
84 Ibid., p.87.
85 Ibid., p.75.

greatly facilitated by the Toynbee Trust. Set up as a memorial to Toynbee, the trust subsidized extension economics courses delivered by resident lecturers who were expected, in addition to teaching, to undertake research into an aspect of local economic conditions and report their findings to the trust, which would help with publication. The trust was not specifically meant to engage Oxford men, but with the decline in economics lecturing in the Cambridge extension, all the trust's lecturers except the first, W. R. Sorley, were Oxford extension lecturers whose courses for the trust were delivered under Oxford auspices. They included L. L. Price (twice), H. Ll. Smith, and W. A. S. Hewins.[86]

Not unlike Cambridge, political economy and related subjects, such as economic and social history, were taught by extension lecturers whose formal acquaintance with the subject was limited, as was their interest in advancing beyond the reading of Adam Smith and J. S. Mill that they had done for Greats or modern history. Such was the case with J. A. R. Marriott;[87] Charles Henry Roberts, then fellow and tutor at Exeter College, and Cosmo Gordon Lang, who lectured mainly to northern co-operative societies.[88] But as demand for political economy decreased, as it had at Cambridge, and many of the early lecturers drifted into other, more promising, jobs, the teaching of the subject was left largely in the hands of the more committed Oxford economists – H. Ll. Smith (until 1890), Price, Hewins, and J. A. Hobson. Even so, the demand for political economy proved insufficient to offer them full employment, forcing them to teach additional subjects, such as history and, in Hobson's instance, English literature, a subject with which he began his extension lecturing in 1887.

The ideological bias of the young Oxford economists, as well as the peculiarities of the Oxford curriculum, are in evidence in the extension syllabuses. To begin with, the employment of economic history to explain current conditions, and the relativist approach to economic theory, were more evident than elsewhere. Some of the courses, especially Price's and Ll. Smith's, contain some elementary theory, but even then it is quickly brought to bear on current problems.[89] The same was true of Hobson, who stated in 1891:

---

86 Kadish, *Apostle Arnold*, pp.230–1, and *Oxford Economists*, pp.88–94.
87 See Sir John Marriott, *Memories of Four Score Years*, London and Glasgow: Blackie & Son, 1946, p.55.
88 J. G. Lockhart, *Cosmo Gordon Lang*, London: Hodder & Stoughton, 1949, pp. 7–8.
89 H. Ll. Smith, *Wealth and Industry*, Oxford: University Extension Lectures, 1888, and *Makers of Political Economy*, Oxford 1888; L. L. Price, *Making and Division of Wealth, Trades Unions, Co-operation and Free Trade*, Oxford: Extension, 1886.

Surely the unpopularity of Political Economy is really due to the fact that it has been too commonly approached from the abstract, metaphysical point of view, instead of from that concrete, present-day statement of living facts and forces which would recommend it to the attention of students whose interests are not purely academic, but in the first and fullest those of citizens.[90]

Hobson suggested that courses should commence with the inductive approach, to be followed rather than preceded by theory:

First, let the student learn to group for themselves those present industrial facts, and watch the movements of those industrial forces which must have a direct personal interest for each of them as workers and citizens. Then turn the light of the past upon those facts by a study of industrial history. Then last of all let them enter the study of the principles of the science of Political Economy that they may inform with the true order of scientific law the loose or partially related facts they have gathered so as to learn the meaning of progress from the industrial point of view.

This was a position that Hobson was to modify as he came to lay greater importance on the value of deductive theory, both in his own work and in his extension teaching.[91] Hence, while the Oxford extension lecturers were as adamant as their Cambridge contemporaries that the proper teaching of economics did not allow short cuts and that the pressure for 'clearness and simplicity' be resisted wherever 'scientific accuracy does not admit it', their methodological position suggested an approach to the teaching of elementary political economy that was not purely, or even mainly, theoretical.

The logic of the historical/empirical approach was further enhanced by the adoption of the relativist view of economic theory. Past theories were not taught as timeless abstract constructions, but, as Hewins pointed out when lecturing on mercantilism,

There were circumstances which justify or explain the appearance of such a system: it arose in the struggle of men to grapple with the practical difficulties of the time. In economics we must constantly bear in mind that we are for the most part dealing with the

90 *Oxford University Extension Gazette*, March 1891.
91 See his *The Economics of Distribution*, New York: Macmillan, 1900, based on lectures delivered at the LSE in 1897 and his extension course, 'The making and sharing of wealth' (1896). On Hobson's extension teaching see A. Kadish, 'Rewriting the *Confessions*: Hobson and the Extension Movement', in M. Freeden (ed.) *Reappraising J. A. Hobson. Humanism and Welfare*, London: Unwin Hyman, 1990, pp.137–66.

ordinary business of ordinary men and women; and if we wish to explain the origin or understand the development of any particular theory, we must find out what was going on at the time in the world of ordinary people.[92]

The reasons for studying past theories were also summed up by W. J. Ashley, who produced a syllabus for advanced students as part of an unsuccessful attempt to encourage systematic home reading at an advanced level:

> Two courses are open to the more advanced student of Economics. He may take some two or three recent treaties of repute, such as those by *F. A. Walker, Sidgwick* and *Marshall*, compare their conclusions where they differ and endeavour to think out for himself some decision on the questions at issue; or he may seek to trace the broad outlines of the historical development of Economic doctrine . . . Either course will supply a useful mental discipline, – but the latter will probably be found more fruitful for the understanding both of modern social problems, and of the nature of economic enquiry.[93]

As might be expected, the Oxford extension lecturers were, as a rule, more emphatic about the practical application of economics. 'Political Economy', Price taught, 'is said by some to be *neutral* in the matter of social reform . . . this view is often *exaggerated*. Theory and practice are closely connected. The best theorist is the most practical man.'[94] They had all been taught the standard formula – as stated by Ll. Smith, for example – that the 'Political Economist does not profess to approve or disapprove of the things which he describes. He is in the position of an investigator, not a judge.'[95] But at the same time, they did not keep back their ideological views. Many of them were favourably disposed towards some form of collectivism, and their criticism of socialism was usually qualified: 'Contemporary scientific socialism', Price declared, 'is vague in its schemes for the future but positive in its criticism of the present.'[96] The radical measures called for by the socialists were unnecessary and dangerous. But, Price believed, the future may well see the adoption of a combination of the best features of state socialism,

92 W. A. S. Hewins, *Economic History chiefly in the Seventeenth Century* (1889).
93 W. J. Ashley, *Home Reading in Economics (for Advanced Students)*, Oxford: Extension, 1889.
94 L. L. Price, *Great English Economists: Their Life and Teaching*, Oxford: Extension, 1888, lecture 6.
95 H. Ll.Smith, *Elementary Course of Reading in Political Economy*, printed at Oxford 1889.
96 L. L. Price, *Some Social and Industrial Movements in England*, Oxford: Extension, 1893.

co-operation, and trade-unionism.[97] Unionism was regarded as a progressive movement likely to advance rather than impede the cause of industrial peace and productive co-operatives were still seen, despite their unimpressive record, as 'means of permanently consolidating the interest of labour and management, of lessening unnecessary friction between various parties in production and of avoiding the waste caused by industrial war'.[98] 'The truths of political economy or of economic history', according to the *Oxford Magazine* following the extension's 1889 summer meeting, 'ought to be capable of treatment apart from the disputes of the day; but the abstraction necessary is difficult, and especially difficult to young and enthusiastic Bachelors of Arts, whose success or failure is measured for all political purposes by the appreciation of their audiences . . . [I]t is well to spread the light so long as the light is not coloured.'[99]

However, Oxford failed to sustain a significant demand for courses in economics. The same problem at Cambridge meant that the few economics scholars who were associated with the extension, such as Arthur Berry (1862–1929), Alfred William Flux (1867–1942),[100] David Hutchison MacGregor (1877–1953),[101] and Arthur Lyon Bowley (1869–1957),[102] were rarely given the opportunity to lecture on economic theory. The same cannot be said of economic and social history. While Marshall was struggling to separate the study of economic theory from that of other subjects, and have it recognized as an autonomous discipline, the extension continued to teach economic theory as part of a more comprehensive programme. And although it had failed to create

97 L. L. Price, *Three Chapters of Economic History,* Oxford: Extension, 1890, a course taught at the summer meeting.
98 M. E. Sadler, *The Economic Force of Combination,* Oxford: Extension, 1890, delivered at the summer meeting. See also W. A. S. Hewins, *The English Labourer Past and Present,* Oxford: Extension, 1889.
99 *Oxford Magazine,* 6 November 1889.
100 Holder of the Marshall Prize (1889), and fellow of St John's (1889–95), Flux taught extension courses on 'Electricity and magnetism', 'The Solar System', and 'Sound, light, and colour'.
101 Having gained a first in moral sciences Part I in 1900 and Part II in 1901, Macgregor was a university teacher in political economy from 1904–8. He offered to teach for the extension any 'Economic subject, or . . . one of a few Moral Sciences subjects, or on Lord Macaulay': BEMS 55/21. He taught mainly economic and social history.
102 Holder of the Cobden and Adam Smith Prizes, Bowley applied for extension work in 1899 at the time he abandoned his short career as a schoolmaster. In his initial application, dated 21 May 1899 (BEMS 55/9), he enquired about 'any present opening for Political Economy courses at any of your centres'. After receiving the extension's reply, he offered courses on 'The Growth of England's Foreign Trade and The Progress of the Working Classes, and he would also be prepared to lecture on Astronomy': BEMS 55/1, 5 June 1899.

demand for systematic economic studies, the extension preserved its ideal in its summer meetings, which, following the Oxford example, were established as a means of supplementing the work already done in the regular courses.[103] A series of lectures in modern English history delivered during the summer meeting of 1893 included 'The Influence of the Early Socialists on English Social Reform (by M. E. Sadler), 'The Industrial Revolution' (Cunningham), and a special class on elementary economics (Berry). It was the conclusion of one of the participants that

> we all felt the fundamental connection between the various subjects, and realized more vividly than we had done before how many apparently unconnected causes had been quietly working together to produce our present civilization. We also became more impressed with the difficulties, social, economic, and political of our own times, and we caught from many of the lecturers some of that keen enthusiasm which alone can aid in the solution of complex problems, and some of that patient faith in the ultimate triumph of truth over error, or good over evil which has been the mainstay of reformers in the past and must be the essential of effective work in the future.[104]

Another statement concerning the status of economic theory in the study of economic phenomena may be found in an outline of a course on economic history which Edward Jenks (1861–1929) delivered at Hull (1893–4). Jenks had read law (first, 1886) and history (first, 1887) at King's,[105] and, at the time of his extension teaching, had also taught as Professor of Law at University College, Liverpool, where he is said to have 'championed the cause of humanism in legal education in opposition to the view that a lawyer . . . is perfectly equipped if he has learnt the technique of his trade'.[106] In his introduction Jenks suggested 'three chief ways in which economy may be studied':

> (i) *Ethically*: – i.e. we may lay down certain objects to be attained, and examine actual or proposed economic practices to see if they tend towards attainment of these objects.
> (ii) *Analytically*: – i.e. we may take existing economic phenomena

103 Roberts, *Eighteen Years*, p.88.
104 The *Cambridge Review*, 12 October 1893.
105 Jenks had previously qualified as a solicitor (1883), and upon graduating from Cambridge, he was called to the Bar. At Cambridge he won the La Bas and the Thirwall Prizes, and following his degrees, he was appointed director of studies in law and history at Jesus College, lecturer at Pembroke, and fellow of King's (1889–95). On his later career, see R. W. Lee's article in the *DNB 1931–1940*, Oxford University Press 1949.
106 Ibid.

as facts, and endeavour to find out their causes and to understand the relations between them.

(iii) *Historically*: – i.e. we may trace the gradual development of our system from its earliest beginnings to the present day. The last will be our plan here. But even this plan is capable of more than one treatment. We may make our history either

(i) *Topical*: – i.e. we may take special departments of the economy, such as *money*, *agriculture*, etc., and trace the history of each separately. This treatment ensures, perhaps, exactness; but it is apt to be dry and to lend to overlapping.

(ii) *Periodic*: – i.e. we may divide our history into more or less definite periods, and endeavour to get a *general* idea of the economic condition of each, giving more time to the more important features.

We will adopt the last.[107]

Jenks then implied that current economic conditions could be analysed without separate recourse to economic theory. The establishment of the economics tripos resulted in the opposite approach. The empirical/ inductive and the historical methods became primarily associated with the study of history, whereas current economic phenomena were studied from a primarily theoretical point of view.

Jenks's choice was in keeping with the importance attached in the history tripos to 'special periods', and the growing recognition of the relevance of economic and social history.[108] Another important stage in the historian's training, the 'topical' or monographic approach, became the standard form of the initial works of many of Marshall's students, who, having accepted the *Principles* as virtually the final statement on general economic theory, turned to the study of its verification in various sectors of the economy. The monographic approach is evident, for instance, in Bowley's courses, which reflect his early work on wages. Carefully analysed empirical data and complex interrelated factors replaced the dogmatic theoretical statements of the 1870s; for example, in Bowley's lecture, 'Historical Causes of the Growth of English Wages during the XIXth Century', delivered at the 1900 summer meeting:

General movements of wages are connected with broad changes in the demand for or supply of labour and with important changes of retail and wholesale prices. At those dates at which workers in a trade have been organized, wages have risen or hours have been

107 Edward Jenks, *Syllabus of a Course of Lectures on the Outlines of English Economic History*, Cambridge: Extension, 1894.

108 See also G. H. Leonard in the *Cambridge Review*, 12 October 1887; and J. H. Clapham, *Syllabus of a Course of Twelve Lectures on England before the Norman Conquest*, Cambridge: Extension, 1898.

reduced. Wages have often risen in unprogressive trades through the influence of progress in wages in neighbouring industries. A rising standard of living has tended to steady wages, while hours of labour have very generally been reduced without causing any fall in weekly earnings.[109]

As for ideological content, the spirit of radical reformism may be found in the Cambridge extension mainly in the statements of its economic and social historians, such as John Holland Rose (1855–1942).[110] In referring to the social consequences of industrialization and their effect on the political system, Rose described misery as the 'chief propelling power of democracy in England'. 'Our commerce and agriculture were apparently never so flourishing as in the year of Waterloo, but the shew of prosperity was gained at the expense of industrial and social changes which were deeply resented by our own working-classes.' In a manner reminiscent of Toynbee and the later works of the Hammonds, Rose wrote of the 'social system warped and strained by an industrial revolution', and 'the industrial and agricultural changes which rendered the first half of this century forever memorable depressed the status of the poor even while they enhanced the wealth of the community'.[111] Not that the young Marshailian economists were necessarily less committed to reformism, but the language accepted as appropriate for scientific statements in economics had become increasingly technical and value-free compared with the rhetoric still relatively common amongst economic and social historians.

The decline in the demand for courses in economic theory in the Cambridge and Oxford extensions did not affect the London Society, where the ideological content was more pronounced than elsewhere.

---

109 In *Life and Thought in England in the Nineteenth Century: Syllabus of Lectures and Time Table*, Cambridge: Extension, 1900, pp.31–2. Other lectures at the 1900 summer meeting included J. H. Clapham, 'The Rise of the Great Cities'; Ernest Aves, 'Trade Unions'; and A. C. Pigou, 'The Growth of Life and the Growth of Wealth'. See also A. L. Bowley, *Syllabus of a Short Course of Six Lectures on the Progress of the Working Class in the Nineteenth Century*, Cambridge: Extension, 1900.

110 After a long and successful association with the extension, Rose was appointed the first Cambridge Reader in Modern History in 1911, and in 1919 the first Vere Harmsworth Professor of Naval History. See *The Times*, 4 March 1942; and John Peile, *Biographical Register of Christ's College, Vol.II 1666–1905*, Cambridge, 1915, p.642.

111 J. Holland Rose, *The Rise and Growth of Democracy in Great Britain*, Chicago and New York: H. S. Stone, 1898, pp. 19, 21, 38, and 218. For an even stronger statement, see Jenks's editorial in the *Independent Review*, August 1903.

The policy of the Technical Education Board (TEB) was to encourage local education institutes to become regular customers of the society. Consequently, after 1890 an increasing number of extension courses on a wide variety of subjects were delivered in such institutes as Royal Holloway College, Morley College, Regent Street Polytechnic, Borough Polytechnic, etc., to which were added the university settlements as permanent local extension centres.

Since most of the above were situated within working-class neighbourhoods, the society's lecturers were spared the frustration experienced elsewhere of insufficiently regular contact with the lower classes. Not that the experience was uniformly encouraging. At one end of the scale there were courses such as George Armitage Smith's at Poplar in Michaelmas 1886 (tickets 2s. 6d.). The audience, the lecturer informed the society,

> as in the case of the other East End centres, was drawn largely from the working classes, and included workers engaged in shipbuilding, boiler-makers, coopers, sawyers, and dock-labourers. The class following the lecture was so thoroughly appreciated by the audience, as often to be protracted to a late hour. Questions were freely asked of the lecturer, and animated and vigorous discussions took place which showed how real was the interest taken by the students and their anxiety to test the principles of political economy by the facts of everyday life.[112]

At the other end of the scale there were courses such as Hobson's five lectures on 'Industrial Problems' at Mansfield House in Canning Town (Michaelmas 1896). Hobson identified two major handicaps to lecturing in such a neighbourhood:

> One is the difficulty of getting men and women wearied with heavy manual labour to give serious study to any subject which cannot be ... recommended to their interest by magic lantern or other sensational approach. The other, especially applicable to lectures upon economic and social subjects, is the fact that most persons possessed of some initial interest in these topics are accustomed to a far more dramatic and, as they think, more practical treatment by propagandist lectures in various kinds of political societies to which they belong.[113]

By then Hobson had begun to recognize the utility of approaching the analysis of current economic problems from a theoretical point of departure, hence his annoyance with the 'popular prejudice against

---

112 *Report of the Council* (1886). See also Roberts, *Eighteen Years*, p.36.
113 Lecturers' reports: EM 2/23/23.

abstract economics'[114] which he detected in some of his audiences. Other lecturers, however, failed to undergo a similar conversion. Armitage-Smith's courses, for instance, became increasingly polemical in content. His mid-1880s course on political economy consisted of a fairly straightforward introduction to theory,[115] whereas his 1890s courses – 'The Industrial Revolution in England' (Cambridge, 1896), and 'Social and Economic Problems: Being a Discussion of Some Economic Aspects of Socialism' (London, 1892) – dealt largely with liberal alternatives to state socialism, and especially the principle of state intervention, which in effect constituted a rationale for a welfare state with a mixed economy.

The relative popularity of extension economics in the metropolitan area may well reflect, at least in part, the quality of the lecturers. The Oxford and Cambridge extensions found it extremely difficult to hold on to their more experienced lecturers, who, in order to make a living from extension lecturing, had to travel extensively during the winter and enjoy a robust constitution without the prospect of permanency or promotion beyond senior staff lecturer.[116] Whereas the society's main economics lecturers – Hobson, Armitage-Smith, and Philip Henry Wicksteed – lived and worked in London. They taught and lectured extensively, and were not dependent on their extension work either as their sole or even their main source of income, or as the only venue available for their lecturing. There were other institutes, such as Essex Hall, with which both Wicksteed and Hobson were associated.[117] During the late 1880s and early 1890s Essex Hall housed the headquarters of the British and Foreign Unitarian Society, and the Ethical Society of which Hobson was an active member (as was Bonar). The Ethical Society sponsored Sunday lectures, with Hobson as a frequent and regular speaker, and from 1891 it ran an extension centre where courses were given by A. W. Flux, John Rae, Wicksteed, and Hobson.[118] Not surprisingly, the London lecturers' extension careers were longer and busier. Hobson lectured for the London Society during every season but one from Michaelmas 1887 to Michaelmas 1897, sometimes

---

114 Lecturers' reports: EM 2/23/24, Lent 1897, report on a course at Westbourne Park on 'The Making and Sharing of Wealth'. For the new place of theory in Hobson's courses, see his *Syllabus of a Course of Ten Lectures on the Making and Sharing of Wealth*, London, 1896.

115 G. Armitage Smith, *Political Economy: Syllabus of a Second Course of Lectures*, London, 1886.

116 See Roberts, *Eighteen Years*, p.105; and Mackinder and Sadler, *University Extension*, pp.96–7.

117 On Essex Hall, see Mortimer Rowe, *The Story of Essex Hall*, London: Lindsey Press, 1959.

118 For details, see the Annual Reports of the London Ethical Society in the British Museum.

up to six and even seven courses a term. After his father's death and consequent economic security, the frequency and number of his extension courses diminished, but he continued lecturing until 1909–10 (his lecturing for the Oxford extension was from 1887 to 1896).[119] Wicksteed began lecturing for the society in 1887–8, and continued to do so for nearly every term until 1915–16 (he taught his last course in economics in 1903–4). He also lectured for the Oxford extension (1895–1918), Cambridge (1896–1916), Liverpool, and Manchester, mainly on literary subjects (Dante, Wordsworth, etc.) but also some economics.[120] Their reputations were such that they could count on a steady demand for their courses, which in any event were not confined to economics.

The London lecturers were largely self-taught, which could prove a problem, as in the case of Hobson. In spite of the fact that Hobson had been given a free hand to teach economics for the Oxford extension, Foxwell for a number of years refused to allow Hobson to add economics to the subjects on which he lectured for the society, for fear that he would teach that 'thrift is morally and socially a vice'.[121] Foxwell also thought that Armitage-Smith, who succeeded him in 1898 as lecturer for the Institute of Bankers, was a mere hack,[122] but that Wicksteed's lack of formal training was an actual advantage in teaching for the extension. In writing to Roberts in 1901, he described one of Wicksteed's courses as

a model of what a University Extension Course should be. It is a kind of study in common sense and moral wisdom the purpose of which is to teach the students to apply exact thought and high principles to the ordinary conduct of life. I might call it a discourse on practical wisdom, a sort of ethical sermon, but preached by a man with the keenest scientific interest, exceptionally wide culture, and a most attractive personality, and brilliantly illustrated from the whole range of ordinary experience, and from many literatures. I cannot imagine any course more genuinely stimulating and educative to ordinary folks, and yet it could hardly take its place in the formal curriculum of a University. This is what I mean when I say that it appears to me a typical Extension course.[123]

119 The figures are from the London Society's lecturers' reports and the Oxford Extension's Historical Register, DES/RG/7/1.
120 For the full list, see C. H. Herford, *Philip Henry Wicksteed: His Life and Work*, London: J. M. Dent & Sons, 1931, appendix I.
121 Note appended to draft of letter from Foxwell to Muirhead, 11 December 1891: Foxwell papers, 87/122.
122 Foxwell to Keynes, 20 January 1898: Keynes papers 1/38, Marshall Library, Cambridge.
123 Foxwell to Roberts, 12 April 1901: BEMS 55/29. Foxwell knew Wicksteed from the Economic Circle. See Herford, *Wicksteed*, pp.206–7.

Thus, as if stating the obvious, Foxwell had dismissed the extension's original ideal of ensuring that its work resembled as closely as possible university studies; or it may be seen as a judgement on the evolution of the study of economics, which had developed to such a point that it was practically unteachable outside the universities.

4

THE TEACHING OF ECONOMICS AT THE QUEEN'S COLLEGES IN IRELAND (BELFAST, CORK, GALWAY), 1845–1900

Thomas A. Boylan and Timothy P. Foley

After the establishment of the Whately Chair in 1832 at Trinity College, Dublin, the most important contribution to the teaching of political economy in Ireland was the foundation of the Queen's Colleges in 1845. Each of the three colleges at Belfast, Cork, and Galway, had, from the outset, a Chair of Jurisprudence and Political Economy. The founding of the colleges was followed five years later by the establishment of their degree-granting institution, the Queen's University. The decision to establish the Queen's Colleges at this time was not an isolated event. It was, in fact, an integral part of a new policy of conciliation, implemented by Peel in 1843, to counteract Daniel O'Connell's campaign for repeal of the Union between Great Britain and Ireland. The problem which Peel sought to solve by the establishment of the Queen's Colleges – the inadequate provision of higher education in Ireland – had a long history, and involved not only questions of education, but also of religion, politics, and economics. It was a source of profound periodic conflict in Irish public debate and in Anglo-Irish relations throughout the nineteenth century. To understand the particular circumstances surrounding the establishment of the Queen's Colleges and their subsequent development requires an examination, albeit brief, of the troubled and protracted history of university education in Ireland. Part I, therefore, provides an outline of the Irish university question as historical background to the founding of the Queen's Colleges, the actual establishment of which is described in part II. Part III examines the structure and evolution of the teaching of political economy within the Queen's Colleges from 1849, their first year of operation, to the 1890s. Part IV contains a brief biographical profile of the holders of the Chairs of Political Economy in each of the three colleges.

111

IRISH UNIVERSITY EDUCATION: THE HISTORICAL BACKGROUND

The modern university question in Ireland emerged in the last quarter of the eighteenth century. At this time the only university institution in Ireland was the University of Dublin, centred on its single constituent college, Trinity College, which had been established 'for the education . . . of youths . . . that they may be the better assisted in the study of the liberal arts and in the cultivation of virtue and religion'.[1] The religion in question was that of the Anglican Church, and a central role of Trinity College was to provide a supply of clergy to that Church. Its members comprised the bulk of the landed aristocracy and the professions, and they were unquestionably dominant socially and politically throughout the nineteenth century. Trinity College was overwhelmingly Anglican, and its Provost and fellows had to be of that faith. In addition, with the accession of Charles I, students were required to attend Anglican services, and all candidates aspiring to degrees had to take the Oath of Supremacy along with a number of other anti-Catholic declarations. Admission to the college was never, in fact, formally denied to either Catholics or Protestant dissenters, but they were, in effect, legally excluded. In the course of the 1780s public debate in Ireland about the university question centred on a number of possible solutions which were put forward for consideration. These included: (i) the 'opening' of Trinity College to Catholics and Protestant dissenters by the abolition of religious tests; (ii) the establishment of a new college or colleges within the University of Dublin; and (iii) the foundation of new university institutions independent of the existing university. In the event nothing was to emerge from the deliberations of the 1780s, but in the following decade, under the impetus of external events, a number of important developments were to take place.

The external events in question were the French Revolution and the ensuing war between Great Britain and the new revolutionary regime. One of the results of the French Revolution was the closing down of the Irish Colleges in France and Flanders, which had been the principal locations for the education of the Irish Catholic clergy. With the closure of these colleges the Irish bishops regarded the continued education of Irish clerical students on the continent with grave apprehension; the bishops feared the students would be exposed to the prevailing revolutionary ideas.

The government was equally enthusiastic about inhibiting the importation of revolutionary notions into Ireland, so they made a number of major concessions to Catholics. The first was contained in a

1 *Charta et Statuta Collegii Sacrosanctae et Individuae Trinitatis Reginae Elizabethae juxta Dublin* (1884), p. 2.

section of the Catholic Relief Act of 1793, which, along with the letters patent granted to Trinity College the following year, permitted Catholics legally to enter and graduate from Dublin University. They were not entitled, however, to enter for fellowships, professorships, scholarships, or prizes, which greatly devalued the concession, since most Catholic students were unable to finance their way through the degree course.[2]

However, the Catholic hierarchy, while acknowledging the concession of 'opening' Trinity College to Catholic laymen, did not view it as a solution to the problem of educating the Catholic clergy. They pressed for the establishment of a special seminary, which, for all practical purposes, would be under their exclusive control. The government, for their own strategic reasons, based primarily on their desire to secure the services of the Catholic clergy in maintaining the established order, granted permission for the foundation of a college at Maynooth, to be supported by an annual grant from Parliament.[3] Parliament imposed no restrictions on the entry of students other than that they should be Catholics, but the bishops did not favour the admission of lay students, even though for a short period between 1810 and 1817 a lay college was maintained in addition to the seminary. Within a short period Maynooth became one of the most powerful national institutions in Ireland.

As a result of the establishment of Maynooth College, the Protestant dissenters, who were mainly Presbyterian, comprised of middle-class tenant farmers, business men, industrialists, and shopkeepers, and who were concentrated geographically in Ulster, were now motivated to demand a similar arrangement for the education of their clergy. Traditionally, the Ulster Presbyterians had maintained strong cultural links with Scotland, and many of their clergy were educated there. Politically, however, they were out of favour with the government of the day as a result of their espousal of radical and republican principles, and their continued demands for a second university in Ulster fell on unresponsive ears. A plan for a more broadly based university in Ulster, to be accessible to all Protestants, including Anglicans and dissenters, and financed by a sum of £5,000 bequeathed by Lord Rokeby, a former primate, was unequivocally rejected by Parliament in London in 1799. This, in effect, marked the end of an important decade in the history of Irish university education, for the problem would not receive any further serious attention, at Westminster at least, until the 1840s.[4]

2 T. W. Moody, 'The Irish university question of the nineteenth century', *History*, Vol.42 (1958), pp.90–109.
3 M. R. O'Connell, 'The political background to the establishment of Maynooth College', *Irish Ecclesiastical Record*, Vol.85 (1956), pp.325–34 (Pt. I), pp.406–15 (Pt. II); Vol.86 (1956), pp.1–16.
4 T. W. Moody and J. C. Beckett, *Queen's Belfast 1845–1949: The History of a University*, Vol. 1, London: Faber and Faber, 1959, pp.xli–xliv.

The intervening period, from the close of the eighteenth century to the 1840s, was not marked by lack of activity with respect to higher education in Ireland, north or south. The Presbyterians, whose demands had been firmly rejected by Parliament, proceeded, in 1810, to establish a college in Belfast – the Belfast Academical Institution – which went a considerable way towards satisfying their educational needs. The college was the result of the combined efforts of the local commercial and industrial interests who were anxious to provide a focal point for Ulster and Irish Presbyterianism, a centre of education at school and university level for both their clergy and laity. The structure of the new institution reflected these concerns, and contained both school and college departments. The former contained schools of English, French, mathematics, classics, writing and drawing; while the latter contained a Faculty of Arts, with professorships in logic, mathematics, classics, *belles-lettres*, natural philosophy, moral philosophy, Irish, Hebrew and Oriental languages, and divinity, and a medical faculty which was established later in 1835.[5] The college was, in effect, totally free from religious tests, and was founded on the principle that a distinction could be made between secular and religious education, and that students of whatever denomination should receive their secular education in common. The establishment of chairs of divinity was not incompatible with the avowed secular stance of the institution, since the professors were appointed and financed by their respective Churches and taught only members of their own faith. For over thirty years the collegiate department of the institution helped to solve the practical difficulties of providing university education for Ulster Presbyterians. But it suffered from two major difficulties: an inadequate level of financial support from the state; and the emergence of a sectarian controversy between orthodox and non-subscribing Presbyterians. Although the first problem affected both faculties of the institution, it was less damaging than the second, which was centred exclusively on the arts faculty. It was this latter problem which finally led orthodox Presbyterians to sever their connections with the college in 1844, when Sir Robert Peel, in July of that year, announced in Parliament his intention to introduce legislation on the Irish university question.

Meanwhile, in the south of Ireland the agitation for educational reform, particularly for the Catholic laity, intensified during the 1830s and into the 1840s under the leadership of Thomas Wyse, MP.[6] It was this agitation, rather than events in Ulster, which finally provoked Peel into addressing the question of university education in Ireland. Wyse,

5 Ibid., pp.xliv–liii.
6 J. J. Auchmuty, 'Sir Thomas Wyse, 1791–1862', *Dictionary of National Biography*, vol.XXI.

who belonged to the Catholic upper class, was an enthusiastic supporter of O'Connell in the struggle for Catholic emancipation. When this emancipation was granted in 1829 he was one of the first Catholics to enter the Westminster Parliament, having been elected as a Liberal in the general election of 1830. He immediately committed himself to achieving a number of major reforms in Ireland, especially in the area of education, where his plans embraced all three levels – primary, secondary, and higher education. By the end of 1830, Wyse had presented a scheme for a national system of education in Ireland, which, though rejected, exerted a decisive influence on the programme introduced the following year by Stanley, the Irish Chief Secretary, on behalf of Grey's Whig administration. In 1835 Wyse introduced his second education bill, this time dealing with secondary and higher education. The government of the day, under Lord Melbourne, appointed a Select Committee, with Wyse as chairman. This committee reported in 1838, and, in an impressive document, written by Wyse, it provided the government with a detailed blueprint for the future of Irish education.[7] The Report envisaged five different levels:

(i)   an elementary school level based on the parish;
(ii) a secondary school, or academy system, at the county level;
(iii) agricultural and professional schools;
(iv) four provincial colleges;
(v)   the provision for additional or 'supplementary' education, which would be supplied through the work of literary and scientific societies, libraries, and Mechanics Institutes.[8]

The different levels envisaged in the Wyse proposals were to be under the direction of a Board of National Education. A central concern of the proposed scheme was the emphasis on the provision of education for the middle classes. This argument was based on the premiss that the upper classes were catered for by the university, that the lower classes, by this time, had access to the state-financed national school scheme, but that the middle classes were largely neglected by the state. It was to rectify this deficiency that the Wyse Committee proposed the establishment of county secondary schools or academies, and, more particularly, the provincial colleges.

The publication of the Wyse Committee's Report gave rise to considerable agitation in Munster for a college along the lines suggested. This agitation was led by Wyse himself, with the assistance of another

7 Moody and Beckett, *Queen's Belfast*, vol.1, pp.liii–lix.
8 The latter were to play an important role in the popular dissemination of political economy throughout the nineteenth century. K. R. Byrne, 'Mechanics' Institutes in Ireland before 1855', M. Ed. diss., University College, Cork 1976.

member of the committee, William Smith O'Brien, MP. A Munster College Committee was formed in Cork in September 1838, and later Limerick was also involved in the agitation. Between 1838 and 1840 considerable pressure was brought to bear on the government of the day, but by this time the administration of Lord Melbourne was in retreat, and the Munster college movement was a spent force by the time Parliament was dissolved in June 1841. But, despite the government's overall lack of response to the Wyse Committee's Report, its recommendations provided the basis for educational reforms throughout the nineteenth century, with its principle of mixed or united education, its advocacy of hierarchical structure, and its emphasis on providing an integrated system of education for the whole country.[9] The establishment of the Queen's Colleges, and later of the Queen's University, based on non-sectarian principles, was profoundly influenced by the system of provincial colleges proposed by Wyse. The later history of the Queen's Colleges was also to substantiate his theory that the educational problem required an integrated approach, as the college scheme was greatly hindered by the lack of a secondary school system, which was not introduced until 1878. This, however, was in the future; the decision to establish the Queen's Colleges was yet to be negotiated.

II THE FOUNDING OF THE QUEEN'S COLLEGES, 1845

Peel's administration faced in 1845 the issue of the higher education of the Catholic laity in Ireland. By this time Wyse's long campaign for educational reform, particularly university reform, had convinced Peel that government action was necessary, and that Wyse's scheme of provincial colleges based on the principle of mixed education was attractive. Peel's motivation in pursuing educational reform was, among other things, based on his belief that 'mere force, however necessary the application of it, will do nothing as a permanent remedy for the social evils of Ireland'.[10] In particular, he feared that he would lose the support of the middle and upper classes among the Roman Catholics, and he wished to retain this loyalty at what some members of his administration regarded as too high a price.[11] This was certainly the view of De Gray, Peel's Lord Lieutenant in Ireland, who disagreed fundamentally with his Prime Minister's views. De Gray was removed from office in July 1844, and replaced by Heytesbury, who shared Peel's approach to Irish policy. The same year Peel embarked upon his policy

9 Moody, 'The Irish university question', p.95.
10 Quoted in Moody and Beckett, *Queen's Belfast*, Vol.1, pp.liii–lix.
11 R. B. McDowell, *Public Opinion and Government Policy in Ireland, 1800–46*, London: Faber and Faber, 1952.

of conciliation for Ireland, with a view 'of weaning from repeal the great body of wealthy and intelligent Roman Catholics by the steady manifestation of a desire to act with impartiality and to do that which is just'.[12] Specifically, the policy of conciliation consisted of three measures implemented over the next few years, which included the establishment of the Queen's Colleges, and later the Queen's University.[13] The first, enacted in 1844, was the foundation of a Board of Charitable Bequests, which effectively replaced an almost exclusively Protestant body which had been established in 1800. The new Board was to consist of thirteen commissioners, five of which were to be Roman Catholics, and reaction to this was very unfavourable, especially amongst the Catholic hierarchy, led by Dr MacHale, Archbishop of Tuam in Galway. Three bishops eventually consented to act, and the Board came into operation in August 1844. Both Peel and Heytesbury regarded this as a substantial victory for the process of conciliation.

The second measure in Peel's policy of conciliation was to increase substantially the financial grant to Maynooth College, which was in serious financial difficulties and for which the Catholic bishops had privately appealed for help to the government. The Maynooth Act of 1845 increased the annual grant from £9,000 to £26,000, and decreed that in future this grant was to be drawn from the consolidated fund, which meant that it was no longer necessary to vote on it annually. In addition, a capital grant of £30,000 was provided for the enlargement of the college.[14] The Act caused considerable political furore in its passage through Parliament, leading, amongst other things, to Gladstone's resignation from the Cabinet. In Ireland, the passing of the Act, though popular, evoked little by way of change in attitude to the government on the part of the Roman Catholic population, though arguably the Act was most effective in removing Maynooth as a source of friction in the Irish university question for the rest of the century.

As the Maynooth grant was being debated, Peel and his Home Secretary, Sir James Graham, were devising a scheme of immense importance to the future of higher education in Ireland: the provision of a system of university education which would be acceptable to all the major religious groups in the country – Catholics, Presbyterians, and Anglicans. Initially, the possibility of making Catholics eligible for scholarships in Trinity College, or of founding new colleges in the University of Dublin, was investigated, but this was quickly abandoned given the hostility of the Anglican Church of Ireland. Consequently, it

12 Moody and Beckett, *Queen's Belfast*, Vol.1, p.1.
13 J. C. Beckett, *The Making of Modern Ireland 1603–1923*, 2nd edn, London: Faber and Faber, 1981, pp.328–31.
14 J. Healy, *Maynooth College: Its Centenary History*, Dublin: Browne & Nolan, 1895.

was decided to leave Trinity College untouched, and to establish three new colleges, at Cork and Galway, intended mainly for Catholics, and at Belfast, primarily for Presbyterians. The first reading of the Bill to enact this development was introduced by Graham on 9 May 1845; the second reading was carried by a large majority on 30 May; and, after a number of amendments at the committee stage, the Bill was passed in the House of Commons on 10 July 1845. It went through all its stages without a division in the House of Lords, and received the Royal Assent on 31 July as the Colleges (Ireland) Act.[15]

The Act, Graham explained, was to improve the social conditions of Ireland by providing the benefits of higher education, particularly to 'the middle and higher classes of society'.[16] The problem of educational reform, as perceived by the administration, centred on the fact that the legally established religion was not that of the majority of the people. A similar problem had been encountered – and overcome – at the national (primary) school level, through the provision of a system of national schools based on the principle of mixed secular education, and separate religious instruction, for children of all denominations. The working of that system was deemed sufficiently satisfactory, in the peculiar Irish circumstances, to justify its extension into higher education. In addition to this source of support for their scheme, the administration pointed to the experience of the Scottish universities, and to University College, London. The new colleges, therefore, which were incorporated in December 1845, were to be undenominational and free from all religious tests. They were forbidden to use their endowments from public sources to fund theological teaching, but private bequests for the purpose on a voluntary basis were permitted. As in the Scottish universities, the new colleges were to be non-residential, and all teaching was to be conducted by professors, who were to be appointed, and dismissed, by the Crown.[17] To complete the scheme, the granting of university degrees to the students of the colleges had to be considered. The 1845 Act did not, in fact, settle this issue, and considerable discussion ensued in an attempt to find an acceptable solution.

The Queen's Colleges scheme was completed in 1850 by the establishment of a new university, the Queen's University in Ireland. After Peel and Graham had abandoned their idea of linking the new colleges to the existing University of Dublin, they looked to the University of London as a suitable model, so that the new university would be primarily an examining body with a number of affiliated institutions.

---

15 G. O. Tuaithaigh, *Ireland before the Famine 1798–1848*, Dublin: Gill, Macmillan, 1972, pp.107–8.

16 Moody and Beckett, *Queen's Belfast*, Vol.1, p.8.

17 Tuaithaigh, *Ireland before the Famine*, p.107.

Under this arrangement, they envisaged students from Maynooth competing with Presbyterians from Belfast, and with Catholics and Anglicans from Cork and Galway. Under the new administration, now in office, the example of the autonomous Scottish universities was canvassed by the Prime Minister, Lord John Russell. But Lord Clarendon, his Irish Viceroy, argued against both options as being unsuitable for Ireland. He thought that the London University structure would lead to a lowering of standards, and would merely facilitate the Catholic hierarchy in their demand for a Catholic university. Clarendon's thinking prevailed, and the Queen's University was established within a federal structure and designated as a teaching university, in that only students educated in one of its three colleges could obtain its degrees. It was empowered to prescribe all courses for the award of degrees and diplomas, and to direct all examinations. The Queen's University exercised a powerful control over the colleges, and maintained a high and consistent standard of instruction.

Outside Parliament, the passing of the Ireland (Colleges) Act received a very mixed reception, extending from enthusiastic support to relentless hostility. This scheme, which Peel intended as a measure of conciliation, became a source of bitter controversy and contention. It is virtually impossible to understand the history of the Queen's Colleges, their acceptance in Irish society, or their role in the dissemination of certain subject areas, particularly political economy, without an appreciation of the reactions of the different groups to the founding of the colleges. In Britain, in contrast to the passing of the Maynooth Act, the college scheme provoked little reaction, but in Ireland opinions differed sharply. Those who supported the principle of mixed education, mainly non-subscribing Presbyterians, enthusiastically supported the measure. Nationalist opinion was divided: one section, represented by Daniel O'Connell, condemned it vehemently when he spoke of the 'godless colleges', echoing the idiom of the militant Tory, Sir Robert Inglis, who had earlier denounced the Bill as 'a gigantic scheme of godless education'.[18] In contrast, the Young Ireland Movement welcomed the colleges as promoting and facilitating two of their most desired objectives – an educated and independent-minded laity, and union between Irishmen of different religions. The Catholic hierarchy was also divided. A minority, led by the primate, Dr Murray of Dublin, was prepared to give the colleges a fair chance, but others, led by Archbishop MacHale of Tuam, were utterly opposed to the scheme. It was under the influence of MacHale that the hierarchy, initially withholding their outright condemnation, insisted that certain amendments be made to the scheme if their co-operation was to be secured. These included:

18 *Hansard* 3rd. Series Vol.LXXX, cols 1155–8 (30 May 1845).

(i) That a fair proportion of the professors and other officers should be Catholics and approved by the bishop.

(ii) All officers should be appointed by a Board of Trustees, which should include the Catholic prelates of the province, and should have the power to dismiss any officer convicted of undermining the faith or morals of students.

(iii) There should be Catholic professors of history, logic, metaphysics, moral philosophy, geology, and anatomy for Catholic students.

(iv) Catholic chaplains should be appointed at suitable salaries to supervise the religious and moral instruction of Catholic students.[19]

These demands would effectively have undermined the scheme of mixed education and were rejected by Peel. A protracted struggle ensued between the hierarchy and the administration, which involved missions to Rome by both sides. The hierarchy, under MacHale's leadership, triumphed, and three papal rescripts in 1847, 1848 and 1850 (the latter coinciding with a National Episcopal Synod held in Thurles) formally condemned the Queen's Colleges, and warned the laity to avoid them as subversive to their faith and morals.[20] Thereafter, the hierarchy acted in unison against the colleges and set about establishing a university of their own, which emerged in 1854 as the Catholic University, with John Henry Newman as its first Rector. The bishops' hostility to the Queen's Colleges had an unquestionable effect on their development, particularly in Cork and Galway, and these colleges, while far from being failures, nevertheless did not succeed in realizing their potential or the purpose of their foundation.

In Belfast the position was radically different, but even there the creation of alternative institutions to the Queen's College was not avoided. The essential difference between Belfast and the rest of the country was that the population from which potential university students could be drawn was almost totally Protestant, and the Presbyterian Church, which was comparable in influence to the Catholic Church elsewhere, co-operated with the new Queen's College in Belfast. However, the Presbyterian General Assembly, whose main concern was the education of its clergy, did not present a totally unified front on the question of the Queen's College. Notwithstanding the establishment of a Presbyterian theological college at Belfast in 1853, which worked in harmony with the Queen's College, a minority in the General Assembly insisted on establishing a completely independent college in Ulster to provide instruction in arts and theology and to be totally under their

19 Beckett, *The Making of Modern Ireland*, p.331.
20 W. J. Hegarty, 'The Irish hierarchy and the Queen's Colleges (1845–1850)', *Cork University Record* No.5 (1945), pp.35–55.

control. This they did in 1865 at Derry, with the help of a sizeable bequest from a Mrs Magee, when they established Magee College.[21] Queen's College, Belfast, in contrast to those at Cork and Galway, and in the different circumstances of Ulster, was immediately successful, and shortly after its opening had as many students as Cork and Galway combined.

It was in these circumstances that the Queen's Colleges were launched. The next fifty years were to prove just as turbulent as the years of their launching, and the 'Irish university question' was to remain a continuing source of grievance to Roman Catholics, and an unsettling issue for successive British administrations.

III POLITICAL ECONOMY IN THE QUEEN'S COLLEGES

The structure of teaching within the Queen's Colleges was centred on the three major faculties of arts, law, and medicine. Of these, the arts faculty was deemed the most important from the point of view of providing a general education, in contrast with the professional orientation of the law and medical faculties. Shortly after the passing of the Queen's Colleges Act in 1845, a Board, consisting of the newly appointed Presidents and Vice-Presidents of the three colleges, was set up. Over the next four years, from 1846 to 1849, it was this Board, under the direction of the government, which grappled with the problems of organization, curricula, and appointments for the new colleges. In their first documents, produced at the end of January 1846, the Board drew up a detailed course of studies in arts. The arts course was to be of three years' duration, with the academic year divided up into three terms, each lasting three months. According to its charter, each college was allocated twelve professorships, and these were divided equally between

(i) a Department of Science, which had professorships in mathematics, natural philosophy, chemistry, anatomy and zoology, botany and rural economy, geology and physical geography; and

(ii) a Department of Literature, consisting of chairs in Latin, Greek, English, German and cognate subjects, French and Italian, logic and mental philosophy.

In addition entrance requirements were specified, and the course of studies to be pursued in each year was also formulated. At this stage no mention was made of the provision of political economy in the arts faculty. In terms of the rigour of the entrance requirements and the extensiveness of the subjects included for study, the course differed

21 Moody, 'The Irish university question', pp.98–9.

from most of the contemporary models available, including those of Trinity College, Dublin, the Scottish universities, and Oxford and Cambridge. It approximated most closely to the arrangement of London University. One evaluator of the proposed course of studies in arts summarized it as follows:

> In general that scheme was most closely akin to the London curriculum in its range of subjects and to the Dublin arts course in its orderly sequence of studies: in all respects it stood at the opposite extreme to the undergraduates of Oxford and Cambridge.[22]

During the remainder of 1846 and into 1847, a number of events conspired to interrupt the work of the Board. These included a change of administration in England, the continuing battle in Parliament over the Corn Laws and, in Ireland, the trauma of the Famine. However, in October 1847 the Board reassembled to revise their earlier work on study courses and statutes, and also to draft courses in law and medicine. A number of changes were introduced in the Board's work during 1847–8. First, the quota of professorships was increased from twelve to twenty for each college, of which thirteen were now to be located in the Faculty of Arts, five in Medicine, and two in Law. Secondly, a number of changes in the original professorial arrangements were implemented. The Chair of English became that of History and English Literature; the two modern languages chairs were replaced by one Chair in Modern Languages and one in Celtic Languages; zoology and anatomy were amalgamated into a Chair of Natural History; botany and rural economy were replaced by a Chair of Agriculture; while geology and physical geography were reorganized into a Chair in Mineralogy and Zoology. In addition, a Chair in Civil Engineering was established within the Faculty of Arts. The establishment of this latter chair, along with the Chair of Agriculture, represented the setting-up of schools of engineering and agriculture within the Faculty of Arts.[23] Thirdly, the arts faculty was divided into a literary division and a scientific division. The former contained the Chairs of Greek, Latin, History and English Literature, Modern Languages, and Celtic Languages; while the latter included the Chairs of Natural Philosophy, Chemistry, Natural History, Mathematics, Logic and Metaphysics, Mineralogy and Geology, Civil Engineering, and Agriculture. Finally, certain changes were made in the number of subjects to be studied over the course of the three years, and it was under this revised plan that

22 Moody and Beckett, *Queen's Belfast*, Vol.1, p.44.
23 W. K. Sullivan, *University Education in Ireland*, Dublin: W. B. Kelly, 1866.

political economy was included for the first time in the course of studies in the Faculty of Arts.

The Chair of Political Economy was located not in the Faculty of Arts, but in Law. The Board's decision to include political economy here was influenced largely by the recommendations of a committee of the House of Commons which had considered the issues of legal education.[24] This committee had been established in April 1846 and had reported by August of that year.[25] The committee commented on the fact that the charter of the Queen's Colleges envisaged the establishment of chairs of law, and pointed to the opportunity which this represented for the introduction of courses in law, which the committee felt that existing universities had failed to supply. However, the committee also felt that since the demand for these courses might be meagre, the Professor of Jurisprudence should also have responsibility for political economy. As a result, one of the two chairs in the Faculty of Law was to be in jurisprudence and political economy, the other in English law.

In the Faculty of Arts the principal courses prescribed were the degree of Bachelor of Arts and of Master in Arts, along with diplomas in civil engineering and in agriculture. Candidates for the BA were required to attend lectures in one of the three colleges for a minimum period of two full terms in each of the three sessions, had to pass the requisite college examinations, and had to be recommended by the President of the college for entry to the degree examination. The three-year course consisted in the first year of English language, classics, a modern language, and mathematics; the second year courses included logic, chemistry, zoology, botany, and either classics or higher mathematics; and the final year courses contained physics, history and English literature, geography, and either metaphysics or jurisprudence and political economy. After graduation, students could proceed to the degree of MA by examination in any one of the three groups of subjects: languages; history, metaphysics, and jurisprudence; or mathematics and physical science.

In the Faculty of Law the prescribed courses were for the diploma in elementary law and the degree of Bachelor in Laws. The diploma was a three-year course, in the first year of which property, conveyancing, and jurisprudence were studied. In the second year equity, bankruptcy, and civil law were covered, and in the final year common and criminal law. On completion of this course students were admitted to the diploma examinations, after which they were entitled to proceed to the LL B

---

24 Moody and Beckett, *Queen's Belfast*, Vol.1, p.52.
25 'Report from the Select Committee on Legal Education', House of Commons, 1846 (696), p.x.

examination, which was taken after a further year of study in any one of the three colleges. Bachelors in Law, after a period of three years, could also proceed to the degree of Doctor in Law by examination.

It was within this organizational framework that political economy evolved in the newly established Queen's Colleges, and this structure remained largely intact during the course of the nineteenth century. In Queen's College, Belfast, William Neilson Hancock was appointed the first Professor of Jurisprudence and Political Economy in 1849, while still Whately Professor at Trinity College, Dublin, and he retained the post until 1853. The number of students taking jurisprudence and political economy during Hancock's term of office fluctuated from a high of twelve during 1851–2 to a low of two in 1852–3. His prescribed reading for the academic year 1850–1 included Whately's *Lectures*, Smith's *Wealth of Nations*, Senior's *Political Economy* and Burton's *Social and Political Economy*.[26] In 1853 Cliffe Leslie was appointed to the chair in succession to Hancock, and held it until 1882. In the early years of Leslie's term of office, political economy was clearly subservient to jurisprudence within the prescribed course structure, which is evident from his entry in the President's Report for the academic year 1856–7:

> The subjects which a course of lectures on Political Economy must embrace are fewer and more definite than those classed under the less advanced and more complicated science of Jurisprudence. It is the Professor's endeavour to illustrate the principles of Economic Science by the help of these practical applications which will be most interesting and useful in a large commercial town.[27]

That this was a view Leslie retained can be seen from his various contributions to the annual Presidential Reports over most of his term of office. After 1862–3 the number of students recorded as taking political economy increased, and by 1871–2 the extra work-load which this entailed is reflected in the entry under 'Political Economy' in the President's Report for that year:

> The Professor of Jurisprudence and Political Economy (Mr T. E. Cliffe Leslie) fills in reality two distinct and important chairs, in the two distinct Faculties of Law and Arts. As Professor of Jurisprudence, he lectures, teaches, and examines in the general philosophy and history of law, in Roman Law, and in Constitutional Law and International Law. As Professor of Political Economy, he lectures, teaches, and examines Arts Students in that great subject. His instruction in Jurisprudence has the twofold

26 British Parliamentary Papers, Vol.L (1851), p.790.
27 'Report of the President of Queen's College, Belfast, for 1856–57', 'British Parliamentary Papers', Vol.XXI, (1857–8), p.591.

purpose and result of teaching legal philosophy and history, both as a branch of higher University Education, and as a preparation for the legal profession; and the duties of the Professor in this Department, discharged as they are by Professor Leslie, would be sufficiently arduous if he had not also to fill the Chair of Political Economy, to which he devotes as much time and labour as though he had no other collegiate duties. The stipend and emoluments attached to this double chair are altogether disproportionate to the abilities, attainments, and exertions it demands on the part of the Professor.[28]

This was not a new theme as far as Leslie was concerned. As early as 1858, when Leslie provided evidence to the Queen's Colleges Commission[29] of that year, he argued for substantial reorganization of the teaching of jurisprudence and political economy. His principal recommendations to the Commission focused on the need to reduce the volume of material provided by the Professor of Jurisprudence and Political Economy. As Leslie outlined to the Commission, the incumbent of the chair was responsible for the following course of lectures: 24 lectures on the principles of jurisprudence, 24 lectures on civil law, and 24 lectures on constitutional, colonial, and international law – to law students; 24 lectures on political economy and 24 lectures on jurisprudence – to third year arts students; and 24 (higher) lectures on jurisprudence and political economy – to fourth year arts students, when required. Leslie's objections to these arrangements were fourfold. The first was that the provision of a suitable course of instruction on such a wide spectrum of subjects was not within the capacity of any one professor, particularly as the 'present emoluments of the chair were settled upon the supposition that its occupant would always be a practising barrister'.[30] This interesting observation would help to account for the fact that all of the professors of political economy in both the Queen's Colleges and Trinity College in the nineteenth century were law graduates. The second point argued that the course in law was oppressive, and, in Leslie's view, it militated against the law student. Civil law and colonial law were particularly troublesome, as was the absence of adequate textbooks on the general principles of jurisprudence. Third, the inclusion of Roman law as part of scientific jurisprudence, however valuable for purposes of comprehensiveness in

28 'Report of the President of Queen's College, Belfast, for 1871–72', British Parliamentary Papers, Vol.XXVI (1873),' p.10.
29 The Queen's Colleges Commission, *Report of Her Majesty's Commissioners Appointed to Inquire into the Progress and Condition of the Queen's Colleges at Belfast, Cork and Galway; with Minutes of Evidence, Documents, and Tables and Returns*, Dublin 1858.
30 Ibid., p.327.

a student's legal education, was unlikely to be either 'useful or interesting' to potential students of law at the Queen's Colleges. Finally, the present arrangement, in Leslie's view, prevented the incumbent of the chair from devoting adequate time to 'Economical Science', which 'is capable of being so treated as to prove a useful and profitable study, even in a commercial respect, in such a town as Belfast'.[31]

Leslie's recommendations sought the omission of both civil and colonial law from the course. In fact, at an earlier stage in his submission, Leslie had argued that jurisprudence should be abandoned completely, and that the duties and titles of the chair should be confined to political economy. However, he later conceded that the total abandonment of 'the original design, as far as jurisprudence is concerned, would be for many reasons, to be deplored', and settled for a modification of the existing arrangements. His second main recommendation concerned the arts courses available in the Queen's Colleges. These, he argued, were also excessive in the range of subjects offered, and he called for a rearrangement of subjects into more orderly and logical groups. Specifically he suggested that political economy, logic, and metaphysics should be grouped together, given that they belonged to the moral sciences and, in his view, 'Economic studies furnish the most rigorous exercises in logical reasoning and the detection of fallacies'. Associated with this recommendation was his call for the creation of special degrees in mental and political sciences, along with special diplomas for industrial knowledge.

Leslie's proposal for the provision of courses in industrial knowledge had been canvassed at some length in earlier evidence to the Commission. Here Leslie argued the case for what he called another 'kind of education', which was predicated on 'the necessity of introducing the physical sciences into the practical operations of life'. In reply to a question from the Commission about the 'subjects which you would comprise in your Commercial and Mercantile education', Leslie singled out instruction in the 'Physical and Mathematical Sciences' as the 'most necessary part of it', citing the arrangements at the Trade Institute of Berlin, which represented for him something of a prototype model.[32] He later elaborated on this theme in a supplementary statement which he submitted to the Commission, entitled 'The Demand for Scientific Industrial Instruction in the Queen's College, Belfast',[33] and in which he defended two propositions. First, that there was a demand for a kind of education which the Queen's Colleges were not supplying; and, second, that continental countries provided ample evidence of institu-

31 Ibid.
32 Ibid., p.100.
33 Ibid., pp.325–7.

tions which represented 'nearly complete models of the kind of additional instruction wanted'. In defence of these propositions Leslie offered a number of arguments, including his concern for the fact that although the Queen's Colleges in Ireland and 'Universities and Colleges generally throughout the kingdom' provided education primarily for the middle classes, there 'was no proportionate increase in the aggregate number of students'. Leslie attributed this to the growing recognition by the middle classes – and particularly by the merchant and commercial classes – of the poor remuneration from the 'learned professions' when compared with the rewards from commercial activities, for which the available education provided no particular training. In addition, Leslie pointed to the productive superiority of the continental countries, and cited at length the French example of centralized schools for the training of civil engineers. For Leslie all wealth was 'the result of a knowledge of the laws of nature, and that where this kind of knowledge is stationary, the modes of production must remain unimproved'.[34] In response to this situation Leslie recommended the establishment of an industrial school, and outlined what he considered to be a suitable curriculum. Political economy would be a significant part of this curriculum, taking its place among such subjects as mathematics, descriptive geometry, linear drawing, chemistry, experimental physics, mechanics applied to the arts, botany, and modern languages. His defence of the inclusion of political economy consists of an interesting account of how, on the basis of a judicious selection of topics, it could be made to serve the mercantile and commercial interests of society. According to Leslie,

> The importance of Economical Science, as a part of Industrial Education, may not at once appear obvious, and it has been overlooked in the Continental Institutions. It is sufficient, on this head, to observe that a knowledge of the causes on which the rate of profit, the present and future prices of labour, raw materials, manufactures, and the precious metals depend, and of the kinds of enterprises suited and unsuited to large partnership and not joint-stock companies, together with an acquaintance with the theories of banking, currency, the foreign exchanges, and taxation, must be of immense value to the heads or managers of factories and commercial establishments. Many of the most disastrous failures in business have occurred from an ignorance of the operation of those laws with which the Economist must be conversant, and could not have occurred under the direction of a person uniting this kind of knowledge to the other requisite qualifications.[35]

34 Ibid., p. 326.
35 Ibid.

Leslie's promotion of the merging of political economy with the interests of commercial society must have been largely influenced by his location in Belfast, which, at this time, was the undisputed industrial capital of Ireland. Outside of the north-east region of Ireland, centred on Belfast, economic activity was dominated by a largely under-developed agrarian economy.

The concerns expressed by Leslie with respect to political economy are not paralleled in the evidence from the other Queen's Colleges at Cork and Galway. In Queen's College, Cork, Richard Horner Mills was appointed Professor of Jurisprudence and Political Economy in 1849, a position he held until his death in 1893, a period of forty-four years. The position of political economy within the BA degree structure was similar in all of the Queen's Colleges, with political economy and jurisprudence constituting a third arts optional course to metaphysics. In Cork and Galway the number of students attending courses in law in general and jurisprudence and political economy was particularly small compared with Queen's College, Belfast. Apart from the opposition of the Catholic hierarchy to the colleges (the background to which was described in Part II), a more mundane set of reasons for this state of affairs was given in evidence to the Queen's Colleges Commission in 1858 by the Professors of Jurisprudence and Political Economy at both Cork and Galway. Both acknowledged that since candidates aspiring to the Bar had in any event to attend either the Benchers own Law School in Dublin or the Law School in Trinity College, Dublin, the provision of legal education in the provincial cities was of little use to them. Neither did the other branch of the legal profession – the attorneys – see the value of the law faculties in the Queen's Colleges. The only potential clients, therefore, were the apprentices to attorneys who were located in Cork or Galway, and even their attendance was not a necessary requirement. Both professors argued that the small numbers studying in their respective faculties was the result of the number of attorneys practising in their respective cities. This prompted Professor Mills to recommend to the Commissioners that the law faculty in Queen's College, Cork, should be abolished, but that legal instruction should be retained on a more modest scale.[36] D. C. Heron from Queen's College, Galway, did not agree with this suggestion, and expressed surprise that either Belfast or Cork, given their relative size compared with Galway, should have experienced difficulty in acquiring students.[37] Mills was also of the opinion that political economy suffered greatly by virtue of its association with jurisprudence, combined as they were in one chair. Indeed, part of his motivation for seeking the abolishment of the

36 Ibid., pp.228–9.
37 Ibid., p.289.

Faculty of Law would appear to be his desire to develop the teaching of political economy. For Mills 'the time allotted to the study of political economy is entirely too small for its due cultivation. It appears to me to constitute one of the most important branches of education'.[38] In the course of providing evidence to the same Commission, Heron proposed a somewhat similar view to Cliffe Leslie in Belfast, that a number of new diplomas should be established in Galway, of which one should be a diploma of commerce. Heron envisaged this as a means of meeting the educational needs of the personnel from the various branch banks throughout the country, but he quickly conceded that this suggestion 'would be more useful in Cork and Belfast than in Galway – especially in Belfast, because the system of banking is more extended in the North of Ireland than in any other part of Ireland'.[39] As suggested earlier with regard to Leslie's proposed role for political economy, the effects of location were not inconsiderable in their influence on the place and function of that subject in relation to the wider society.

The contents of the political economy courses taught in the Queen's Colleges were broadly similar. In Galway, D. C. Heron's course in political economy consisted of a series of topics which included: history of political economy, elements of political economy, taxation, capital, labour, pauperism, and colonization. The required reading material included Smith's *Wealth of Nations*, Senior's *Political Economy*, Buron's *Political and Social Economy*, Heron's *Lectures on Taxation*, and Bastiat's *Popular Fallacies*.[40] In Queen's College, Cork, Mills' course in political economy included such topics as: the nature and distribution of wealth, the principles which regulate rents, profits and wages, the principles of commerce, taxation, the funding system, and the principles of currency and banking. The reading material for this course included Smith's *Wealth of Nations*, Senior's *Political Economy*, Longfield's *Political Economy*, Longfield's *Lectures on Commerce*, Huskisson's *Questions Stated*, and John Stuart Mill's *Principles of Political Economy*.[41] The course, as in the other Queen's Colleges, consisted of twenty-four lectures, which were delivered during the months of December, February, and March of each session. By 1866–7 Mills had added to the reading lists Fawcett's *Manual of Political Economy*, McCulloch's *Taxation and Funding*, and Goschen's *Foreign Exchanges*. In the same year the reading material in Queen's College, Galway, centred on the work of Smith and John Stuart Mill, and by 1871–2 this was extended to include Ricardo's

38 Ibid., p.230.
39 Ibid., p.290.
40 'Report of the President of Queen's College, Galway, for 1851–52', 'British Parliamentary Papers', Vol.XLIII (1852–3), p.474.
41 'Report of the President of Queen's College, Cork, for 1856–57', 'British Parliamentary Papers', Vol.XXI (1857–8), p.632.

Principles of Political Economy, Cairnes's *Logical Method of Political Economy*, Goschen's *Foreign Exchanges*, and Price's *Currency*.[42] Over the period from the 1840s to the turn of the century no major changes in the position and status of political economy within the Queen's Colleges can be discerned. Those changes that did occur were marginal; substantial alterations were not introduced until the early twentieth century.

In this chapter we have outlined the historical background to the foundation of the Queen's Colleges and traced in some detail the difficulties which attended their inception and evolution. These difficulties were to a large extent inevitable, given the complex political and religious circumstances within which the colleges were to operate. Indeed, the establishment of the Queen's Colleges was viewed as a pivotal instrument in the Administration's negotiation of, and solution to, these very difficulties. To have anticipated a successful outcome for the new colleges would have been unduly optimistic; and that they never reached their full potential, with the possible exception of Queen's College, Belfast, should come as no great surprise. However, it cannot be argued that the Queen's Colleges were a failure. From their inception in 1849 they attracted very distinguished scholars, and, as reflected in the evidence to the Queen's Colleges Commission of 1885, their graduates compared very favourably with – and on occasion surpassed – their counterparts from universities in the United Kingdom. The Queen's Colleges undoubtedly represented the 'establishment' view as far as the majority of the population was concerned. Their foundation not only failed to solve Peel's problem of providing higher education for the Catholic majority, but in fact stimulated the establishment of the Catholic University in the mid-1850s, largely to counteract their influence.

Viewed from the narrower institutional perspective of providing instruction in political economy, Part III of this chapter demonstrates the extent to which the Queen's Colleges were hampered by combining political economy with jurisprudence. This development, together with the explicit assumption that the holders of the chair would be practising barristers, acted as a major constraint on the expansion of instruction in political economy within the Queen's Colleges. This contrasted with the Whately Chair in Political Economy at Trinity College, Dublin, where no corresponding impediment existed. On the other hand, there was considerable mobility between the holders of the Whately Chair at Trinity College, Dublin, and the Chairs of Jurisprudence and Political Economy at the Queen's Colleges. Hancock, Cairnes, and

---

42 'Report of the President of Queen's College, Galway, for 1871–72', 'British Parliamentary Papers', Vol.XXVI (1873),' p.263.

Bastable held chairs in both institutions at various stages in their careers. In addition, most of the incumbents of the chairs in the Queen's Colleges were graduates of Trinity College, Dublin. Whilst this mobility ensured at least a certain homogeneity in course content and reading material between the two universities, it could also be argued that it contributed to the widely held view on the part of the Catholic majority that political economy was primarily the intellectual preserve of the 'establishment' class, a view that was to evoke a hostile indigenous response from different sources during the course of the troubled nineteenth century in Ireland.

Acting on the advice of Rome, the National Synod of Thurles in 1850 decreed the foundation of a Catholic University in Ireland. There were to be five faculties: theology, law, medicine, philosophy and letters, and science.[43] The philosophy and letters faculty included classical literature and languages, ancient and modern history and geography, English literature, modern languages, logic, metaphysics, ethics, Irish language, archaeology, and political economy.[44] The fact that political economy was on the syllabus marked an advance for Catholic higher education. It was to take a further 130 years or so for the first Chair of Economics to be established in Maynooth, the national seminary for Catholics which was funded and endowed by the government in 1795. But, in fact, very little political economy appears to have been taught at the Catholic University of Ireland. Indeed, its first Rector, John Henry Newman, described political economy as 'a science at the same time dangerous and leading to occasions of sin'.[45] No doubt this secular science, with its morals of the market place, mocked spirituality, and propagated values unbecoming to a gentleman. It is significant that the old Oxford friends, Newman and Whately, never met in the four years in which Newman lived in Dublin.[46]

In October 1854 the provisional appointment of a 'Lecturer in Political Economy' was announced.[47] The following year, the appointee, John O'Hagan, was made Professor of Political Economy.[48] In the *Calendar* of 1857 O'Hagan was still listed as Professor, but by 1869 there was no incumbent. From 1897 to 1900 W. P. Coyne was lecturer in political economy, and from 1900 to 1930 the Jesuit T. A. Finlay was Professor of Political Economy at what had become, in 1908, University

43 *Constitution and Statutes of the Catholic University of Ireland*, Dublin 1869, p.9.
44 Ibid., p.10.
45 J. H. Newman, *The Idea of a University*, London: Longman's, Green and Co., 1901, p.86.
46 F. McGrath, *Newman's University: Idea and Reality*, London: Longman's, Green and Co., 1951.
47 Ibid., p.322.
48 Ibid., p.356. See also *University Gazette*, June 1855, p.356.

College, Dublin, a constituent college of the National University of Ireland, including the former Queen's Colleges of Cork and Galway. But the actual teaching of political economy at the Catholic University seems to have been minimal: O'Hagan pursued a successful legal career and eventually became a Justice of the High Court. It is possible that occasional series of lectures were delivered in the university by guest lecturers. Frank Hugh O'Donnell, for instance, a former student of Cairnes's at Galway, and later to become a Parnellite MP, delivered a series of three lectures 'On Economic Science'.[49]

In November 1873 a *Memorial Addressed by the Students and Ex-Students of the Catholic University of Ireland to the Episcopal Board of the University* was published. Amongst other things, it regretted the neglect of the teaching of science, the lack of a proper scientific library, and the absence of exhibitions and prizes in science. There was, the *Memorial* claimed, too much emphasis on classics, whereas 'the distinguishing mark of this age is its ardour for science',[50] and the bishops were informed that the 'absence of Political Economy from the course of studies in the University' had 'excited many unfavourable comments'.[51] One of the signatories, William Dillon, a son of the MP John Blake Dillon, was later to write a Ruskinian critique of political economy called *The Dismal Science* (1882).

IV BIOGRAPHICAL NOTES ON PROFESSORS OF THE QUEEN'S COLLEGES

Queen's College, Belfast

William Neilson Hancock (1820–88) was Professor of Jurisprudence and Political Economy from 1849 to 1853. He was called to the Irish Bar in 1844. Hancock's remarkably prolific career was characterized by a commitment to what he called 'Applied Political Economy'. It was this commitment which led him to establish the Dublin Statistical Society in 1847, and the Belfast Social Inquiry Society in 1851. Among Hancock's many publications the following represent some of his more significant contributions: *The Tenant-Right of Ulster, Considered Economically* (1845); *Three Lectures on the Questions, Should the Principles of Political Economy be Disregarded at the Present Crisis? And if not, How can they be Applied Towards the Discovery of Measures of Relief?* (1847); *Introductory Lectures on Political Economy* (1849); *Report on the Supposed Progressive Decline of Irish Prosperity*

---

49 *Irish Ecclesiastical Record*, vol.11 (1875), pp.145–56, 252–66, 355–68.
50 *Memorial addressed by the Students and Ex-Students of the Catholic University of Ireland to the Episcopal Board of the University*, 1873, p.16.
51 Ibid., pp.24–5.

(1863); *Report on the Landlord and Tenant Question in Ireland from 1860 till 1866* (1866); and *The State of Ireland* (1874).

Thomas Edward Cliffe Leslie (1825–82) was born on 21 June 1825 in County Wexford, the second son of Reverend Edward Leslie, Annahilt, County Down, and Margaret Higginson. He was educated at King William's College, Isle of Man, and Trinity College, Dublin, where he graduated in 1847 with a gold medal in ethics and logic. In 1851 he took the degree of LL B at Dublin. In 1850 he was called to the Irish Bar, and after further legal studies at Lincoln's Inn, to the English Bar in 1857. Leslie was appointed Professor of Jurisprudence and Political Economy at Queen's College, Belfast, in 1853, a position he retained until his death on 27 January 1882. Despite the fact that Leslie resided mainly in London, he was an active member of the Statistical and Social Inquiry Society of Ireland between 1851 and 1863. He was appointed Barrington Lecturer in Political Economy, under the auspices of this society, for 1852 and 1853, and acted as one of the Honorary Secretaries from 1857 to 1863. He read a number of papers to the Society between 1851 and 1855. He was a member of both the Political Economy Club and the Athenaeum Club in London. His principal publications included; *The Military Systems of Europe Economically Considered* (1856); *Land Systems and Industrial Economy of England, Ireland and Continental Countries* (1870); and *Essays in Political and Moral Philosophy* (1879), the second revised edition of this work was entitled *Essays in Political Economy* (1888).

William Graham (1839–1911) was born in 1839 at Saintfield, County Down. He was educated at the Dundalk Institution, and later at Trinity College, Dublin, where he graduated in 1867 with a BA, and in 1870 obtained an MA. While at Trinity, Graham was elected Scholar in Mathematics and Mathematical Physics, Wray Prizeman in Logic, Ethics and Metaphysics, and Vice-Chancellor's Prizeman in English Prose. During 1873–4 he was private secretary to Mitchell Henry, and engaged in literary and private tutorial work in London between 1875 and 1882. He was called to the Bar at the Inner Temple in 1892. He was examiner in political economy and philosophy for the Indian Civil Service Examinations, and was examiner for the Royal University of Ireland in 1893–4 and 1900–9. He was appointed Professor of Jurisprudence and Political Economy at Queen's College, Belfast, in 1882, and retained this position until 1909. He died on 19 November 1911. His principal publications were: *Idealism: An Essay* (1872); *The Creed of Science* (1881); *The Social Problem* (1886); *Socialism, New and Old* (1890); *English Political Philosophy from Hobbes to Maine* (1899); and *Free Trade and the Empire* (1904).

Queen's College, Cork

Richard Horner Mills (1815–93) was born in Dublin in 1815, the first son of Francis Mills, a merchant, and Anne Horner. He was educated at Trinity College, Dublin, where he graduated in 1838 with a BA, and in 1841 with an MA. He worked as a merchant until he was called to the Irish Bar in 1847. In 1849 he was appointed the first Professor of Jurisprudence and Political Economy at Queen's College, Cork, a position he retained until his death in London on 24 August 1893. His principal publication was *The Principles of Currency and Banking; Being Five Lectures Delivered in Queen's College, Cork* (1853).

George Joseph Stokes (1859–1935) was born in Sligo on 3 March 1859, and was educated at the Diocesan School, Sligo, Trinity College, Dublin, and the Universities of Heidelberg and Berlin. He held the Hibbert Travelling Scholarship between 1881 and 1883. He received an MA degree from Trinity College, Dublin, and was called to the Bar at Lincoln's Inn. He was for a time a member of the Senate of Dublin University. He was Professor of Mental and Social Science in Queen's College, Cork, from 1894 to 1909, and Professor of Philosophy from 1909 to 1924. He died on 6 March 1935. His publications, which are mainly philosophical, include: *The Objectivity of Truth* (1884); 'Gnosticism and Modern Pantheism', *Mind*, 4 (1895); and 'Logical Theory of the Imagination', *Mind*, 9 (1900).

Queen's College, Galway

Denis Caulfield Heron, (1824–81) the first Professor of Jurisprudence and Political Economy at Queen's College, Galway, was born on 16 February 1824 in Dublin, the first son of William Heron of Newry, County Down and Mary Maguire. He was educated at St Gregory's, Downside, and in 1840 he attended Trinity College, Dublin, where, in 1843, he qualified for a scholarship, but as a Catholic he was refused election. He graduated in 1845, and in 1857 he was awarded an LL B and LL D. In 1849 Heron was appointed to the Chair of Jurisprudence and Political Economy at the newly established Queen's College, Galway, a position he held until 1859. Heron was one of the original members of the Dublin Statistical Society, later to become the Statistical and Social Inquiry Society of Ireland. He was also one of the first four Barrington Lecturers appointed in 1849, and was a Vice-President from 1871 until his death in 1881. After he resigned his chair at Queen's College, Galway, Heron devoted himself to his legal career, with a short interlude in active politics. He became a Queen's Counsel in 1860, a Bencher of King's Inns in 1872, and third Sergeant-at-law in 1880. Between 1870 and 1874 he was a Member of Parliament for County Tipperary, having narrowly won the seat from Charles Kickham. Heron died while salmon fishing on Lough Corrib at the age of 57, on 15 April 1881. His major publications included the following works: *The Constitutional History of the University of Dublin* (1847); *Should the Tenant of Land Possess the Property on the Improvement Made by Him?* (1852); *An Introduction to the History of Jurisprudence* (1860); and *The Principles of Jurisprudence* (1873).

John Elliot Cairnes (1823–75) was Professor of Jurisprudence and Political Economy at Queen's College, Galway, from 1859 until 1870. Cairnes was educated at Trinity College, Dublin, where he graduated in 1848, and received his MA in 1854. He held the Whately Chair of Political Economy at Trinity College, Dublin from 1856 to 1861. In 1857 he was called to the Irish Bar, but he never seriously practised; for the remainder of his life he was a full-time academic economist. In 1859 he was appointed Professor of Jurisprudence and Political Economy at Queen's College, Galway, a position he held until 1870. Meanwhile, in 1866, he was appointed Professor of Political Economy at University College, London, but was forced to resign in 1872 because of ill health. At his death, Cairnes was regarded as one of the most outstanding economists of his time. His principal publications included: *The Character and Logical Method of Political Economy* (1857); *The Slave Power* (1862); *Essays in Political Economy, Theoretical and Applied* (1873); and *Some Leading Principles of Political Economy Newly Expounded* (1874).

William Lupton (1830–76) succeeded Cairnes at Queen's College, Galway. He was educated at Queen's College, Belfast, where he graduated with first class honours in mathematics in 1852. The following year he obtained his MA in mathematics and mathematical physics with first class honours. He was a member of the Inner Temple. From 1853 to 1870 he was Registrar of Queen's College, Galway, and in 1870 he was appointed to the Chair of Jurisprudence and Political Economy at Queen's College, Galway, a position he held until 1876. He was the author of *The Reform Bill and the Queen's University in Ireland* (1860) and a series of articles, 'Industrial progress: its causes and conditions', *The Irish Industrial Magazine* (1866).

Robert Cother Donnell (1839–83) was born on 25 June 1839 at Ballina-mallard, County Tyrone. He was educated at Queen's College, Belfast, and was the first gold medallist in jurisprudence and political economy in the Queen's University in Ireland. He graduated in 1860, received the MA in 1863 and the LL D in 1882. He was called to the Irish Bar in 1864. He was Barrington Lecturer for the years 1871–73. In 1872 he was appointed ninth Whately Professor of Political Economy at Trinity College Dublin, and held the post until 1877. In 1876 he was appointed Professor of Jurisprudence and Political Economy at Queen's College Galway, a position he held until his death in 1883. His principal publications included: *Practical Guide to the Law of Tenant Compensation*

135

and Farm Purchase under the Irish Land Act (1871); *Chapters on Lease-holder's Claim to Tenant-Right, and Other Tenant-Right Questions* (1873); *A Scheme of Land Transfer for Small Proprietors, by Local Registry of Title* (1874); and *Reports of One Hundred and Ninety Cases in the Irish Land Courts* (1876).

Charles Francis Bastable (1855–1945) was born in Charleville, County Cork. His early education was at Fermoy College. He entered Trinity College in 1873, and graduated in 1878 with first-class honours in the senior moderatorship in history and political science, which included some study of political economy. After graduation he read law and was called to the Irish Bar in 1881. In 1882 he obtained an MA, and in 1890 an LL D. In 1882 Bastable was appointed to the Whately Chair for the statutory five-year period. On completion of the five-year term, the conditions for holding the Whately Chair were altered, permitting it to be held for longer periods. Bastable was re-elected under the new conditions and retained the chair until his retirement in 1932, by which time he had spent fifty years as Whately Professor. During this period Bastable held a number of positions, both in Trinity itself and in other institutions. In 1883 he was appointed Professor of Jurisprudence and Political Economy at Queen's College, Galway, a position he retained until 1903. In 1902 he was appointed Professor of Jurisprudence and International Law, and then in 1908 Regius Professor of Laws, at Trinity College, Dublin. He played an active part in the Statistical Society, and he was one of the original Fellows of the British Economic Association, later the Royal Economic Society. In 1894 he was elected President of the British Association, Section F, and in 1921 he was elected a Fellow of the British Academy. When the Irish Free State was established in 1921 he served on the Fiscal Inquiry Committee, which reported in 1923. Bastable retired in 1932. His principal works include: *An Examination of Some Current Objections to the Study of Political Economy; Being an Introductory Lecture Delivered in Trinity College, during Trinity Term, 1884* (1884); *The Theory of International Trade; With Some of its Applications to Economic Policy* (1887); *The Commerce of Nations* (1892); and *Public Finance* (1892).

5

MARSHALL AND THE CAMBRIDGE ECONOMICS TRIPOS

Alon Kadish

The state of economic studies at Cambridge at the time of Marshall's appointment to the chair vacated by Fawcett's death in 1885 was not much different from that at Oxford. Papers in political economy were included in the moral sciences and the history triposes, whereas the general interest in the subject was largely due to extraneous factors. The advent of new liberalism did not bypass Cambridge, and the martyrdom of Arnold Toynbee affected young Cambridge as well as Oxford. Following the example of Sidney Ball's Oxford Social Science Club,[1] a number of Cambridge dons and young graduates with an active interest in social and economic matters founded the Society for the Study of Social Questions in late November 1883.[2] The Society's first subjects for debate were socialism and land reform.[3] Its first meeting was addressed by H. S. Foxwell, who read a paper on Hyndman and Henry George followed by a general discussion. In its next issue, the *Cambridge Review* reported: "'What a very liberal speech Mr Sedley Taylor made [in the debate]", said one enthusiastic young under-graduate to one of our best political economists with whom he was returning from the debate . . . "One might almost suppose he was a Socialist." "A Socialist?" was the reply, "Of course he is a Socialist, we are all Socialists!"'[4]

The Society's meetings consisted of addresses delivered by speakers from the University and elsewhere on some subject of general interest, followed by a discussion and, in the course of the next few days, by informal meetings at which the subject was further debated amongst the members. By 1885 it appears that the follow-up meetings were generally abandoned,[5] leading to the establishment of a small study group – the

---

1 *Cambridge Review,* 11 November 1885.
2 The first meeting was held at J. R. Tanner's (1860–1931) rooms at St John's, with H. S. Foxwell (1849–1936) presiding.
3 *Cambridge Review,* 13 and 27 February 1884.
4 Ibid., 27 February 1884.
5 Ibid., 11 November 1885.

Cambridge Economic Club – which aimed to produce, print, and discuss papers on economic subjects more thoroughly and in greater detail than the meetings of the Society for the Study of Social Questions had done. Initially the Club's primary interests coincided with the Society's, i.e. the challenge of socialism and its possible alternatives. The Club's first papers included a critique of Marx's use of the evidence contained in blue books by J. Tanner and its first president, F. S. Carey, 'The Alternative to Socialism in England' by W. Cunningham, 'The Emancipation of Labour' by J. H. Stone, and 'State Interference' by H. N. G. Bushby.[6]

The founding of the Society for the Study of Social Questions and the Cambridge Economic Club may serve as indicators of the nature of the interest in policy-oriented economic questions prevalent at Cambridge throughout the 1880s and 1890s. Many active members of these societies also lectured and examined for the Cambridge Extension, promoted university settlements, supported the Workmen's Social Education League, and became involved in Liberal politics. Their economics were admittedly normative. 'For substantial guidance', Foxwell wrote in the late 1890s, 'in that work of social reorganisation which will be the true business of the next century, and is the real aim to-day alike of socialists and economists, we must look . . . to a conception of social ends.'[7] The purpose of economic investigation was to ensure the welfare of society as a whole, i.e. a more equitable distribution of wealth, hence Foxwell's condemnation of classical economics: 'In its spirit, it was strongly materialistic, sacrificing national welfare to the accumulation of individual wealth.'[8]

Criticism of the ideological bias of classical economic theory often took the form of an attack on abstract theory based purely on deductive reasoning. The 'higher' the theory, the less applicable it became to real conditions. The falsity of Ricardian economics was due not only to its method, but also to its choice of moral premises, thereby implying that the validity of economic theory was necessarily linked to morality. The applicability of any prescriptive policy depended on its practicality and its moral soundness. The Ricardians, on the other hand, had 'set up and worshipped their ill-determined hypothesis of Competition as the natural goal and ideal of social progress'.[9] Their definitions, 'though

6 Volumes of the Club's papers can be found at the University of Cambridge Library, Cam.c.291.28, and in the Marshall Papers, Marshall Library, Large Brown Box.
7 H. S. Foxwell, 'Introduction' to Anton Menger, *The Right to the Whole Produce of Labour*, London: Macmillan, 1899, p.cvii.
8 'The economic movement in England', *Quarterly Journal of Economics*, Vol.2, (October 1887), pp.84–103.
9 'Review of W. Bagehot, *The Postulates of English Political Economy*' in *Cambridge Review*, 18 November 1885.

undoubtedly derived from a review of the facts, as seen by Ricardo, cannot be taken back to the facts, and so made of any use: without which a definition in political economy, as in any other science, has no value in real life'.[10] Even Fawcett, Mill's popularizer, stated in 1883 that he would discuss in his lectures 'the great social questions of the day which demand rather application of that science [political economy] than the examination of its theory',[11] implying that, at least for immediate practical purposes, the two were not quite compatible.

At the same time, there were dons, some of whom taught economics, who took a far less radical view of the aims and method of political economy. Mill's *Principles*, condemned by Foxwell for its soporific influence on English economics,[12] was still widely regarded as the definitive statement of economic principles – subject to occasional minor modifications. H. Sidgwick, for one, was even prepared to protect Mill against himself. In an article published in 1879, Sidgwick attempted to rehabilitate the wages fund theory by arguing that its flexible adaptation to current conditions could provide answers to the main objections of its critics, who in turn were unable to forward a comparably satisfactory alternative.[13] The defenders of theory were prepared to concede that in itself it could not be regarded as an adequate key to the understanding of economic phenomena, but it did offer an invaluable tool without which little sense could be made of empirical evidence. In the words of V. H. Stanton in a review of the Marshalls' *The Economics of Industry* (1879): '[I]t is difficult to see how the helpfulness of abstract theory can be denied, which traces the laws of the forces that are most considerable or most uniformly present, and thus give us a clue to follow amid the maze of individual facts, and enable us to go some way at least in sorting and comparing them.'[14]

As the newly appointed Professor of Political Economy, Marshall was faced with two distinct, if not conflicting, tasks. As the University's paramount authority on the subject, his was the task to enhance its scientific and academic status. The prevailing attitude towards the nature of science, entailed the defence of the importance and value of the existing corpus of works in the classical tradition (hence 'neo-classicism') while underlining theory's claims for objectivity.[15] At the

10 'Review of J. Bonar (ed.), *Letters of David Ricardo to Thomas Robert Malthus*', in the *Reflector*, 12 February 1888.
11 *Cambridge Review*, 14 November 1883.
12 Foxwell, 'Introduction' to A. Menger, p.lxxviii.
13 H. Sidgwick, 'The wages fund theory', *Fortnightly Review*, February 1879.
14 *Cambridge Review*, 3 December 1879.
15 On the application of the positivist definition of science to economics, see A. Kadish, *The Oxford Economists in the Late Nineteenth Century*, Oxford: Oxford University Press, 1982, pp.131–3.

same time, Marshall hoped to attract more students to a systematic study of economics by drawing on the general interest in current economic problems, which, in turn, had little to do with the pursuit and development of economic theory for its own sake. As a means of dealing with the latter objective, Marshall joined the Society for the Study of Social Questions,[16] and chose issues of general interest as the subjects of his first courses.[17] Rather than begin with the principles of economics, Marshall's first course was advertised as 'adapted to the wants of those who expect to be concerned with economic questions in the after life, but are not able to give much time to them while at Cambridge'.[18]

In choosing to lecture on subjects of general interest, Marshall, at least temporarily, adhered to the educational ideology which maintained that the main purpose of a Cambridge training was to prepare young men, by means of a general education, for future positions of responsibility and leadership. The University's task, asserted in *Granta* in 1892, was

> to train the mind that a man shall be able not only to hold his own in any of the liberal professions, but shall be fitted afterwards to apply himself with an enlarged and disciplined habit of mind to any special subject into which he may be forced. General cultivation strictly and rigorously pursued should be our aim and object.[19]

Early specialization, according to this view, was contrary to the objective of a general education,[20] a view Marshall was at pains to disprove in the later stages of his campaign for the economics tripos.

In his simultaneous efforts to promote the scientific status of economics, Marshall began by emphasizing its neutrality. That in itself did not necessarily clash with the 'general education' view of a Cambridge training. It was widely assumed that the university was there to teach

---

16 *Cambridge Review*, 11 February and 11 March 1885.
17 *Cambridge University Reporter* (hereafter *CUR*), 21 April 1885. Marshall's first course was entitled 'Distribution of wealth with special reference to the causes that determine the incomes of different classes in England now, and to the inquiry how far the existing inequalities are unavoidable'.
18 See in addition P. Groenewegen, 'Alfred Marshall and the establishment of the Cambridge economics tripos', *History of Political Economy*, Vol.20 (1988), pp.627–67; and his 'Teaching economics at Cambridge at the turn of the century: Alfred Marshall as lecturer in political economy', *Scottish Journal of Political Economy*, Vol.37 (1990), pp.40–60.
19 'A modern tripos', *Granta*, 23 January 1892. See also H. Montagu Butler in *The Times*, 26 May 1900.
20 See E. A. Parkyn in *Cambridge Review*, 3 March 1880 and 14 June 1882, and F. Pollack, ibid., 5 December 1883.

rather than to indoctrinate. It was better 'that a man should not suffer under the proud consciousness of having attained to the truth of all things before he has taken his degree'.[21] However, there were those who believed that inapplicability was the best guarantee of neutrality. Science was best pursued for its own sake.[22] Therefore the study of social questions – with its direct and obvious relevance to current problems – was best suited for mature minds, and should not be encouraged amongst undergraduates.[23] In choosing the middle ground, Marshall attempted in his inaugural lecture to project an image of economics as a neutral theoretical discipline of only limited application to current matters, while extolling its value in training young men to deal with any economic and social problems they might meet in their future careers. On the one hand there was, according to Marshall, 'scarcely any limit to the developments of theory which are possible: but of those which are possible only a small part is useful in having a direct relation to practical issues'.[24] Economic theory, therefore, could not claim to displace common sense as the only practical resource for dealing with social problems.[25] On the other hand, Marshall stressed the importance of a training in economics in joining 'in the great work of inquiring how far it is possible to remedy the evils of the present day. For indeed the work is urgent.'[26] 'The great scientific strength of Cambridge', Marshall complained, 'is not indeed indifferent to social problems: but is content to treat them in an amateur fashion.' It was time the University mobilized its scientific resources in the struggle to redress social misery.[27]

In institutional terms, Marshall's initial objective was to establish an option of systematic training in economics beyond that offered by the existing curriculum. Economics, he argued, was not the type of subject a student could pick up on his own. In the particular instance of its relation to the study of history, it was best that the student should master theory before turning to the interpretation of facts – an

21 B. H. Holland, 'Parties at Cambridge', *Cambridge Review*, 26 November 1879. See also E. L., 'The Universities and public life', ibid., 13 October 1880.
22 See T. Beck, 'London Positivism', ibid., 12 May 1880.
23 See A. T. F., 'Party politics and undergraduates', ibid., 24 May 1882; and 'Cambridge from without', ibid., 12 May 1886: 'the notion has very generally gone abroad that we are unpractical here, and given over to mathematical abstractions'.
24 Alfred Marshall, 'The present position of economics', in A. C. Pigou (ed.), *Memorials of Alfred Marshall*, Macmillan, London 1925, p.162.
25 Ibid., p.164.
26 Ibid., p.172.
27 Ibid., p.173. On Marshall's social ideology, see David Reisman, *Alfred Marshall: progress and politics*, Basingstoke: Macmillan, 1987 and *Alfred Marshall's Mission*, Basingstoke: Macmillan, 1990.

opposite approach to the practice adopted by W. Cunningham in his courses:[28]

> In order to be able with any safety to interpret economic facts, whether of the past or the present time, we must know what kind of effects to expect from each course and how these effects are likely to combine with one another. This is the knowledge which is got by the study of economic science, while, on the other hand, the growth of the science is itself chiefly dependent on the careful study of facts by the aid of this knowledge.[29]

As an *ex officio* member of the History Board, Marshall was able to enforce his view of the separation of economic theory from the study of economic history, and its placement in front of the latter in the order of studies, without in any way suggesting that economics had no place in the history tripos.

At Cambridge, unlike Oxford, professors wielded considerable power in university affairs. The intercollegiate system developed more slowly than the Oxford combination system, and was not as powerful. Within the history tripos, J. R. Seeley, the Regius Professor of History, led a camp which regarded the tripos as a school of statesmanship which should consist mainly of the study of politics, including political economy.[30] The opposing view was represented by G. W. Prothero of King's College, who maintained that the proper focus of history was the 'whole evolution of human society'. History 'embraces not political evolution alone, but the history of religion and philosophy, of literature and art, of trade and industry'.[31] Seeley and his allies, including Cunningham, tended to emphasize the value of relatively recent history to the understanding of current affairs, a view to which Marshall subscribed [32] but was careful not to stress, in order not to alienate Prothero's camp which underlined the importance of a wide chronological perspective and the principle of historical continuity. Nor did Marshall challenge the auxiliary position assigned to economics within

---

28 Audrey Cunningham, *William Cunningham: Teacher and Priest*, London: SPCK, 1950, p.64.
29 Marshall, 'Present position of economics', p.168.
30 See Seeley's inaugural lecture, 'The teaching of politics', in J. Seeley, *Lectures and Essays*, London: Macmillan, 1870; and D. Wormell, *Sir John Seeley and the Uses of History*, Cambridge: Cambridge University Press, 1980.
31 G. W. Prothero, *Why Should We Learn History?*, Edinburgh: James Thin and Cambridge : Deighton Bell & Co., 1894, p.8.
32 Marshall, 'Present position of economics', p.169. See also A. Marshall, *A Plea for the Creation of a Curriculum in Economics*, Cambridge 1902, p.4, reprinted in C. W. Guillebaud's edition of Marshall's *Principles*, London: Macmillan, 1961.

the history tripos, so as not to add to Prothero's fears of the tripos becoming predominantly theoretical.[33] Hence when Marshall, the University's foremost authority on economics, suggested some relatively minor changes in the teaching of his subject within the history tripos, neither camp saw any reason to refuse him.

The status of economics, then, was not a major issue in the debates leading up to the 1885 reform of the history tripos.[34] The joint economic theory and history paper was retained, although Marshall had managed to separate the teaching of the two subjects. In addition, students were offered the option of a paper in political economy, plus a paper in the general theory of law and government and international law, as an alternative to one special subject. This optional paper was to consist largely of questions concerning the theory of government action in matters of finance and industry, and it was subsequently pointed out that it required considerably more extensive reading than the compulsory joint paper, forcing the students to master a more advanced level of theory than Fawcett's *Manual* and, later, Marshall's *Economics of Industry*.[35] All history students were therefore required to study some economic theory. And, while the tripos remained solidly empirical on the whole, the option was created of at least some specialization in theoretical subjects.

The arrangements for teaching economics in the history tripos may not have comprised the level of specialization Marshall had had in mind, but at least they provided a steady stream of students, albeit 'kittle-kattle ... intelligent, more or less earnest, but not very profound',[36] whereas the moral sciences tripos suffered from a perennial dearth of students. Marshall may have preferred mathematicians and natural science graduates who chose to complete their Cambridge studies with some economics, but the only tripos to offer anything remotely approximating specialization in theory was the moral sciences. Prior to his return to Cambridge, Marshall had defended the inclusion of economics within moral sciences on the grounds that 'it deals only incidentally with inanimate things'. In the moral sciences, 'a man who confines himself entirely to one narrow branch of inquiry is not likely to make good progress in it. The economist should know something of the history of manners and

33 G. W. Prothero, 'The historical tripos', *Cambridge Review*, 28 January 1885.
34 See Jean O. McLachlan, 'The origin and early development of the Cambridge historical tripos', *Cambridge Historical Journal*, Vol. 9 (1947), pp.78–105.
35 G. W. Prothero, *The Historical Tripos*, Cambridge: University of Cambridge, 1892, pp.5, 15.
36 Marshall to J. N. Keynes, 27 August 1889; Keynes Papers I (90), Marshall Library, Cambridge.

customs and laws of the principles of mental, moral, legal and political science.'[37] Following Mill, Marshall asserted that 'a person is not likely to be a good economist who is nothing else'. In retrospect, however, Marshall stated:

> my main reason for thinking that the association of economics with Mental Science has been so disastrous is that in my opinion it is essential that students should acquire an extensive knowledge of *facts i.e. big facts* [rather than 'detailed facts'], in order that they may understand how a sense of proportion is, after sound reasoning, the most important equipment of an economist.[38]

In forwarding the cause of economics within the moral sciences tripos, Marshall faced a potential conflict of authority. He was the undisputed authority on economic theory on the History Board, but on the Moral Sciences Board he had to accommodate the views of Foxwell, J. N. Keynes, and H. Sidgwick. Marshall soon discovered that Foxwell and Keynes, both of whom were former students of his, were prepared to submit to his authority, despite occasional differences. Both had enthusiastically supported his candidacy for the chair, although, in Foxwell's case, Marshall's appointment meant surrendering his supervision of the honours teaching of economics in the moral sciences tripos.[39] Keynes, it so happened, became increasingly absorbed in university administration, and Foxwell chose to overlook his growing disagreements with Marshall, in keeping with the principle that 'the Professor ought to be Head of the School, and control the arrangements'. 'I do not', Foxwell confessed, 'believe in Committee government.'[40] Sidgwick, however, posed a different problem.

Within the Moral Sciences Board as well as the University in general, Sidgwick had enjoyed considerable influence and commanded wide respect. Prior to leaving Cambridge in 1877, Marshall and Sidgwick had been quite close, but upon Marshall's return a clash of authority became inevitable. In his inaugural lecture Marshall continued to defend the inclusion of economics within the moral sciences, but, he added, 'many of those who are fittest for the highest and hardest economic work are not attracted by the metaphysical studies that lie at the threshold of ... [the moral sciences] Tripos'.[41] Accordingly,

37 Alfred and Mary Paley Marshall, *The Economics of Industry*, 2nd edn, London: Macmillan, 1881, Book I, ch. 1, 2, 3.
38 Marshall to Keynes, 6 February 1902: Keynes I (126).
39 Audrey G. Foxwell, *Herbert Somerton Foxwell: A Portrait*, Boston, Mass: Kress Library of Business and Economics, 1939, p.9: and J. M. Keynes, 'Herbert Somerton Foxwell', *Economic Journal*, Vol. 46 (1936), pp.589–619.
40 Foxwell to Keynes, 6 October 1900: Keynes I (32).
41 Marshall, 'Present position of economics', p.17.

Marshall set out to establish economics as an autonomous course of studies within the moral sciences tripos, requiring a minimum of philosophy and, in particular, metaphysics. A similar intention may be discerned in Marshall's establishment in 1886 of the Marshall Prize, to be awarded by an examination based on the political economy papers set in the moral sciences tripos,[42] thereby, hopefully, encouraging students to attain the level of economics required in the tripos without having to read metaphysics.[43]

One of Marshall's main advantages in dealing with the Moral Sciences Board was Sidgwick's almost obsessive fairness. Following Sidgwick's death, John Reile wrote: 'No man could be more single-minded, but he could see two (or more) sides of a question where the ordinary man saw one: and his fairness in making allowance for the strong points of an opponent's view made him willing to sacrifice whatever he did not think vital to his own.'[44] At this time the Board was considering the division of the tripos into two parts, of which the second would offer advanced training in the moral sciences and related subjects. Marshall's main objection was to making metaphysics compulsory in Part II, although he had no objection to a similar clause concerning Part I – apparently in the hope that Part II could be made attractive to graduates of other triposes. By Michaelmas 1888, Marshall's intransigence had led Sidgwick to offer a compromise, according to which students reading for Part II who wished to take advanced economics might be exempted from the study of metaphysics.[45]

With the 1889 reform in the moral sciences tripos, Marshall had created an option whereby students could read the principles of economics in either moral sciences Part I (two papers out of seven) or history, and then proceed to a more advanced level in moral sciences Part II, with the choice of metaphysics or politics and ethics as additional subjects. In defence of his efforts to exclude metaphysics from the recommended course of economic studies, Marshall stated: 'Looking at the history of economics, one did not find that those who had approached it from a metaphysical standpoint had contributed very much to its progress: almost all economists had worked on lines separate from metaphysics, and many had even indicated a certain distinct severance of their minds from metaphysical questions.'[46] The association of economics with ethics was, in his opinion, far more important: '[E]verybody should look on social questions more or less

42 *CUR*, 4 May 1886.
43 The first winners of the prize were S. M. Leathes (1887), John M. McTaggart (1888), and A. W. Flux (1889).
44 *Cambridge Review*, 25 October 1900.
45 *CUR*, 26 February 1889.
46 Ibid., 19 March 1889.

from the ethical side.' There was a great deal to be said, Marshall concluded, 'for separating to some extent these two branches of moral science, the mental and the metaphysical side, and the social side . . . Ere long a time might come when they would be ready to have a political sciences school.' The last reform, therefore, was merely 'a transitional stage' on the way to a more comprehensive overhaul of the system.

The 1889 reform did not pass unchallenged, but with Sidgwick supporting the Board's report, there was little the opposition, led by Cunningham, could do beyond recording its objections. The new regulations were followed by Marshall establishing a new prize – the Adam Smith – to replace the Marshall. This was a triennial prize of £60, to be awarded for an essay 'on some unsettled question in Economic Science, or in some branch of Nineteenth-Century Economic History or Statistics'.[47] Officially the prize's purpose had remained unaltered – to attract to the study of economics 'men who are able to bring to it highly trained minds and who have gradually acquired, by intelligent observation of what goes on around them, a sound knowledge of contemporary economic conditions: but who, for the present at all events, cannot give their whole time to economic studies'. But instead of an examination, the candidate was to 'choose his own subject and . . . no one should be put at a great disadvantage through the want of extensive literary and historical knowledge'. Candidates – graduates with no more than four years since their first degree – were 'invited to consult the Professor of Political Economy with regard to their choice [of subject], and with regard to a suitable course of reading in connection with it'. The adjudicators – Marshall and an examiner recommended by the Moral Sciences Board – would judge the works for their 'constructive ability and the grasp of scientific principles' rather than for their display of erudition. Marshall, in effect, had followed the prevailing practice in the history tripos, where prize essays were made to approximate mini-dissertations which could then be used in applications for prize fellowships, thereby tightening his hold on prospective economists who might seek to pursue an academic career.

The changes in the triposes instituted in the late 1880s had established economics as a subject worthy of, and requiring, special study. The status of the subject was further enhanced by the publication in 1890 of Marshall's *Principles of Economics*, widely acclaimed as the definitive work upon which the study of economics was to be reconstructed as a strictly scientific discipline. Students were encouraged to believe that the broader problems in economics were safe in Marshall's keeping, leaving them to follow up the *Principles* by concentrating on

47 Ibid., 17 February 1891.

the narrower issues which required detailed monographs.[48] In 1892 Marshall added to the *Principles* his *Economics of Industry*, which in content and arrangement corresponded closely to the curriculum of the economics papers in moral sciences Part I, a worthy substitute, according to the *Cambridge Review*, 'for wrestling with Locke and Aristotle which once used to play so large a part in training English minds at universities'.[49] Economics at Cambridge was increasingly becoming strictly Marshallian, a state approved of by the *Cambridge Review*:

> It is of the utmost importance in a mobile science like Political Economy that students should, from the very first, come into contact with the minds of the masters of the Science . . . Professor Marshall's position as a leader in the development of the Science affixes a first-hand stamp upon this work [*Economics of Industry*] which cannot but cause it to plough deeper into a student's mind than any compiled text-book could possibly do.

By the mid-1890s it became clear that Marshall's confident assertion concerning the potential demand for an advanced course in economics – once its link with metaphysics was made optional – were not borne out by the class lists. Part II of the moral sciences tripos proved far from popular, and few students took up political economy as a special subject. The average class list contained more examiners than students.[50] Marshall found it necessary to continue to offer short advanced courses to students and graduates interested in economics but unwilling to undertake the more systematic curriculum offered in moral sciences Part II. During the early 1890s, therefore, much of Marshall's influence on the future generation of economists was wielded by means of direct supervision, usually at home, rather than through the class-room. The best way to learn to row, Marshall wrote to Gonner in 1894, 'is to row behind a man who is already trained: the learner's body moves by instinctive sympathy with his. And so the trained teacher should, I think, work his own mind before his pupils: and get theirs to work in swing with his.'[51] By such means Marshall succeeded in drawing to economics A. W. Flux, A. L. Bowley, and C. P. Sanger. Not quite a new school, but, as Marshall consoled himself, 'one Sanger, or even one Bowley, is a good recompense for five years work'.[52] Yet even they could rarely look forward to an academic career in economics. Bowley, for

48 See A. C. Pigou, 'Looking back from 1939', in A. C. Pigou, *Essays in Economics*, London: Macmillan, 1952, p.7.
49 *Cambridge Review*, 27 October 1892.
50 See *CUR*, 9 June 1891, 7 June 1892, 6 June 1893, etc.
51 Marshall to Gonner, 9 May 1894, in Pigou, *Memorials*, p.381.
52 Marshall to Keynes, 2 November 1895: Keynes I (108.)

instance, left Cambridge to become a schoolmaster,[53] leading Marshall to complain:

> more than half of those from whom I expected most have been carried off by Headmasters to toil for the good of others: and though the spirit is often willing, the flesh is generally too weak to stand the strain of original work while teaching in a school. Such men of course help to form a sound public opinion in those parts of the country in which they settle: but they do not contribute much to that reward of the teacher's work which he loves best.[54]

Graduates of other triposes who chose to study economics in the 1890s still did so out of largely ideological reasons based on the supposed applicability of their knowledge. The Society for the Study of Social Questions (and, to a much lesser extent, the Economic Club) remained active, joining forces with the Ladies' Discussion Society in 1888.[55] Also in 1888 the Cambridge Ethical Society was formed, with the aim of 'bringing the problem of practical ethics into more definite relation to the philosophic thought of the time, and in that way affording a somewhat clearer insight into the principles on which their solution will depend'.[56] And in 1892 a Cambridge branch of the Christian Social Union was founded, the discussion groups of which were to study current social and economic problems.[57] The spirit which animated all this activity found an expression in a sermon on the Church and the unemployed by the Revd C. W. Stubbs, Dean of Ely, in the course of which he called upon Cambridge students to use their years at the University:

> to study such questions . . . study them carefully and scientifically in your economic text-books, and with the methods you learn in your economic class-rooms, but study them also in the light of Christ's incarnation . . . [F]or the Christian, Christ's law must always be the ultimate authority, and . . . in the last resort therefore in all economic problems, the question is not about wealth but about men.[58]

Those who used economics to seek the means of ensuring a more equitable distribution of wealth found in Marshall a sympathetic guide.

---

53 In 1895 Bowley began lecturing at the LSE, but he did not abandon schoolteaching until 1899.
54 Marshall to Gonner, 9 May 1894, in Pigou, *Memorials*, p.381.
55 *Cambridge Review*, 29 November 1888.
56 Ibid., 1 November 1888. Marshall was a member of the Ethical Society's committee.
57 Ibid., 24 November 1892.
58 Ibid., 28 February 1895.

There were two Marshalls, S. J. Chapman recalled, 'the theorist of genius and . . . the economic watcher and the social meliorist'.[59] F. W. Lawrence (later Pethick–Lawrence), who won a Trinity prize fellowship in 1897 with his Adam Smith prize essay on local variations in wages, remembered Marshall's lectures as

> not only illuminating but inspiring. While he insisted that the 'laws' of economics were statements of fact like the 'laws of nature', and not commands to be obeyed like Acts of Parliament, he really cared passionately that a knowledge of economics should be applied to bettering the lot of humanity and in particular of the underdog. He held strong political views and every now and again expressed them.[60]

In a similar vein, Marshall called in 1896 upon the members of the revived Economic Club to take a firm stand in favour of greater material equality. The academic economist, he stated,

> has no class or personal interest to make him afraid of any conclusions which the figures, when carefully interpreted, may indicate: he accepts the premises of the working classes that the well being of the many is more important than that of the few. He is specially trained to detect the falsity of the mirage which is caused by the fact that the comfort of a few rich men sometimes has higher bidding power in the market than the more urgent needs of many poor, and will outbid them in the market.[61]

At the same time, enthusiasm was no substitute for systematic training. During the early 1890s, economics had begun to acquire some of the trappings of a recognized scientific profession.[62] In 1890 the British Economic Association was founded, and in 1891 its organ, the *Economic Journal*, commenced publication. Marshall, however, appears to have placed greater value on founding an institutionalized school of economics which would ensure an orderly development of the discipline along generally uncontroversial lines by means of establishing some continuity of generations of teachers and students. The issue emerged during a debate in 1894–5 on the question of post-graduate degrees, in the course of which Marshall expressed his concern that

59 S. J. Chapman, unpublished autobiography, LSE Coll Misc. 664, p.24.
60 F. W. Pethick-Lawrence, *Fate has been Kind*, London: Hutchison & Co., 1942, p.34.
61 A. Marshall, 'The old generation of economists and the new', in Pigou, *Memorials*, p.305.
62 On the issue of professionalization, see especially John Maloney, *Marshall, Orthodoxy and the Professionalisation of Economics*, Cambridge: Cambridge University Press, 1985.

There was at present a danger that the teaching should be in the hands too exclusively of the older men and that the supply of younger teachers preparing for more responsible work should be deficient. What was wanted was some system analogous to the German one by which the older teachers gave much of their attention to the *Seminar* while the more elementary teaching was mainly in the hands of younger men – *Privat Docents* [University teachers paid only by students' fees][63]

On another occasion Marshall expressed the view that the strength of German universities lay in 'having a class of *Privat Docents* to understudy the parts of the older teachers who were also learners, and to learn while teaching'.[64]

Marshall, then, envisaged the ideal state of economic studies as a centralized discipline whereby recruitment was internalized, with prospective academic economists following a course of training determined by Marshall, teaching his general courses, and going on to do research under his supervision. Such a school would ensure methodological unity and concentration of effort, thereby eliminating disruptive controversy on both method and aims.

During 1896–7 the History Board initiated the division of the history tripos into two parts. By then Prothero had left to take up the history chair at Edinburgh and Seeley had died. Political science and, in particular, political theory had lost considerable ground, although the value of economic theory to historians appears to have remained uncontested. Planning the reform was one instance in which Marshall and Cunningham were in agreement.[65] The Board's initial recommendations[66] called for an option in Part I of either two papers in English economic history, including questions on economic theory, or two papers on a special historical subject. Part II was to offer an option of two papers (to be taken together) in political economy, while allowing graduates of other triposes reading history II to add the economic history papers of Part I, thereby enabling them to sit for four out of seven papers (of which three were in any event compulsory) on economic subjects. As Tanner stated in the Senate, it could no longer be argued 'that Political Economy was treated cursorily and inadequately, and suffered if the Examiner was not a specialist'.

The creation of a new course of specialization in economics was

---

63 *CUR*, 20 February 1894.
64 Ibid., 6 November 1894.
65 Marshall to Foxwell, 18 January 1895 [1896]: Foxwell Papers, 14/190. Details on the location of the Foxwell Papers may be obtained from the National Register of Archives.
66 *CUR*, 1 December1896.

defended by Marshall on the grounds of greater freedom of choice allowing 'more intense' study as an alternative to the more traditional curriculum of general studies:

> What was wanted was as far as possible to allow each student to develop his own idiosyncrasy, provided only that whatever work he did was thorough ... The true function of University education was to develop a man's faculties that they might continue to develop to the fullest extent in after life: and in this respect, though not in all respects, the German system was superior to ours. For it gave the student a freer choice of work and therefore a keener interest in it and one more likely to remain active in after life. The proposed change would be a step towards combining the advantages of the German system with our own.[67]

Following the debate in the Senate, some changes were made in the Board's report, including the addition of two papers in economic theory as an alternative to the economic history papers in Part I. Marshall's concern that economics students should not be burdened with too much pre-industrial, i.e. irrelevant, history led to the additional stipulation that the economic theory papers require knowledge of recent economic history only.[68] These final changes created yet another option of early specialization in economics, i.e. history I followed by moral sciences II, while at the same time increasing the likelihood that most history students would at one point or another acquire some proficiency in economic theory and/or economic history. The historians had acknowledged economics as constituting 'without doubt the most instructive and valuable of the Theoretical Subjects. The more scope given to it the better.'[69] In turn, Marshall adopted the History Board's policy of multiple options as a likely model for future reforms.[70] For, despite the historians' generosity, Marshall still was not satisfied: 'In my view,' he wrote to Keynes in 1897, 'historical economics, though infinitely more important than philosophical economics, because infinitely more real, is yet not economics proper. That I take to be a scientific study of existing economic facts and contemporary changes, of course not neglectful of their historical antecedents.'[71]

While the History Board was working out the details of its final report, the Moral Sciences Board had entered a new round of discussions concerning further changes in the 1889 regulations. These

67 Ibid., 9 February 1897.
68 Ibid., 10 May 1898.
69 *Cambridge Review*, 25 February 1897.
70 Marshall to Foxwell, 11 February 1902: Marshall III (44).
71 Marshall to Keynes, 30 August 1897: Keynes I (102).

were deemed necessary in view of the paucity of candidates for Part II, which was proving unattractive even to graduates of Part I.[72] The Board proposed to render Part I more comprehensive by adding a paper on ethics, thereby bringing the total of papers to eight, and to develop further the specialization option in Part II by dividing it into two entirely separate parts – 'philosophical' and 'politico-economical' – with the emphasis in the latter on the 'economical'. For the first time Marshall was given a virtually free hand to develop his own programme of advanced economic studies.

According to the new regulations, Part II could only be taken as a second tripos. Marshall could therefore assume that the candidates for Part II group B (economics) had already read some economic theory. This was certainly the case with graduates of Part I, in which the study of economics had been considerably extended. Marshall had divided the economics curriculum of Part I into four major subjects: (i) consumption; (ii) production; (iii) value (i.e. relations between the two); and (iv) policy or applied economics.[73] Students were advised that there 'will be required throughout a study of fundamental notions and their appropriate definitions: of the scope and method of the science: and of its relations to other branches of social science'.[74] The reading-list was changed accordingly. Marshall's *Principles* replaced his *Economics of Industry*, and Mill was relegated to the list of recommended additional reading. As for the rest of Part I, it consisted of papers in psychology (two), logic and methodology (two), ethics (one), and a paper of essays.

In discussing the proposed extension of economics in Part II, Marshall outlined his concept of an advanced course as consisting of: (i) unanalytical acquaintance with leading facts as a basis (i.e. a groundwork in the description and simple history which set forth records of events and conditions and circumstances of life and action – most people know enough from the ordinary course of life to be able to pass by this stage); the study of facts from the (ii) elementary qualitative, (iii) compound qualitative, and (iv) quantification (of *some* but not all facts) point of view; and the use of (v) simple general, (vi) complex general, and (vii) detailed and technical synthesis or 'applied economics' in subordination to ideals and aims.[75] In other words, Marshall saw the empirical and policy-oriented aspects of economics as vital, although not much was intended in the way of training in empirical fact-gathering. Students were expected to demonstrate proficiency in high theory and especially in 'a more careful and exact study

72 *CUR*, 18 May 1897.
73 Marshall to Foxwell, 26 April 1897: Marshall III (28).
74 *CUR*, 18 May 1897.
75 Marshall to Foxwell, 25 January 1897: Marshall III (26).

of the mutual interaction of economic phenomena, especially in recent times: and to have grappled with the difficulties of disentangling the effects of different causes, and of assigning to each as nearly as may be its relative magnitude and importance'.[76] The paper on political science in Part II remained unaltered.

Marshall had hoped for even greater specialization, but even so he had succeeded in establishing economics, with political science as a junior partner, as a semi-autonomous discipline requiring special training, preferably by specialist teachers. Whereas elementary economics was still taught in Part I in association with other subjects, advanced economics had been allowed glorious isolation in Part II, group B. At the same time, Marshall had succeeded in enhancing the subject's image of cohesion and unity, replacing the confusion of methods and theories evident in the late 1880s. According to S. J. Chapman, who had read moral sciences Part I after having graduated from Owens College, Manchester (1891), Marshall had established

one simple principle of value, which ran up and down, from wants through production and exchange to distribution and vice versa ... Moreover, he introduced an apparatus of analysis, founded on the differential calculus, by means of which it could be presented within the long-period and the short-period which he abstracted for the purposes of his investigation ... In short, Marshall, by furnishing a unifying conception and a method, raised economics to a higher scientific level.[77]

Although the students reading moral sciences Part II showed distinct promise, they were not quite what Marshall had hoped for. His heart was set, he told Foxwell, on capturing students fresh from school,[78] their minds still uncluttered by the material of previous university studies. Instead, most of his moral sciences students were graduates of other universities or other triposes, and most of them regarded economics as a means of rounding off their education rather than a vocation.[79] It may well have seemed as if no amount of tinkering could ever transform the moral sciences tripos into a sufficiently attractive school of economics. Consequently, Marshall came to the conclusion that the continued association of economics with the moral sciences would mean the former's inevitable stagnation. The study of

76 *CUR*, 18 May 1897.
77 Chapman, unpublished autobiography, p.22. See also S. J. Chapman, *Political Economy*, London 1912, pp.19–20: 'to Dr Marshall belongs the distinction ... of having presented economic phenomena unified for the first time in an all-embracing theory'.
78 Marshall to Foxwell, 23 February 1902: Marshall III (46).
79 Marshall to Foxwell, 14 February 1902: Marshall III (44).

philosophy contributed little, or so he now claimed, to the training of economists, and the small intake of students resulted in little demand for trained young economists as tutorial fellows, thereby hampering the development of a permanent faculty.[80] It was not as if economics as such was inherently unattractive. The recently founded London School of Economics (1895)[81] had proved that a different arrangement of economic studies could be popular, thereby strengthening Marshall's belief that an alternative institutional approach to the study of economics 'will strengthen the demand in Cambridge for a bona fide economics school, under a Board which shall regard it as a study worth having in itself and not as an "inferior study"'.[82] As for the recently reorganized history tripos, while popular, it still was '*not* economics proper'. Nor did Marshall wish to have economics permanently associated with the history school.[83] The regulations it seemed would have to undergo another round of changes. The current situation was intolerable in Marshall's view. Through 'causes for which no one is – in the main – responsible', he wrote in 1902, '*the curriculum to which I am officially attached has not provided me with one single high class man devoting himself to economics during the sixteen years of my Professorship*'.[84]

In the meantime, Marshall concentrated his efforts on raising a cadre of committed young scholars – the foundation upon which a future school of economics might be erected. With the German model in mind, Marshall intended to transfer the responsibility for his general elementary courses to younger men who had been trained by him, leaving him greater freedom to concentrate on more important work.[85] His choice fell on A. C. Pigou, a graduate of the history tripos who had chosen moral sciences Part II for his second school. Pigou, a Harrovian and a King's scholar, had already acquired something of a reputation as a Union orator, while expressing distinctly safe views tending towards political and economic conformism.[86] Apart from his Union career,[87] Pigou was elected honorary secretary of the revived Cambridge Economic Club in February 1898, while still reading history, and by November 1898 he had replaced Chapman as its president.[88] As of early

80 Marshall to Keynes, 30 August 1897: Keynes I (102).
81 Referred to in Marshall to Keynes, 16 August 1897: Keynes I (111).
82 Marshall to Keynes, 30 August 1897: Keynes I (102).
83 Marshall to Keynes, 16 August 1897: Keynes I (111).
84 Marshall to Keynes, 30 January 1902: Keynes I (125).
85 See Marshall to Keynes, 23 February 1899: Keynes I (115).
86 See reports of Union debates in *Cambridge Review*, 20 January 1898 and 30 May 1901.
87 Secretary, June 1899: Vice-President, October 1899.
88 *Cambridge Review*, 24 February and 10 November 1898. See also ibid., 19 October 1899, and 1 February 1900.

1900, Marshall began to take an active interest in Pigou's career. He supported his application for an extension lectureship, describing him as showing 'in some respects exceptional genius'.[89] In 1900 Marshall decided to use £100 out of the £200 added to his annual emolument from St John's to establish a university lectureship in economics.[90] The position was initially filled by Bowley and, from 1901–2, by Pigou. Marshall wished Pigou to teach 'one general course of lectures suitable for high-class beginners, and treated from the scientific as distinguished from the historical [Cunningham] and literary [Foxwell] point of view',[91] leaving Marshall responsible for the advanced courses. Not everyone, least of all Foxwell,[92] was happy with Marshall's choice, but no one was prepared to challenge him.

Meanwhile, Sidgwick's death in 1900[93] improved the chances of pushing through yet another reform in the status of economics. Marshall took the currently most attractive course – history I followed by moral sciences II, the combination chosen by Pigou – as the basis for his programme of economic studies with which he approached the History Board. In May 1901 a committee consisting of Marshall, Ward, and G. L. Dickinson was appointed in order to discuss the development of economics and political science within the history tripos. At the time, Marshall hoped that discussions might lead to the constitution of a semi-autonomous tripos, run by a special committee within the history tripos on lines similar to physics or biology in the natural sciences tripos.[94]

In his advocacy of greater autonomy for economics, Marshall introduced a variation on the more general demand for greater attunement of higher education to national needs.[95] According to Marshall, a restructured course in economics would greatly benefit not only

> professional students of economics and politics: but also . . . those who are preparing for: (a) Work in Parliament, or on local Representative bodies: (b) The Home or Indian Civil Service: diplomacy and the consular service: (c) the higher work of large

89 BEMS 55/24, University of Cambridge Library. Marshall's reference is dated 23 February 1900. I am grateful to Mr M. J. Allen for permission to study file 55.
90 Marshall to Keynes, 4 March 1900: Keynes I (116).
91 Marshall to Keynes, 8 January 1901: Keynes I (122).
92 See Foxwell to Keynes, 6 October 1900: Keynes I (40), quoted in full in Maloney, *Marshall, Orthodoxy and Professionalisation*, p.57 n.
93 See the reference to Sidgwick in Marshall, *A Plea*, p.3.
94 Marshall to Foxwell, 8 May 1901: Marshall III (41).
95 On the specific case of economics, see O. Lodge's statement in *The Times*, 22 December 1901, and the LSE's calendar for 1900–1, quoted in *The London School of Economics Register*, London, 1934, pp.viii–ix.

businesses, public and private, including railways, shipping, foreign trade and those branches of manufacture that do not require a long study of engineering and physics: (d) the duties of a country gentleman: (e) the service of the poor.[96]

Should the university persist in ignoring the needs of the business community, Marshall warned, it was likely to lose its financial support in favour of the new civic universities. Yet Marshall had no intention of following the LSE's example of vocationally-oriented studies. Cambridge should aim, in his view, to develop a student's general faculties rather than his technical skills.[97]

Marshall's discussions with his colleagues led to a proposed two-part curriculum resembling history I and moral sciences II without the additional subjects of psychology, logic, pre-industrial history, etc. However, by then it had become clear that a considerable number of historians were unwilling to allow Marshall to repeat in the history tripos what had already been done to moral sciences. In a later statement, F. W. Maitland, who had already expressed his misgivings concerning the 1897 regulations, argued that

the friction between History and Economics has increased, is increasing and will not diminish for a long time to come. Each desires to make the other an ancillary science. In this respect our little world in Cambridge is only a faithful copy of the big world. Let both sides go their own ways and they will someday come to a good understanding. Unprincipled 'deals' in bewildering 'options' are the only alternative.[98]

Marshall, then, was either forced or encouraged by some members of the History Board to produce a more ambitious plan for a new autonomous tripos.

Accordingly, Marshall devoted a considerable part of his *Plea* for the new tripos to an exposition of the desirability of separating economics from history, while careful not to belittle in any way the importance of the latter.[99] The economist was mainly concerned with the present, and 'in spite of the great advance of historical knowledge, the present age has to resolve its own economic problems for itself, with less aid from

96 Scheme appended to Marshall to Foxwell, 8 May 1901: Marshall III (41).
97 See Marshall's letter, 'Education for business men', *The Times*, 18 December 1905.
98 F. W. Maitland, 'Economics and history', signed 2 June 1903, in Marshall Papers, Large Brown Box (31). See also J. R. Tanner and S. Leathes, 'The proposed new tripos', signed 28 May 1903, ibid.
99 Cf. his comment to Foxwell that the moral sciences could not, on their own, 'afford a good training for young men'. Marshall to Foxwell, 29 January 1902: Marshall III (43).

the experience of the past [i.e. pre industrial history] than has been available for any other age'.[100]

Marshall's main theme, however, was the national need for a new approach to the training of the country's future leaders by means of placing greater emphasis on subjects more closely related to current problems. Not, he hastened to add, that the principle of general studies should be abandoned. A balance between the two approaches could be struck whereby both would be realized. 'I myself think,' Marshall wrote, 'that the higher study of economics gives as good a mental training, its breadth and depth being taken together, as any other study: and that, in addition, it develops the human sympathies in an exceptional degree.'[101] At the same time, 'economic issues are growing in urgency and intricacy, and . . . economic causes exert an increasing control on the quality of human life'. Economic studies 'offer abundant scope for the training and the exercise of those mental faculties and energies which it is the special province of a university to develop'. In view of the subject's dual appeal, 'those who are looking forward to a business career or to public life are likely to prefer a residential university which offers a good intellectual training and opportunities for distinction in subjects that will bear on their thoughts and actions in after life',[102] rather than one of the new civic universities where greater stress was placed on vocational training. 'I do not ask,' Marshall emphasized, 'that room be made here for technical studies . . . It may be right that the university of a great city should offer to some classes of business men as direct a training for earning their livelihood as we do to schoolmasters and physicians. But the proper work of the older English universities in relation to business seems to lie in another direction.'[103]

In his efforts to present the prospective tripos as potentially attractive to future business men, Marshall played down the place of pure theory in the curriculum, while underlining the treatment of empirical data which would ensure that 'the study would become truly realistic'.[104] In fact, the history papers in the projected Part I were reduced from four to two,[105] and students who wished to specialize in politics were advised to read history or law instead.[106] Nevertheless, Marshall's presentation of his view of economic studies as primarily realistic proved sufficiently convincing to warrant a protest from J. N. Keynes in favour of assigning greater importance 'to a sound knowledge of economic theory and of

100 Marshall, *A Plea*, p.4.
101 Ibid., p.8.
102 Ibid., p.11.
103 Ibid., p.8.
104 Ibid., p.15.
105 Logic and most of the philosophy papers were omitted entirely.
106 Marshall, *A Plea*, p.16.

the right methods of economic reasoning' rather than to a detailed knowledge of economic facts.[107]

The publication of the *Plea* was followed by a memorandum submitted to the Council of the Senate, requesting the appointment of a syndicate to enquire into the matter.[108] The request was granted, and the syndicate's report on the whole adopted Marshall's position, but added some options to Part II, thereby extending it to fourteen papers, of which only four – three on general economics plus one of essays – were to be compulsory. Like Marshall, the syndicate envisaged the new tripos as essentially non-technical, offering instruction suitable for students 'looking forward to a career in the higher branches of business or public life', as well as 'those who are proposing to devote their lives to the professional study of Economics'[109] – a class of students previously hardly mentioned in the debate.

In the discussion of the report in the Senate, Marshall made it clear that, contrary to earlier impressions, the training of professional economists was his main objective. It still remained true that economists were vitally needed for the 'diagnosis of social maladies' and for the management of the Empire.[110] The provision of a more appropriate education for future business men was surely an important cause, but it was 'not the main object of the movement [to establish the new tripos]: the main object was to render possible a thorough scientific and therefore realistic study of economics'. The subject should be treated on similar lines to physics and mathematics in order to ensure thoroughness. And it was only through early specialization that a sufficiently professional standard could be attained. There was no other way in which economics could be made to develop into a fully-fledged scientific discipline. 'There had been,' Marshall told the Senate, 'in the whole of the eighteen years since he returned to Cambridge, only two men who had had in their third year a knowledge of the realities and a grasp of the machinery of their science, such as a tolerably able student of Physics had in his third year.'

Despite the support of many historians eager to rid their tripos of too much theory, a considerable body of Senate members remained unconvinced. Cunningham, with McTaggart, both members of the syndicate, refused to sign the report and questioned virtually every point raised by Marshall in favour of a new tripos, including its suitability for training future business men, and the value of isolating economics from subjects with which it had previously been

---

107 Keynes to Marshall (copy), 29 January 1902: Marshall I (110).
108 *CUR*, 29 April 1902.
109 Ibid., 10 March 1903.
110 Ibid., 14 May 1903.

associated.[111] McTaggart objected to Marshall's demand for special status for economics while disregarding the University's limited means. Many subjects were forced to share triposes, a state which often proved to be to their benefit in preventing unnecessarily early specialization. Similar objections were raised by Gwatkin, Creighton's heir as the Dixie Professor of Ecclesiastical History, who thought that economics should remain part of the history tripos, to which Marshall replied that 'history to the economist was a means towards his ends, and they must consider what his ends were'.

Following the Senate meeting, the debate was continued up to the vote on 6 June 1903 by means of flysheets and letters to the *Cambridge Review*. As an alternative to a separate tripos, Cunningham suggested the transformation of the special examination (the pass) in political economy into a post-graduate programme of specialized studies – a solution similar to the Oxford diploma.[112] Cunningham's suggestion was further developed by G. E. Green and W. F. Reddaway, who recommended the adaptation of the special examinations to the training of business men.[113] The idea was later mentioned by Marshall in a letter to *The Times* (18 December 1905) in defence of the new tripos, but he appears to have done nothing in the way of its adoption in 1903, probably in order to avoid its possible undermining of his appeal for an independent tripos. Otherwise the discussion mainly reiterated points already made in the Senate, while bringing into relief the very different notions Marshall and his supporters had of the new tripos. Foxwell, for instance, rejected Cunningham's criticism of the dangers of early specialization. Economics, he argued, offered as good a general education as any other tripos. It was 'intimately related to Ethics, Politics, Law, History and even to Philosophy ... Economics, when adequately treated, must include a reference to almost all the aspects of the citizen's life. ... [F]rom the educational point of view ... the study cannot fairly be called narrow.'[114] Marshall, on the other hand, defended rather than denied early specialization on the grounds that 'if a man has not learnt to be thorough before he is twenty-two, he will never learn.'[115]

Marshall's view was defended by Pigou, who wrote in the *Cambridge Review*:

---

111 For Cunningham's position, see ibid. and *Cambridge Review*, 7 May 1903.
112 W. Cunningham, 'Draft resolutions', 9 March 1903: Marshall Papers, Large Brown Box (31).
113 G. E. Green and W. F. Reddaway, 'The proposed new tripos', n.d., ibid.
114 H. S. Foxwell, 'The proposed new tripos', 30 May 1903, ibid.
115 A. Marshall, 'The proposed new tripos', 5 June 1903, ibid.

I am anxious to record my own vivid impressions of the immense time that it takes to get even a rudimentary understanding of general economic theory. It is not a question of the acquisition of detailed information: that is a different matter altogether. The thing that takes time is the realization of the general drift and broad principles of the subject, and it is hardly too much to say that all the work of the first half of the new tripos will be necessary to make candidates see that it has any broad principles or general drift at all.[116]

Economics was raised by Pigou to the level of a mystery. A proper economist was one who had been initiated in the proscribed manner by a recognized master.

On 6 June 1903 the Senate adopted the syndicate's report in favour of a new tripos by 103 votes to 76.[117] Having finally established economics as an independent tripos, Marshall still hoped to preserve the subject's position within the other triposes, probably as a secondary means of student recruitment (i.e. graduates of other triposes reading economics as a second tripos). However, despite his protests, economics was soon excluded from both parts of moral sciences,[118] although it was not until 1909, shortly after Marshall's retirement, that economics was reduced to a sole optional paper in history II[119] (economic history was made a compulsory special subject in Part I). By then the economics tripos had gained sufficient self-confidence to allow the reform in the history tripos to pass without protest. Although the initial student enrolment was small, it had been increasing steadily. In 1908 Pigou was appointed as Marshall's successor, thereby establishing teacher–student continuity. 'I hold', Marshall wrote to Clapham in 1912, 'that the University should be represented to the world as German Universities are, mainly by their chief students being also their chief teachers.'[120] By the same token, Pigou's appointment over Foxwell's head[121] ensured a continued emphasis on Marshallian high theory and policy-orientation, and in turn largely determined the course of the development of economics in the United Kingdom, and their relation to both economic history and business studies. In 1923

116 A. C. Pigou, 'Is an economic tripos necessary?', *Cambridge Review*, 4 June 1903.
117 *CUR*, 9 June 1903.
118 Ibid., 23 February and 8 March 1904.
119 Ibid., 4 May 1909.
120 Marshall to Clapham, 17 May 1912: Marshall III (90)
121 E.g. see S. Webb to W. J. Ashley, 10 June 1908: University of Birmingham Archives, 9/iv/5: 'Marshall seems to have moved Heaven and Earth to exclude . . . Foxwell. I happen to have quite accidentally learned a couple of years ago, that Marshall intended and expected Pigou to succeed him.'

Keynes wrote in his introduction to the *Cambridge Economic Handbooks*:

> the writers of these volumes believe themselves to be orthodox members of the Cambridge School of Economics. At any rate, most of their ideas about the subject, and even their prejudices, are traceable to the contact they have enjoyed with the writings and lectures of the two economists who have chiefly influenced Cambridge thought for the past fifty years: Dr Marshall and Professor Pigou.[122]

For a more detailed account of the subject see Kadish, *Historians, Economists and Economic History*, and 'University Reform and the *Principles*' in *Quaderni di Storia dell'Economia Politica*, Vol.ix, 1991, nos. 2–3, pp. 289–309.

122 In D. H. Robertson, *The Control of Industry*, London and Cambridge 1923.

6

JEVONS'S CONTRIBUTION TO THE TEACHING OF POLITICAL ECONOMY IN MANCHESTER AND LONDON

R. D. Collison Black

At the beginning of the nineteenth century none of those thinkers in Britain who were advancing the study of political economy were doing so from academic chairs in the subject – with the sole exception of Malthus after 1805. At the beginning of the twentieth century almost all such British thinkers held chairs of economics or political economy. Understanding of the process by which this change came about may be helped by a study of the way in which one leading nineteenth-century economist came also to be an academic.

W. Stanley Jevons (1835–82) provides a good subject for such a study. He holds a well-defined and accepted place in the history of economic thought as one of the makers of the 'Marginal Revolution', and there is a strong case for regarding him as one of the pioneers of modern economics.[1] At the same time Jevons was one of the first English economists whose career was mainly centred upon academic appointments outside the ancient universities of the United Kingdom. In this chapter, the three main phases into which that career was divided will be examined in sequence. The first deals with his early years, detailing the process by which Jevons came to be first an economist and then an academic; the second covers the period of his appointments at what was then Owens College, Manchester, from 1863 until 1876; and the third examines the last period of his life in London, during most of which he held the Chair of Political Economy at University College, London.

---

1 R. D. Collison Black, 'W. S. Jevons, 1835–82', in D. P. O'Brien and J. R. Presley (eds), *Pioneers of Modern Economics*, London: Macmillan, 1981, p.1.

I

The facts of Jevons's biography are well known and documented and need not be repeated here,[2] but certain features need to be stressed if his development as an academic economist is to be fully understood.

Although generally 'not in academic bowers but oppressed by mercantile and senatorial cares',[3] the classical economists nevertheless contrived to be curiously detached from the Industrial Revolution which was going on all around them, although in that struggle the captains of industry appealed frequently to 'the principles of political economy'. London, Edinburgh, Oxford, and Cambridge formed the economists' personal milieu, and the background of their studies was moral philosophy, not the natural philosophy which was finding practical applications in the 'dark satanic mills'. By contrast, Jevons's whole background was that of the industrial north of England at the height of its development; he was born and reared in Liverpool, where his father's family were engaged in the iron trade. His mother was a daughter of William Roscoe, who had combined a career as a banker with distinguished contributions to botany and the history of the Renaissance. Jevons thus grew up in a family where the idea of obtaining a living by working in industry or commerce was taken for granted, but in which there was also a remarkable breadth of culture, both literary and scientific.

The Jevons and Roscoe families were Unitarians, and as such were part of the Nonconformist community of the north of England which played so large a part in the social and economic development of the country in the Victorian era. Their outlook was always liberal, some-times almost radical, and they always preserved a sturdy independence of mind: 'we Unitarians don't pray by Command of any human auth-ority', wrote Thomas Jevons to his son William Stanley, when a day of prayer for peace was decreed by Royal Proclamation in 1855.[4] Through a wide circle of Nonconformist relations and friends the Jevons family mixed with some of the leading intellectual families of the time, such as the Martineaus[5] – but only with those who shared their dissenting outlook.

2 R. Konekamp, 'Biographical introduction' in R. D. Collison Black (ed.), *Papers and Correspondence of William Stanley Jevons*, Vol.I, London: Macmillan, 1972, pp.1–52.
3 From Thomas de Quincey's comment on Ricardo in *Confessions of an English Opium Eater* (1821), quoted in M. Blaug, *Ricardian Economics*, New Haven: Yale University Press, 1958, p.v.
4 R. D. Collison Black (ed.), *Papers and Correspondence of William Stanley Jevons*, 7 Vols., London: Macmillan, 1972–81, Vol.II, p.132.
5 Konekamp, 'Biographical introduction', pp.2–3.

To people from such a background, the idea of sending their sons to public school and thence to Oxford or Cambridge simply did not occur at this time. Nonconformists were not allowed to graduate from Oxford until 1854, and from Cambridge until 1856, and all religious tests were not abolished at these universities until 1871. W. S. Jevons began his education at the Mechanics Institute High School in Liverpool, but in 1850 he was sent to University College School in London, founded in 1830 and 'remarkable for its originality . . . The aim throughout was mental discipline and as it contributed to that, so each subject was judged. There was no religious teaching, and the boys were of many creeds and denominations'.[6] Jevons left the school in 1851, at the age of sixteen, as was then normal, and entered University College, London.

During the two years which he spent there, 1851–3, Jevons's main interest was in chemistry, although he also took courses in botany, mathematics, classics, and history. In his spare time he took long walks through the commercial and manufacturing parts of the East End of London, and it seems to have been as a result of these that he became interested in what he called 'the industrial mechanism of society'.[7] Political economy in the formal sense formed no part of his studies, and indeed courses in it were not being offered at University College in those years.[8]

In the second term of the academic year 1852–3 Jevons had already 'firmly fixed not to enter a profession but rather to go into business of some kind'.[9] It appears to have been accepted without question by both Jevons and his family that he would not complete a third year at college, and the idea of leaving without a degree seems to have caused him no concern at this stage. His father suggested that he might use his interest and ability in chemistry to make a career as a manufacturing chemist, but that could not have been done in Liverpool, and at this time Jevons's preference was to live at home, working in some commercial concern and pursuing his scientific and literary interests in his spare time.[10] Neither the boy nor his family considered that any specific education for commerce would be necessary; that would all be a matter of learning on the job.

No sooner had these plans become settled in Jevons's mind than they were upset by an unexpected turn of events. His cousin, H. E. (Harry) Roscoe, with whom he lodged in London, was already a student at

6 H. Hale Bellot, *University College, London 1826–1926*, London: University of London Press, 1929, p.171.

7 W. S. Jevons, *The Principles of Economics and other Papers*, London: Macmillan, 1905, p.vii.

8 Bellot, *University College, London*, p.252.

9 Black, *Papers and Correspondence*, Vol.II, p.37.

10 Ibid., Vol.I, pp.78–9.

University College and determined to devote his life to the study of chemistry. According to Roscoe, Thomas Graham, the Professor of Chemistry at University College,

> sent for me one day and offered me the post of Assayer in the Mint at Sydney, which had just been established. It was worth £600–700 a year, and was a post which many young men would have jumped at. I felt, however, that I could not leave my mother and sister, as they did not wish to go to Australia, so I declined it with thanks, but told him that I knew a young man who was singularly well fitted for the position, and who I believed would accept it. This young man was Stanley Jevons.[11]

Jevons's first reaction to this proposal was that it was 'perfectly impossible'; nevertheless he consulted his father about it and was somewhat dismayed when the latter advised him to accept the post. It is not relevant to the subject of this chapter to examine why Thomas Jevons gave this advice and why Stanley followed it. For the latter, it might simply have meant that he traded the uncertain prospect of a business career in Liverpool for a lucrative but obscure post, or series of posts, as a gold assayer in Australia. Eventually though, Jevons had simply too much intellectual curiosity and originality to allow this to happen. Once he had settled in Sydney and established the Assay Department of the new Mint, his duties were light enough to enable him to devote a good deal of time to pursuing his own studies.

At first, these were mainly concerned with meteorology, culminating in a major study of *The Climate of Australia and New Zealand*,[12] but Jevons also published the results of his research into the geology of New South Wales. He recorded in his personal journals how his scientific interests had moved from chemistry to geology and then to meteorology,[13] but from late 1856 onwards, Jevons began to read widely in political economy, finding it, as he declared to his sister Henrietta, 'deeply interesting'.[14] By February 1858, the view of the relationship between economic theory and other social sciences to which he always adhered was clearly formulated in his mind, and he had firmly decided to devote himself to their study. 'You may feel assured', he told Henrietta,

> that to extend and perfect the abstract or the detailed and practical knowledge of man and society is perhaps the most useful and necessary work in which anyone can now engage. There are

11 H. E. Roscoe, *The Life and Experiences of Sir Henry Enfield Roscoe*, London: Macmillan, 1906, p.39.
12 Black, *Papers and Correspondence*, Vol.I, pp.22–5.
13 Ibid., p.114.
14 Ibid., Vol.II, p.292.

plenty of people engaged with physical science, and practical science and arts may be left to look after themselves, but thoroughly to understand the principles of society appears to me now the most cogent business.[15]

'I think that it is my mission to apply myself to such subjects', he told her, 'and it is my intention to do so.'

Once having formed that intention, Jevons was soon equally clear in his mind that to carry it into effect he must leave Australia, return to England, and extend his education. 'I do not know whether I have before explained why I desire at once to leave Sydney', he wrote to his sister Lucy in July 1858. 'It is because I believe my education is but now continuing, and that by staying here it is checked, and irretrievably deferred.'[16] At home in Liverpool, some of the older generation of his family were appalled by the folly of young Stanley's decision to leave a well-paid position with excellent prospects in order to come back to London as a student, condemning himself and his sisters to living in near penury on his savings without any assurance that his studies would lead to secure or profitable employment in the future. To himself and his immediate family, Jevons justified his decision in terms which have often been interpreted as foreshadowing the theory of capital which he later developed; 'You do not duly appreciate', he told Henrietta,

> the comparative importance of *preparation and performance*, or perhaps as I may illustrate it, of *Capital* and *labour*. You desire to begin and hammer away at once, instead of spending years in acquiring strength and skill and then striking a few blows of immensely greater effect than your unskilled ones, however numerous, could be. We enter here into one of those deeply laid and simple propositions of Economy which I hope someday to work out into a symmetrical and extensive manner hitherto unattempted even by Mills [sic] or Adam Smith. [17]

Six months earlier he had explained his position to Lucy with the words: 'Will the future be better than the present to one who makes no present sacrifices? Granting that a given position is good, may it not be wisely relinquished if a happier one may be attained, even after much trouble?'[18]

Harry Roscoe, who had been a student with Jevons at University College in 1851–2, had graduated in 1853 and gone on to carry out research for a doctorate in chemistry at Heidelberg under the great

15 Ibid., p.322.
16 Ibid., p.332.
17 Ibid., pp.359–60.
18 Ibid., p.331.

Robert Wilhelm Bunsen, who had just taken up his appointment as professor there. Returning to London in 1856, Roscoe had begun to practise as a consulting chemist, but when the Chair of Chemistry at the recently established Owens College in Manchester fell vacant, he applied for and was appointed to it in 1857.

Owens College, the forerunner of the present University of Manchester, had opened its doors to its first students in 1851. It had been founded as a result of a bequest by John Owens, a Manchester manufacturer, 'for the purpose of affording to youths of the age of fourteen years and upwards instruction in the branches of education taught at the English universities, free from the religious tests which limit the extension of university education'.[19] Since Roscoe came from the same Unitarian background as his cousin Stanley Jevons, Owens was one of the few colleges in England at which he was likely to obtain an appointment at this time. Roscoe was elated by his appointment and wrote to Jevons that he hoped 'in time to succeed in making this the school of Chemistry in the North',[20] but his initial prospects were uncertain enough, as the college had only thirty-five students and 'was at that time nearly in a state of collapse'.[21]

Nevertheless, Jevons saw Roscoe as a fortunate example of what could be achieved by study: 'I often think with pleasure of your agreeable position in England', he wrote to his cousin while still in Sydney,

> indeed if there is any man I envy it is a Professor. Still when I knew you in London, you devoted all your prospects to a pursuit of which the primary results are never very brilliant and often long deferred. Even well off as you now are, you may perhaps be considered to have better luck than many Scientific men. Do not blame me therefore, for abandoning a good salary because it interferes with other desirable things, even if I starve in consequence, as is not improbable.[22]

In spite of this, it seems clear that Jevons did not return to his studies at University College with any definite expectation that they would open the door to an academic career for him. At the start of the second term of his resumed studies, he wrote to his brother Herbert:

> I have no definite plan of earning money, but after my B.A. will try what can be done in the way of writing or teaching, so as to keep myself while working for my M.A. which I have a great desire to take

19 J. Thompson, *The Owens College: its Foundation and Growth*, Manchester 1886, pp.16–17.
20 Black, *Papers and Correspondence*, Vol.II, p.322.
21 Roscoe, *Life and Experiences*, p.102.
22 Black, *Papers and Correspondence*, Vol.II, p.347.

in the Political Economy and Mental Philosophy branch – as these are entirely the subjects I should follow in any case. Harry Roscoe whom I saw in London at Christmas is rather indignant that I am no longer a Chemist and wants to know how I shall get my bread, which perhaps is quite a pertinent question.[23]

Pertinent the question certainly was, and it gave Jevons a fair amount of anxiety, but in the years 1860 to 1862 it must have been forced to the back of his mind by the sheer volume of intellectual work he was undertaking. During this period Jevons was not only studying a wide range of subjects, some for the first time, to meet the course requirements of his BA and then of his MA, but he was also doing wholly original and pioneering work in both theoretical and applied economics.

In July 1860, in a letter to his brother Herbert, he set out the catalogue of work which he was about to 'attack in earnest' for the BA examination in October, in which he gained a first: 'Latin, Greek, Mathematics, Roman History, Greek History, English History, French, Animal Physiology, Logic, Natural Philosophy, Moral Philosophy, all of which require looking up seriously and many to be learnt from the beginning'.[24] He had already taken the college examinations in June in mental philosophy and political economy and was still smarting from the 'sad reverse' which he had suffered in the latter subject by being placed equal third with another student, when he had confidently expected first place. 'However', he consoled himself, 'I shall fully avenge myself when I bring out my "Theory of Economy" and re-establish the science on a sensible basis'.[25] For it was only in February of that year that Jevons had 'fortunately struck out what I have no doubt is *the true theory of Economy* so thorough-going and consistent, that I cannot now read other books on the subject without indignation'.[26]

Since he attributed his sad reverse 'to a difference of opinion which is perfectly allowable having prejudiced the Professor against my answers', Jevons feared that he would not succeed in winning the Ricardo Scholarship in Political Economy. But his fears were groundless, and he was awarded the scholarship in December 1860, adding a useful £60 to his income for the following year. By this time he was back to work at University College on mathematics and Greek, and attending James Martineau's lectures on mental philosophy.

Throughout 1861 Jevons went on with his studies for the MA degree and took the final examination in June 1862. He was awarded the

23 Ibid., p.406.
24 Ibid., p.415.
25 Ibid., p.416.
26 Ibid., p.410.

degree with honours and a gold medal. A letter which he wrote to his younger brother Tom, in December 1861, gives an indication of the range and depth of study which Jevons undertook to achieve this:

Only lately the *additional* subjects for the M.A. were published – and are as follows:- 'On the nature and principles of Social order and Social progress, or of Civilization' and in the History of Philosophy, 'Greek Speculation – the Theaetetus and Gorgias of Plato and the Nicomachean Ethics of Aristotle'. Is not this a pretty prospect ... Then there is the whole of Mental and Moral Philosophy, Logic, Political Economy etc.[27]

In the spring and summer of 1861 Jevons had also been 'very busy at present with an apparently dry and laborious piece of work', the collection and compilation of data for his proposed Statistical Atlas. The Atlas itself was never fully completed, because Jevons could not find a publisher who would take it on, and could only afford to pay for the publication of two of the diagrams, which appeared in June 1862. This work formed the foundation of the paper 'On the Study of Periodic Commercial Fluctuations', which Jevons submitted to Section F of the British Association for the Advancement of Science in 1862, along with his 'Brief Account of a General Mathematical Theory of Political Economy'. It also led on to his classic work, *A Serious Fall in the Value of Gold Ascertained*, which was to appear in 1863. Thus, as one recent authority has put it, 'Jevons' statistical work was far-ranging, and in the early 1860's almost compulsive'.[28] What is really remarkable is that in 1862, he not only completed successfully the formidable programme of study required for his MA, but he also carried out what the same authority has rightly called 'his immense labour on banking and price statistics', and set out in his 'Brief Account' the essentials of the theory which has earned him a place in the history of economics as a pioneer of the Marginal Revolution.

Despite this prodigious effort and achievement, the autumn of 1862 saw Jevons in the same sad position as too many of our graduate students today – he was highly qualified, but he had no regular employment and little prospect of any. Beyond that superficial similarity, however, the comparison cannot be sustained; for one thing, the range of academic and other appointments open to Jevons was very small. The number of professorships of political economy in England at the time could still be counted on the fingers of one hand, and appointments below professorial level were almost unknown. It is not

27 Ibid., p.437.
28 S. M. Stigler, 'Jevons as statistician', *The Manchester School*, Vol.50 (1982), pp.354–65.

surprising, therefore, that Jevons did not at first think in terms of an academic post. His initial plan seems to have been to support himself by journalism, writing mainly for weekly reviews, and to carry on his research for publication in books and pamphlets which might gain him a reputation.

He had before him the example of another cousin, Richard Holt Hutton (1826–97), who had been associated with Walter Bagehot as joint editor of the *National Review* and assistant editor of *The Economist.* Hutton had left *The Economist* in 1861 to become editor of the *Spectator.* He helped Jevons by giving him the opportunity to write some articles for this periodical in the autumn of 1862; but Jevons, who had dashed off many pieces for the Sydney newspapers with apparent ease, now seemed to find 'hack writing . . . destructive of any true thinking',[29] and he made little progress with it. Since the opportunity to stay in London and work in the Reading Room of the British Museum was vital for his own research, Jevons hit on the plan of starting a form of literary agency, offering for a fee of three shillings an hour to look up material for 'Authors and others not at the moment within reach of works or objects to which they may need to refer'.[30]

The possibility of a university appointment first became a reality for Jevons in December 1862, when Harry Roscoe mentioned to him that there was an opening for a tutor at Owens College. It was a post which offered the prospect of hard work for small pay, for it 'involved tutoring students in difficulty from all the subjects taught in the college by the nine Professors who constituted the total teaching staff'.[31] Jevons was at first doubtful about the post itself, and about the wisdom of a move from London to Manchester. He decided to delay a final decision, but his scheme of a literary agency did not prosper, and in a few months Jevons had come round to the view that the tutorship 'will be a step in the right direction. After some experience in teaching, and by degrees in lecturing, I shall be more ready to offer myself for any professorship that may happen – perhaps one at Owens College itself. There is no doubt, I think, that the professorial line is the one for me to take'.[32]

So, late in April 1863, Jevons went up to Manchester 'to arrange or consider the tutorship affair'. Though still conscious of 'the dull nature of the town, and the regret in leaving London and the Museum', he was favourably impressed by the account of the tutor's duties given by the Principal, J. G. Greenwood (who had been one of his teachers at University College School), and by Owens College and its prospects. So

29 Black, *Papers and Correspondence*, Vol.III, p.6.
30 Ibid., Vol.I, p.190.
31 W. H. Chaloner, 'Jevons in Manchester, 1863–1876', *The Manchester School*, Vol.40 (1972), p.74.
32 Black, *Papers and Correspondence*, Vol.III, p.6.

it was agreed that he should go there 'if some 20 or 25 pupils offer to pay 3 guineas each for the Session'.[33] Presumably this condition was met, for Jevons wound up his affairs in London, spent the summer 'practising up my Mathematics, Greek and Latin for my tutoring work at Manchester but . . . chiefly working at my logical system',[34] and took up his duties at Owens College in October 1863.

II

The years which Jevons spent at Owens College, Manchester – from 1863 to 1876 – are perhaps the years of his career of most interest from the point of view of the institutionalization of political economy. For Jevons himself they were the years in which he devoted most time and effort to the teaching of the subject, and which witnessed his promotion from a very junior tutor to a full professor. For Owens College they were years of rapid growth and transition, away from the ailing state in which Harry Roscoe had found it, and towards becoming a major civic university.

In 1863 Owens College had 110 day and 312 evening students.[35] Day students could enter at the age of fourteen; evening students had to be at least sixteen; the only other entrance qualification required of them was an ability to read and write and a knowledge of 'the first four rules of Arithmetic'. With the day students Jevons's basic duties were to consist 'in teaching small classes of six or eight students for some two or three hours per day, as well as giving . . . general assistance',[36] but the number of students prepared to pay the three guinea fee for the tutor's services seems not to have come up to Principal Greenwood's forecast in the first year,[37] and so Jevons also undertook evening classes, for which there was an additional payment of £15 for a course of twenty lectures. His meticulously detailed reports to the Principal on each year's lectures still survive among his papers at the John Rylands Library in Manchester,[38] and show that in 1863–4 he gave a course on logic to twenty-two students, one on political economy to eleven students, and two others on 'Junior Geometry' and arithmetic to thirteen students. In the latter instance Jevons's comment that the attendance of the younger students was 'very uncertain, and their progress consequently could not be ensured', serves as a reminder of the wide range of age, ability, and application of the students he taught.

33 Ibid., p.14.
34 Ibid., p.29.
35 Thompson, *Owens College*, p.245.
36 Black, *Papers and Correspondence*, Vol.III, p.9.
37 Ibid., pp.9, 52.
38 John Rylands University Library of Manchester, Jevons Archives, 6/4/14.

Jevons had expected his first year's work as a tutor to be 'very novel and hard ... and most inadequately paid', and in none of these respects was he disappointed; his income from Owens College in 1863–4 was 'nearly £100'.[39] At the end of his first term of teaching he confessed himself, not surprisingly, 'slightly used up ... probably because my four evening lectures require considerable exertion after the day's work'.[40] Looking back on his first session as a college tutor in June 1864, Jevons admitted to himself that his work had often given him 'intense discouragement', but that he had also 'learned to speak with some composure in public'.[41]

Whatever problems and anxieties teaching may have brought for Jevons – and they were not slight – he did not allow them to interfere with the progress of his own research. At this time he was completing the work for his paper on 'The Variation of Prices and the Value of the Currency since 1782',[42] an important extension of the index number work he had done for *A Serious Fall.* The collection and collation of the data for it was, in Jevons's own opinion, 'a most long and tedious piece of work indeed',[43] but that did not deter him from spending the whole summer vacation of 1864 in London compiling material 'in connection with the question of the exhaustion of Coal, which I look upon as the coming question'.[44]

Jevons undoubtedly chose this because 'a good publication on the subject would draw a good deal of attention. I am convinced that it is necessary for the present at any rate to write on popular subjects', he told his brother Herbert.[45] Why should Jevons have taken this view? Keynes gave the generally accepted answer when he referred to Jevons's

> extreme anxiety that his ideas should not be overlooked. His highly original communications to the British Association (in 1862) had fallen flat. His diagrams for business forecasting ... had been published at his own expense and, barely mentioned in *The Times* and *The Economist*, lost him money. His pamphlet on Gold (in 1863) though it attracted attention a little later on, had sold 74 copies. Yet he had a passionate sense of vocation and of having something valuable to give the world.[46]

All this is true, and Keynes's interpretation of the facts is valid

39 Black, *Papers and Correspondence*, Vol.III, pp.34, 52.
40 Ibid., p.48.
41 Ibid., Vol.I, p.196.
42 *Journal of the [Royal] Statistical Society*, Vol.28, pp.394–420.
43 Black, *Papers and Correspondence*, Vol.I, p.197.
44 Ibid., Vol.III, p.58.
45 Ibid., p.52.
46 J. M. Keynes, 'William Stanley Jevons', in *Essays in Biography*, Vol. 10, *Collected Writings of John Maynard Keynes*, London: Macmillan, 1972, p.115.

enough, but there is a further point which he did not bring out. Jevons had deliberately sacrificed a good income and invested much of his savings in further education because of his passionate sense of vocation. But he still had his living to make, and after five years he had no secure source of adequate income. Had he been firmly established in academic life in 1864 he could have gone on in the knowledge that the works which did not sell widely were nevertheless gaining him recognition among his peers, and that his reputation would grow as his scholarly work progressed. At that time, however, he had no such place and could not be sure of gaining it; the only other way of giving his ideas to the world and making a living out of them was to become a nationally recognized author. Publishers and editors of weeklies, monthlies, and quarterlies would not then reject his productions, theoretical or applied, but, on the contrary, would be competing to pay for them.

So, Jevons spent the hot summer of 1864 researching the material for *The Coal Question* in London libraries. He gave the completed manuscript to Alexander Macmillan just after Christmas, but when the book appeared in April 1865 it was not the immediate success its author had hoped. By the end of the year, however, it was receiving wider attention, and when, in the spring of 1866, both Gladstone and J. S. Mill used it as an authoritative reference in the House of Commons, Jevons's status as a 'national name' was assured.

The price which he paid for this success, in terms of physical effort and mental strain, was considerable. 'I worked throughout one vacation at it', he wrote in his journal in December 1865, 'often writing for 5 or 6 hours at a stretch scarcely leaving my seat. No wonder I was somewhat the worse when college work came on in addition to the work of completing the book. I may well be glad it did not destroy my powers'.[47]

Pushing himself in this way, Jevons carried on with his tutoring at Owens during 1864–5. In January 1865 he applied for what he rightly called 'a small Professorship' in logic, mental and moral philosophy at Queen's College, Liverpool, which had been established in 1857 as an offshoot of the Mechanics Institute and 'was the first serious attempt actually to establish a college of higher education in Liverpool'.[48] Jevons was appointed Professor of Political Economy as well as Logic there in May 1865, but held office for only one year. For all its wide scope, the post was really a part-time one involving mainly evening teaching – for which the Council of the college took the unusual step of guaranteeing Jevons 'as to one lecture a week . . . a minimum payment of five shillings per lecture'. Despite the small pay, Jevons liked 'having such a place in the old town and the old Mechanics', and enjoyed the

47 Black, *Papers and Correspondence*, Vol.I, pp.200–1.
48 T. Kelly, *For Advancement of Learning: The University of Liverpool, 1881–1981*, Liverpool: Liverpool University Press, 1981, p.32.

weekly outing from Manchester which it gave him.[49]

In Manchester itself the academic year 1865–6 brought changes at Owens College which had an important effect on Jevons's position. At the same time as his appointment to Queen's College, Liverpool, Jevons had been asked to act as a substitute lecturer in political economy for R. C. Christie, who since 1855 had been Professor of Political Economy as well as holding the Chairs of History and Juris-prudence. In September 1865, A. J. Scott, who after resigning the post of Principal in 1857 had remained as Professor of English, and of Logic and Mental and Moral Philosophy, fell ill, and Principal Greenwood asked Jevons to take over his logic and philosophy classes. Jevons agreed, and at this point resigned his tutorship.[50]

Scott died on 12 January 1866, and two weeks later Christie, who had intended to resign his posts at the end of the session, brought forward his resignation to facilitate redistribution of the subjects hitherto taught by Scott and himself. The committee appointed to consider this question recommended the creation of a Chair of Logic, Mental and Moral Philosophy, and Political Economy.[51] Jevons was obviously a strong candidate for this, and, indeed, his appointment for one year only as a substitute for Christie had been made precisely because a reorganization of this kind was anticipated.[52] At first the trustees of the college wanted to offer the chair to Jevons straight away, but they then decided on principle that it should be advertised. This was done in April 1866, but the report which the trustees received from the appointing committee was that they had 'found the testimonials in favour of Mr. W. S. Jevons so decidedly superior to those of other candidates, that they [had] no hesitation in at once recommending him to the Trustees for election to the Professorship', and the trustees resolved to appoint him 'from the twenty-ninth day of September next at the yearly salary of two hundred and fifty pounds'.[53]

Thus Jevons finally attained the security of a chair, from which he could teach the subjects to which he had decided to devote his life some nine years previously. Principal Greenwood had 'hinted that in the course of a few years I might fairly look forward to a professorship in Owens College' when Jevons first went there 'to consider the tutorship affair',[54] and once Christie had resigned the Chair of Political

49 Black, *Papers and Correspondence*, Vol.III, pp.68, 76.
50 Ibid., pp.75–6.
51 Archives of the University of Manchester, Minutes of the Trustees of Owens College, 25 January and 22 March 1866.
52 Thompson, *Owens College*, p.254.
53 Minutes of the Trustees, 31 May 1866; for the testimonials, see Black, *Papers and Correspondence*, Vol.III, pp.106–20.
54 Black, *Papers and Correspondence*, Vol.III, p.9.

Economy 'there was never much reason to doubt that he [Jevons] would obtain the appointment', as his widow later wrote.[55] Nevertheless, Jevons was far from confident of the outcome until the final decision was announced – even though he had the support of most of the leading economists of the day – Bagehot, Newmarch, Thorold Rogers, Fawcett, Cairnes, and John Stuart Mill himself.

Jevons remained at Manchester for ten years – a decade which saw the peak of his achievements in both logic and political economy. The books and papers which he published during those years served to consolidate the place he had already begun to establish for himself in the development of both those disciplines. They have been extensively discussed in the history of ideas, and those discussions need not be repeated here. However, from the standpoint of the institutionalization of political economy, there is one aspect of Jevons's contribution to the subject in these years which deserves emphasis.

In *Portrait of a University*, written to commemorate the centenary of the foundation of Owens College, H. B. Charlton pointed out that it was largely through Jevons's cousin, H. E. Roscoe,

> that experimental science became the motive force by which the British idea of a university was revolutionised. Investigation by experiment was a general pattern of research which Roscoe had seen in operation in German universities. As a scientific technique, however, it was capable of adaptation to investigations occupied with problems in other fields of knowledge. To Roscoe's impetus on the scientific activities of Owens College, there was soon joined an ideally appropriate co-adjutator on the Arts side, A. W. Ward.

Ward, who succeeded A. J. Scott as Professor of English Language and Literature in 1866, had spent much of his youth in Germany and knew the German academic approach.

> So, whilst Roscoe was domiciling research as a major function in the academic pursuit of the physical sciences, Ward accepted a similar obligation to pass from a teacher's transmission to a researcher's extension of knowledge in the field of the humanities . . . It was the Roscoe–Ward adoption of research as the directive and formative factor in academic development which took Owens College on its first big step forward towards university status.[56]

Jevons, who had begun his training in the same field as Roscoe, carried many of his ideas on research methodology from the physical

55 H. A. Jevons, *Letters and Journal of William Stanley Jevons*, London 1886, p.221.
56 H. B. Charlton, *Portrait of a University 1851–1951*, Manchester 1951, pp.54–5.

sciences into the social sciences, with striking results.[57] But for Owens College, the content of the work he did was perhaps of less significance than the simple fact that Jevons was intensely motivated towards research and contributed actively to the extension of knowledge in his field. In this respect Jevons made an important contribution to the 'new academic policy of research' which Roscoe and Ward were developing at Manchester, and helped to ensure that the growing college was more than simply a teaching institution.

As regards the transmission of ideas by teaching, Jevons's opportunities at Owens were fairly narrowly restricted. In his application for the chair he had written: 'I have long hoped to have an opportunity of extending the teaching of Economic Science. In addition to a course on Abstract Political Economy, I should desire to give courses of lectures on Commercial History, the Social Condition of the People, &c, in which the truths of Economy would be illustrated and enforced'.[58] These hopes were not realized; throughout his tenure of the Chair of Political Economy Jevons appears to have given only one course in the subject to day students, which was repeated in a somewhat condensed form for evening students. In addition, he gave one course of 'rudimentary instruction in political economy' to pupil teachers, because his professorship was partly endowed by the Cobden Memorial Committee, which had made it a condition of the endowment that all teachers in schools supported by public funds in Manchester and Salford should be admitted to such a course without paying a fee.

One student's notes of the course which Jevons gave to day students in his last year at Owens, 1875–6, have survived and have now been published.[59] They make clear that what Jevons himself said about this course was precisely correct: 'I have generally followed somewhat the order of subjects in Mill's Political Economy in perfect independence, however, of his views and methods when desirable'.[60] They do not, as Keynes claimed, show 'how his repression of his own theories had brought his own feeling against Mill to boiling point'.[61] By this time, in fact, Jevons was teaching his own ideas quite freely to his students, and advised them to read his own *Theory of Political Economy*.

In later years there were worthy Manchester bankers and merchants who had learned political economy in Jevons's lectures at Owens, but

---

57 R. D. Collison Black, 'W. S. Jevons and the Foundation of Modern Economics', in R. D. C. Black, A. W. Coats and C. D. W. Goodwin (eds), *The Marginal Revolution in Economics*, Durham N. C.: Duke University Press, 1971, pp.103–5.
58 Black, *Papers and Correspondence*, Vol.III, p.105.
59 Ibid., Vol.VI.
60 Ibid., p.23.
61 Keynes, 'William Stanley Jevons', p.138.

none of his students there themselves became academic economists. That in itself is hardly surprising; out of one course, covering virtually every aspect of the subject, theoretical and applied, Jevons had little or no opportunity to produce specialists. Yet, even if Jevons did not establish an oral tradition at Manchester as Marshall did at Cambridge, he still had more influence on the teaching of economics than is generally realized. In 1875 he produced what he termed a 'semi-popular' book, *Money and the Mechanism of Exchange*, and in 1878 followed the *Primer of Logic*, which he had written in 1876, with a *Primer of Political Economy*. All these texts had large sales, and 'for a period of half a century practically all elementary students both of Logic and of Political Economy in Great Britain and also in India and the Dominions were brought up on Jevons'.[62]

Reconciling the demands of teaching with those of his own research had been a serious problem for Jevons in his early years as a college tutor at Owens, but after his appointment to the chair he found his work 'much more easy, familiar and congenial'.[63] Even so, it was not long before the old dilemma recurred. After going to London to read his paper, 'On the Condition of the Gold Currency', to the Statistical Society in November 1868, he wrote to his brother Herbert: '. . . these journeys rather knock me up. I had three classes on Monday afternoon and evening, went to London on Tuesday morning, read the paper in the evening and back on Wednesday for two classes in the evening. Now, a thing of this sort knocks me up for the rest of the week'.[64] Nevertheless, Jevons 'was so scrupulous that other engagements should not interfere with his lectures at college that he would go through almost any amount of fatigue rather than fail to meet his class at the appointed time'.[65]

Matters came to a crisis early in 1872, after Jevons had written the *Theory of Political Economy* at great speed and had put immense efforts into the preparation of *The Principles of Science*. This time his health was seriously damaged; 'I have been rather more ill than I like to think of', he told his brother again; 'I seem to have exhausted my nervous system by over-work'.[66] He found evening lectures particularly tiring, and on medical advice he employed a substitute to give them in 1872–3, continuing the day lectures himself. Even with his duties reduced in this way, Jevons did not feel he had regained his strength sufficiently to resume all his classes in the following year, and in June 1873 he offered to resign.

62 Ibid., p.142.
63 Black, *Papers and Correspondence*, Vol.III, p.149.
64 Ibid., p.195.
65 H. A. Jevons, *Letters and Journal*, pp.250–1.
66 Black, *Papers and Correspondence*, Vol.III, pp.249.

As early as March 1872 Jevons and his wife had 'almost come to the conclusion, hastened by [his] present state, to leave Manchester and go and live quietly and economically in or near London'.[67] From 1873 until 1876 Jevons went through a long period of uncertainty about this matter. On the one hand, he felt a strong sense of obligation to the authorities of Owens College, and a great liking for the college and his colleagues there. On the other, he seemed to find the burden of teaching, especially evening teaching, almost insupportable, and he was attracted by the possibility of living near London libraries and being in touch with London institutions such as the Statistical Society and the Political Economy Club, of which he had been made an honorary member in 1874. The balance was further shifted in favour of London in 1875, when it became clear that Jevons could have first refusal of the then vacant Chair of Political Economy at University College.

The Council of Owens College was very reluctant to see Jevons resign in 1873 and readily agreed to the alternative which he proposed – that he should be reappointed for a further year but given leave of absence on condition of finding 'an efficient substitute'.[68] At this time the college had no other staff in political economy apart from the professor; the substitute whom Jevons found was W. H. B. Brewer, who had first completed his MA at London University in 1872 and had been helping Jevons with his bibliography of mathematical economics. This temporary appointment did not lead Brewer into a career of university teaching; he subsequently became an inspector of schools.

Jevons tendered his resignation for a second time in May 1874, but was persuaded to carry on, again on the condition that he could employ a deputy to give his evening lectures. So he continued at Owens for the year 1874–5, but in March 1875, John Robson, the Secretary of University College, London, wrote informing him that the Council was about to recommend him for appointment to the Chair of Political Economy there, 'his duties not to commence until next Session'.[69] Owens College then offered to increase Jevons' salary to £300 per annum.[70] Jevons was

---

67 H. A.Jevons, *Letters and Journal*, p.256.
68 Black, *Papers and Correspondence*, Vol.IV, pp.20–1.
69 Ibid., p.109.
70 His widow wrote: 'Mr. Jevons was very sorry that he did not know, before he withdrew his resignation at Owens College, that the professorship of political economy in University College, London, would become vacant in October' (H. A. Jevons, *Letters and Journal*, p.336). This appears to be inconsistent with the fact that Robson's letter to Jevons informing him that the Council of University College, London proposed to appoint him to the chair was dated 8 March 1875, whereas Principal Greenwood wrote to Jevons saying: 'I suppose the next formal step will be the withdrawal of your letters?' only on 7 May 1875 (Black, *Papers and Correspondence*, Vol.IV, pp.108–9, 112–13).

in a difficult position, not only because of his sense of obligation to Owens, but also because the loss of income involved in going to University College, where the professor's salary was only £100, was more than he could readily accept. He appealed to Robson for a delay of six months before matters were finalized, and later suggested that he might be appointed a temporary lecturer at University College, London for the session of 1875–6 so that he could continue to discharge his duties at Manchester for that year at least.[71] However, the Council of Owens College would not accept this, and Jevons had to look about for a substitute lecturer, this time to do the work in London. He told Robson that he had 'in his eye' Mr Alfred Marshall of Cambridge, but it was eventually Foxwell who agreed to take the temporary post. With this arrangement settled, Jevons finally submitted a formal application for the University College professorship in November 1875, and was appointed in December. The Senate of Owens College received this information 'with deep regret', but its members went on to record that 'they heartily wish you a long enjoyment of the honours your achieve-ments have already secured for you, and all prosperity in your new Chair and home'.[72]

III

The circumstances surrounding Jevons's appointment to University College, London were indeed different from those involved in his appointment to the Manchester chair a decade earlier. Jevons was no longer the promising young man who had to respond to an advertise-ment and await the decision of the appointing committee, filled with uncertainty and anxiety. Now he was a Fellow of the Royal Society, a professor whom Owens College would go to considerable lengths to keep, one 'whose ability and energy have signally helped to advance its progress, and whose literary achievements have shed a lustre upon its reputation'.[73] After discussing the position with the Secretary of University College, he could tell his wife: 'it is quite evident that I have the refusal of it and they want me to apply', but the application itself was merely a formality.[74]

Nor was the chair at University College the only one which Jevons might have had in 1875. The same post which brought him confirmation of the London appointment also contained a letter from W. B. Hodgson, Professor of Political Economy at Edinburgh, saying that he was about to resign and hoping that Jevons might be his successor. The

71 Ibid., pp.123–4.
72 Ibid., p.164.
73 Ibid., p.163.
74 Ibid., p.118.

Edinburgh chair carried a salary of £600 per annum, but Jevons had made his decision and did not seriously consider altering it.[75]

This underlines the fact that, although Jevons was sought after as an academic at this time, his move from Manchester to London was not that of a man who, having secured his first chair at the age of thirty-one and fulfilled his earlier promise, was choosing at forty-one to move from a provincial university to a post of greater prestige and responsibility in the capital. Jevons was seeking less responsibility, not more, and reconciled himself to the loss of income involved because it seemed to him that in trying to accomplish what he had set out to do in political economy and logic, 'one labours under disadvantages in not living, like most of the political economists and literary men, in London'.[76]

This linking of political economists with 'literary men' is a recurrent theme in Jevons's correspondence. It serves to emphasize the point that to him an economist was first and foremost a writer, and it was therefore perfectly possible to function without an academic, or, indeed, an institutional base at all. What he deemed essential was access to libraries and 'literary circles' – editors, publishers, and fellow authors – which could best be had in London.

This is not to say that Jevons considered his position at University College, London to be of secondary importance, or that he took his responsibilities there lightly. There was at that time only one course in political economy there, usually consisting of about twenty-four lectures. In his formal application for the chair, Jevons announced his intention 'to extend the course of lectures considerably, giving from 40 to 50 in the session', and also 'to endeavour to make political economy and connected portions of the social sciences a more important feature in the curriculum of the college'. In the first year of his appointment, Jevons did double the number of lectures, but he then reverted to the previous plan of lecturing only once a week. It would seem that experience in London bore out what he wrote from Manchester: 'my own experience here, and that of other teachers in London and elsewhere, forbid me to be very sanguine as to the success of any extended courses of this kind'.[77] At the time of Jevons's appointment, the numbers taking political economy were disappointingly small; Foxwell had only four students in his class in 1875–6. When Jevons took over in 1876–7 this increased to twenty-three, and for the rest of his period of office he had between twenty-five and thirty students each year. The class lists, which still survive in the archives of University

75 Ibid., pp.150, 173.
76 Ibid., p.134.
77 Ibid., p.144.

College, do not reveal the names of any students who went on to become well known in English economics, but they do include a notable number of overseas students. Among these in 1878-9 was Maggiorino Ferraris, who edited the journal *Nuovo Antologia* from 1897 to 1926, and held ministerial portfolios in three Italian governments between 1893 and 1922. In every year, except 1877-8, Jevons's class included one or more Japanese student; these were among the earliest visitors to the West after the Meiji Restoration, and included members of the *samurai* and others who were to take senior offices in the Japanese government. Notable among them were Yoshitane Sannoniya (1843-1903), and Yoshio Kusaka (1851-1923). Sannoniya was a *samurai* who left Japan in 1870 as one of the attendants of Prince Higashi Fushimi, and stayed in England until 1877 when he was appointed Second Secretary in the Japanese Embassy in Berlin. Sannoniya returned to Japan in 1880 to serve first in the Ministry of Foreign Affairs, and later in the Ministry of the Imperial Household. Kusaka came to London in 1876 with Count Inoue to study economics and public finance. After his return to Japan in 1880 he introduced modern systems of registration of births, marriages, and deaths, and of official statistics, and reformed the postal system. He became a prefectural governor and a member of the Diet.

It would appear that through these and other pupils some of Jevons's ideas were carried back to Japan,[78] but from the standpoint of Western economic thought, perhaps the most important pupils Jevons had in London were those he met outside the classroom. He maintained a close friendship with H. S. Foxwell, who was to succeed him at University College, and who started him on his career as a book collector. Jevons was also a strong formative influence on F. Y. Edgeworth, whom he came to know when the latter was trying to develop his practice at the Bar.[79]

Hale Bellot, the historian of University College, London, pointed out that the Chair of Political Economy had three distinguished incumbents in the 1860s and 1870s: J. E. Cairnes, Leonard Courtney, and Jevons, 'yet none of them managed to put very much spirit into the Department'.[80] He did concede, though, that in those days 'the professors were little more than visiting lecturers', and in the circumstances Jevons could not reasonably have been expected to do much more in the college.

Even with the limited duties of his London professorship, it was not long before Jevons began to feel the old tension between the demands

78 I am indebted to Professors Hiroshi Mizuta and Takutoshi Inoue for providing me with information on the careers of Jevons's Japanese students.
79 Black, *Papers and Correspondence*, Vol.V, pp.98, 202.
80 Bellot, *University College*, p.331.

of the lecture room and those of his writing. In the spring of 1878 he was again in uncertain health as a result of overwork, and that autumn he confided to his brother Tom: 'I have, as usual, got a series of books and articles on hand, all of which want writing immediately, and I sometimes feel desperate about ever getting them done'.[81] His duties as an examiner for London University also interrupted his own writing; in September 1880 he wrote to Foxwell: 'You are quite right in thinking that I hate exams, but I hate lecturing even more'.[82] He had just returned from a seaside holiday with his family at Littlehampton, following a month's tour in Norway, but he had not derived much benefit to his health from either. He began his teaching as usual, but after a week or two he decided that he could not continue and resigned his professorship, after obtaining leave to appoint a substitute to carry on his lectures for the remainder of the academic year.[83]

To terminate his academic career so suddenly and finally was a drastic step which Jevons did not take lightly: 'It is impossible to relinquish the employment of eighteen years without some peturbation of spirits, and when I introduced my deputy to a well-filled classroom, I had some pangs of regret', he wrote. 'But I am nevertheless sure that the step was not only wise but indispensable. It is quite impossible for me to go on with trying fixed duties when I have so much literary work on my mind'.[84] So, for the few years of his life which remained, Jevons ceased to be an academic and became what he had originally intended to be when he was working for his MA – a London-based economist who was a freelance writer.

I have suggested elsewhere[85] that Jevons can be regarded as a transitional figure in both economic theory and economic policy, who broke with the classical approach, yet did not completely fit what has since come to be regarded as the neo-classical mould. Something similar might be said of him as regards the institutionalization of political economy. Jevons was very much in contrast to most of the older political economists – coming out of the Nonconformist middle class of the industrial north-west of England and bringing the methods of mathematics and experimental science to bear on the study of society in which his interest came to centre. He was one of the first economists to be trained outside the ancient universities and to make a living and a career out of teaching political economy in the new university colleges which were developing in nineteenth-century England.

81 Black, *Papers and Correspondence*, Vol.IV, p.291.
82 Ibid., Vol.V, p.106.
83 H. A. Jevons, *Letters and Journal*, p.419.
84 Black, *Papers and Correspondence*, Vol.V, p.110.
85 'Transitions in political economy', Manchester Special Lectures, 1982 (unpublished).

Like his cousin Harry Roscoe he proved that teaching a subject meant contributing to it as well as lecturing on it.

Yet Jevons was not the complete academic economist as the twentieth century would see it. He belonged to an era before economists became a scientific community with their own learned societies and journals. That he spent much, but not all of his career, in academic institutions, and that he finished as he began, a freelance writer, must in large part perhaps be attributed to his own physical and mental make-up, and to his preferences and priorities. Yet it seems also to be accountable in some degree to the fact that in Jevons's time the institutionalization of political economy was advancing, but was by no means complete.

7

POLITICAL ECONOMY IN THE NORTHERN CIVIC UNIVERSITIES

Keith Tribe

Political economy was in later nineteenth-century England more a subject of discussion than a subject for teaching. Despite widespread interest in the topics with which it dealt, and a significant volume of associated publications, it nowhere formed the core of a regular course of study. At most, it formed a small part of ordinary BA degrees, or honours history. There were, it is true, a number of academics in Oxford, Cambridge and London who gave the subject a great deal of their attention; but there were very few by 1890 who either gave it their undivided academic attention, or who could be said to have made their living by teaching it. In Cambridge and London it was securely established as part of a course of study – as a paper in the moral sciences tripos taught by Marshall in Cambridge, and in courses at King's and University Colleges.[1] The actual substance of such teaching varied from course to course, and from teacher to teacher – but the low level of teaching activity provided little stimulus towards the formation of a general consensus on the specific content of a university course in political economy. Instead, the teaching that did take place was not clearly distinguishable in substance and level from that to be found in

1 Since the 1850s Leone Levi, Professor of Commerce and Commercial Law, had taught day and evening classes at King's College: in 1856–7 he taught a course on 'Banking and Commercial Law', from 1858 various courses on 'Economical Science', and from 1872 he also delivered the Gilbart Lectures in Banking – F. J. C. Hearnshaw, *The Centenary History of King's College London 1828–1928*, London: George C. Harrap, 1929, p.308; King's College, *Calendar* 1856–7, p.243; 1858–9, p.229. The Tooke Professorship of Economic Science and Statistics was founded in 1859, each appointment to last five years and the incumbent being required to deliver twenty lectures per year. J. E. T. Rogers was the first appointee, and held the post until shortly before his death in 1890, when he was succeeded by Edgeworth – Tooke Professorship, King's College 1859–1916 College Archives KAS/AC2/F304. At University College Foxwell was appointed Professor of Political Economy as Jevons's successor in 1882.

extension teaching and other, more popular, forms of public dissemination.

This situation was to alter rapidly in the years from 1890 to 1905, with the foundation of the London School of Economics, the establishment of the Cambridge tripos, and the establishment of faculties of commerce at Birmingham and Manchester. These developments represent a definite departure from the pattern of the later nineteenth century, despite their varied success and rate of development – at Cambridge, for example, attention has been focused on the emergence of the tripos, although in fact the great expansion of students reading economics before the First World War was not in the new economic tripos, but in the BA ordinary degree;[2] while Birmingham's fame as a model faculty of commerce, under the leadership of W. J. Ashley, never fulfilled its early reputation, soon being eclipsed in the quality of courses, staff and students by the rapid development of Chapman's faculty at Manchester.[3] In all cases, however, it was not until well into the 1920s that syllabi, staff and organization settled into a path of development that is discernible today as the early history of economics as a university discipline.

It was through the University Extension movement that political economy first gained a wider audience as an academic subject, teachers from Oxford and Cambridge delivering lectures in towns and cities up and down the country. The subject proved initially very popular, attracting large attendances at lectures and, more importantly, the associated classes in which students could study textbooks and write essays. Typically, these political economy courses were held in the evening and were attended by young clerks and working men, whereas courses on history and literature were scheduled in working hours, and were attended by a mixed, more leisured audience, who paid higher fees. Diligent students were able, with the aid of these courses, to sit Oxford and Cambridge Local Examinations, and in this way move towards the completion of the work necessary for a University of London degree. The sporadic nature of the teaching, and the absence of local tutors, meant however that study on this basis was difficult and uncertain. The early success of University Extension as a means of

2 In 1909 seven students sat the Pt.I and four the Pt.II Ordinary BA papers and passed (*Cambridge University Reporter*, Vol.XL No.13, December 1909, p.383); these numbers then rose over the following years, to thirty-five passing Pt.I and seventeen Pt.II papers in 1913 (*Cambridge University Reporter*, Vol.XLIV No.16, 23 December 1913, p.413).

3 Ashley's Faculty of Commerce attracted a great deal of contemporary attention, and this is reflected in more recent literature; Chapman's Manchester faculty on the other hand was, once established, far more successful and influential, but has hitherto attracted very little attention from historians.

introducing the populations of the emergent industrial and commercial centres to university-level study prompted in turn efforts to consolidate on this by the establishment of local colleges, where both full and part-time students might combine to support embryo university colleges.[4]

The foundation of Owens College in Manchester in 1851 predated this movement, but reflected a similar process of development.[5] In its early days Owens College did not flourish, and there was talk in the later 1850s of it having failed. It was only with the expansion of its evening classes in the session 1860–1 that student numbers picked up, rising to 527 in the evening classes and 264 in the day classes in 1870–1.[6] The strong development of evening and day classes through the 1870s indicates that it shared in the same general trend which, in other English provincial cities, was inducing the foundation of new civic colleges. All these institutions, Owens included, fashioned themselves after the model first established by University College, London – secular, open to both sexes, and with teaching across a broad spectrum of classical and modern subjects.[7] The manifest purpose of these institutions was to bring advanced education to the sons and daughters of the middle and working classes of the provincial cities. Classics and mathematics as the basis of study would here have limited appeal; a more strictly vocational imperative ruled. Courses in scientific and technical subjects were especially popular, and the examinations set by the City and Guilds Institute and the University of London provided clear guidelines for the development of teaching.

Political economy, despite its initial strong appeal to extension

4 In fact the Oxford and Cambridge movements differed in their objectives, the former placing far greater emphasis on the establishment of local college centres as the prime objective, whereas in Cambridge this was left to the discretion of local organizers. See above p.89ff.

5 We can safely ignore here the existence of Durham, founded 1833 but moribund; only as a consequence of the linkage with Armstrong College, Newcastle did Durham University develop into a university recognized as such by its contemporaries. Owens College was warranted to grant certificates qualifying students to be examined for University of London degrees in May 1851, and entered its first complete session in October 1851 – see J. Thompson, *The Owens College: Its Foundation and Growth; and its Connection with the Victoria University, Manchester*, Manchester: J. E. Cornish, 1886, pp.133, 138.

6 H. B. Charlton, *Portrait of a University 1851–1951*, Manchester: Manchester University Press, 1951 Appendix V. There was a sustained expansion in daytime male attendances only after 1868.

7 Although in the case of Owens, it was only with the foundation of Victoria University that women were admitted to daytime classes. The northern movement for women's education had been the decisive force during the later 1860s in the development of the University Extension movement, and was reflected in the constitutional structure of the new colleges.

students, soon faced a steady decline in its audience. In the medium term, the demand for extension lectures was sustained primarily by those seeking a career in teaching; courses in literature, history and the sciences directly contributed to the educational foundations for such a career, and in turn prepared students for recognized examinations. Political economy, on the other hand, had no such immediate relevance to existing career paths, nor was certification in the subject recognized as a qualification for any specific employment. Such knowledge of political economy as was required for the Indian Civil Service examinations could be learnt from a book, there was little autonomous demand from the world of business and commerce, and, as a direct result of these two circumstances, there was very little call for teachers versed in its principles. Consequently, when the extension movement of the 1870s rapidly fused into a localized movement for civic foundations, political economy everywhere ranked low among the first subjects of instruction in the resulting institutions. Where it did find a place on the syllabus, it was almost everywhere marginalized, taught as an adjunct to moral philosophy, primarily to evening students.[8] The existing demand for tuition in the elementary principles of political economy could be adequately met in this manner; there was scant demand for any advanced teaching.

Nevertheless, the perception that political economy was a natural subject for these new colleges to include in their curricula remained a strong one, and it was in fact in these institutions, and their successors, that (eventually) many students had their first encounter with the principles of economics, taught by young lecturers who later went on to become professors and academic economists. In many cases, the slow beginning to the inclusion of political economy in the curriculum was not solely due to a lack of demand; it was also a reflection of the financial difficulties of the early civic colleges. Extension lectures were rarely subsidized, and they were provided only if a guarantee fund had been created; but the accumulation of such a fund did not necessarily represent an insuperable obstacle for local organizers. Finance became more obtrusive a consideration when the construction of permanent premises was mooted; and, in fact, it could be said that in most cases, the costs of construction and upkeep of a building for public lectures

8 Although in extension lectures it was the evening class students who were the more vocationally-oriented, in the new civic colleges evening students were representative of the part-time tradition of extension teaching, where individuals were free to pursue their own ends at their own pace. The new institutions could not effectively develop on this casual basis, emphasis therefore shifting to the recruitment of daytime students pursuing structured courses leading to specific external examinations. There was a symbiotic financial and academic relationship between day and evening classes, however, as is shown below with Owens in the 1890s.

and classes revealed the realistic limit of provincial resources and nature of their priorities. Furthermore, extension teaching had space and other requirements different to those needed for regular university work, so that in Sheffield, for example, the internal layout of Firth College turned out to suit it for the former, but not the latter, purpose.[9] The logical transition from the provision of courses by peripatetic lecturers, to the creation of a local college with staff and facilities capable of teaching to the standards required by the University of London was, except in Manchester and Liverpool, a very difficult one indeed. In some cases, such as Leeds, local finance was never forthcoming in anything other than derisory amounts;[10] and the lack of serious financial support for new institutions outside Liverpool, Manchester and Birmingham was a serious impediment to growth in anticipation of future student demand.

The most convenient way in which to approach the differences between these new institutions, and the reasons for their slow pace of development, is via a consideration of the Victoria University, a federal body initially established by Owens College in 1880 (as sole member), chartered to confer its own degrees in arts, science, law and music. The charter of the University provided for the addition of other colleges alongside Owens; University College, Liverpool joined in 1884, and Yorkshire College, Leeds in 1887. The Victoria University gave these three northern colleges a coherence as university-level institutions that was lacking so long as their students studied for examinations set by the University of London – although some continued to study, and sit for, London degrees. The professoriate of the three constituent colleges were free to determine their own courses and examinations, and introduced a system of external examination to assure common standards both between the three colleges, and between Victoria and London degrees. Degrees could also be offered in subjects that did not exist in the London curriculum, such as engineering; and, as we shall see, this autonomy enabled the colleges to develop courses in commercial subjects related to local needs.

Firth College, Sheffield applied to join the Victoria University in 1895, but was rejected in June 1898, a decision provoking a great deal of public controversy. The reasons given at the time for this rebuff related to the disparities in scale of activity between Firth College on

---

9 A. W. Chapman, *The Story of a Modern University. A History of the University of Sheffield*, London: Oxford University Press, 1955, p.18.
10 Failing local support, much of Yorkshire College's endowment was given by the London Clothworkers' Company: A. J. Taylor, 'County college and civic university: an introductory essay', in P. H. J. H. Gosden, A. J. Taylor (eds) *Studies in the History of a University, 1874–1974*, Leeds: E. J. Arnold, 1975, pp.5–6.

the one hand, and Owens College and University College, Liverpool on the other – disparities which were genuine enough;[11] but behind these arguments lay an implicit recognition that the days of the Victoria University were themselves numbered, given developments in London and in the provincial colleges. In 1900 Mason College, Birmingham gained University status with Oliver Lodge, first Professor of Experimental Physics at Liverpool, as its Vice-Chancellor. This in turn prompted popular agitation in Liverpool for autonomy from the Victoria University, which led directly to conferral of the University Charter in July 1903. Owens College simultaneously assumed the name of the Victoria University of Manchester, while Leeds received its charter in April 1904. The dismantling of the northern federal university, combined with the transformation of the University of London into a federal, London-based teaching institution, opened the way for other university colleges to seek university status, and hence control over their own curricula and strategic development.[12] Economic and commercial science belonged firmly to the agenda of these newly-independent institutions, and during the next two decades most of the new universities established departments of economics and faculties of commerce. In this process, the Manchester Faculty of Commerce provided the leading model, as well as providing many of the new professoriate. This gives us a second, auxiliary justification for our approach to the development of political economy in the provincial colleges *via* an account of the Victoria University.

It has been noted above that when first established the Victoria University was a federal body with one member – Owens College. Moreover, the constitution of Owens had by this time undergone several important revisions, moving it progressively away from occasional teaching towards regular university studies. As occurred elsewhere, the successful foundation of the college in 1851 followed upon a variety of educational initiatives aimed primarily at working men,[13]

---

11 But, as was recognized at the time, Sheffield's position with respect to the Victoria University was not at all dissimilar to that of Yorkshire College, Leeds at the time that it had joined – Chapman, *The Story of a Modern University*, pp.138–9.

12 T. Kelly, *For Advancement of Learning. The University of Liverpool 1881–1981*, Liverpool: Liverpool University Press, 1981, pp.127–8.

13 Indeed the terms of the bequest formally excluded women from the college; in 1871 the Owens College Act revised the terms of the bequest and *inter alia* established the principle that women might be admitted, although no effort was made to do so. The Charter of the Victoria University opened its degrees to women, but Owens, the sole constituent college, still refused to admit women students on the grounds that mixed classes were bound to cause trouble; it was not until 1883 that the court resolved to admit women, sixty registering for the academic year 1883–4. See E. Fiddes, 'Admission of women to full university status'. App.IV in Charlton, *Portrait of a University*, pp.156–61.

beginning with the foundation of the Manchester Mechanics' Institution in April 1824. The pattern familiar from similar contemporary foundations was here repeated: the Directors were primarily middle-class Whigs and Dissenters, and among the most active members were clerks, warehousemen and shopkeepers. Initial enthusiasm stimulated by lectures on mechanical philosophy and on chemistry had waned even by the time a building was ready in 1827, it proving difficult to sustain long lecture courses in these subjects without suitable equipment and to an audience unversed in scientific language. By the early 1830s the length of such courses was cut back, no more than six lectures being given on any one subject, with a consequent shift in emphasis from instruction to recreation.[14] Classes in natural history, the sciences, mathematics and geography continued, although a request for a course on history was rejected, on the grounds that it might lead to political debate.

In 1834 a group of Mechanics' Institution subscribers banded together to form a 'Mutual Improvement Society', at which papers of a practico-scientific nature were read before a membership composed almost exclusively of professionals, clerks and small business men. This was soon renamed the 'Literary and Scientific Society', dealing with contemporary issues such as education, taxation, political economy and temperance.[15] The establishment of the Athanaeum in 1836 further emphasized this social bifurcation within popular education, the Mechanics' Institution serving a broader social and recreational need than those foundations frequented by the middle classes.[16] During the 1840s, for example, the Royal Manchester Institution proposed a cycle of instruction intended

> To provide for the younger, and more particularly for the female, branches of the wealthier families of this Town, such a course of higher instruction in Science, Literature and Art, as may form a proper sequel to a liberal school education, and may offer them advantages for mental culture, proportionate to what are now beginning to be extensively enjoyed by other classes.[17]

14 M. Tylecote, 'The Manchester Mechanics' Institution, 1824–50', in D. S. L. Cardwell (ed.) *Artisan to Graduate*, Manchester: Manchester University Press, 1974, pp.58–62.

15 H. M. Wach, 'Culture and the middle classes: popular knowledge in industrial Manchester', *Journal of British Studies*, Vol.27 (1988), pp.383–4.

16 John Seed notes that its efforts turned increasingly to the organization of Christmas parties, concerts, popular lectures and the acquisition of entertaining books: 'Unitarianism, political economy and the antinomies of liberal culture in Manchester, 1830–50', *Social History*, Vol.7 (1982), p.13.

17 Revd John James Anderson, Minister to Unitarian Upper Brook Street Chapel, RMI Minute Book, cited in Wach, 'Culture and the middle classes' pp.387–8.

Political economy found a place in these lectures, notwithstanding the concern recently aroused by use of the term in Liverpool; lecturers dealt with it in the framework of 'The Rise and Progress of Civil Society', in which the extension of wealth with the developing division of labour was argued to result both in general prosperity and moral and intellectual improvement.[18]

Besides these institutional developments, the foundation of University and King's Colleges in London prompted analogous provincial initiatives. A paper read before the Manchester Statistical Society in 1836 proposing the establishment of a university in Manchester led to a preparatory meeting in November of the same year to consider the foundation of a 'College for General Education' linked to the University of London. Six chairs were envisaged, in mathematics, chemistry, natural history, classical literature, English literature and 'History, with economical and political philosophy'.[19] Alongside this, it was proposed that a Medical Department should be formed, although there was no clear consensus on how this would be achieved. As it happened, two medical institutions already existed, and the mutual rivalry of these institutions sufficed to wreck the plans for the proposed college.

A number of other institutional developments and educational proposals of the later 1830s and 1840s strengthened the movement for a permanent college of higher learning in Manchester, but it was only the death of John Owens in 1846, and his bequest of £96,942 for the establishment of a new college, that consolidated these various interests into substantial plans for such a foundation. Owens's estate trustees canvassed a wide range of academics concerning the educational complexion of the proposed foundation, evincing a preference for Scottish institutions, although, as it turned out, few who were so approached deigned to respond. Nevertheless, the trustees favoured the creation of a wide, modern curriculum including commercial studies, which they understood to comprise bookkeeping, commercial geography, the history and progress of arts and manufactures, together with the general principles of commercial jurisprudence.[20] In principle, they followed the teaching plan suggested in 1836, although not all the staff envisaged in that plan were appointed by the time teaching began. The chair in logic, mental and moral philosophy, whose holder might have been expected to be capable of teaching elementary political economy, was combined with the position of Principal; but the appointee, A. J. Scott, who had been formerly Professor of English

18 Wach, 'Culture and the middle classes' p.391.
19 Thompson, *The Owens College*, p.27.
20 Thompson, *The Owens College*, p.121. For an outline of earlier, but similar proposals, see G. W. Daniels, 'Economic and commercial studies in the Owens College and the University', *Manchester School*, Vol.1 (1930), pp.3–4.

Literature at University College, London, was unpractised in such teaching. He was furthermore a leading Irvingite who had played a prominent role in the development of the doctrine of the gift of tongues, and the lack-lustre early history of Owens can to a great extent be reasonably ascribed to the many failings of Scott.[21] He was replaced as Principal in 1857 by the Professor of Greek and Latin, J. G. Greenwood, who remained Principal until 1890, who also, as it happened, represented the main source of opposition to the admission of women to the College.

Greenwood had been responsible for organizing the first evening classes of the College in 1853. Directed at local schoolmasters, fifteen lectures each in classics and mathematics were attended by twenty-eight teachers during the initial session. The programme was expanded in the subsequent session to include history and natural history 'for young men of business and others'; and by 1860, classes were offered in English literature, French, logic, jurisprudence, chemistry and natural philosophy, by which time seventy-seven students were attending.[22]

Greenwood was also involved with other members of Owens College in the movement to provide, within the framework of the Mechanics' Institution, teaching along the lines pioneered in London by F. D. Maurice with the foundation of the People's College in 1854. A Working Man's College was first established at Ancoats in January 1857, followed one year later by Manchester, which held its classes in the David Street Mechanics' Institution. Classes were held six days a week in subjects ranging from arithmetic, algebra and geometry to history, human physiology, Latin and political economy. It was stipulated that:

> Students must be sixteen years of age, must be able to read and write, and must know the first four rules of arithmetic. No class will be formed for less than six students, unless at the desire of the teacher. Each student will pay a permanent entrance fee of two shillings and sixpence, not to be renewed after absence. ... Admission to the Bible class will be free to all members of the college.[23]

Two hundred and thirty students entered the first classes in Manchester, the most popular class being arithmetic and algebra (ninety-eight students), closely followed by English literature with ninety-five stu-

---

21 E. Fiddes, *Chapters in the History of Owens College and of Manchester University 1851–1914*, Manchester: Manchester University Press, 1937, pp.29–30.

22 T. Kelly, *Outside the Walls: Sixty Years of University Extension at Manchester, 1886–1946*, Manchester: Manchester University Press, 1950, p.6. During the 1858–59 session there had been 107 students in the evening classes – Thompson, *The Owens College*, p.223.

23 Thompson, *The Owens College*, p.233.

dents. Political economy was not popular: with nine students it just edged ahead of Common Law, which with eight students was the least popular subject out of twelve. Eighty of the students attending in this session were classified as operatives, with sixty clerks and bookkeepers, fifty-two warehousemen and salesmen, and twenty shopkeepers and assistants. Here too the established pattern for such popular education soon asserted itself: the number of those attending classified as operatives declined sharply, leaving the Manchester Working Man's College dominated by clerks and shopworkers. Furthermore, difficulties also soon emerged with the Mechanics' Institution premises, and this prompted discussions with Greenwood concerning a more direct involvement on the part of Owens. The model of King's College, London was invoked in proposing entry into the evening classes during the winter half-year, and for the session 1861–2 members of the Manchester Working Man's College joined the existing classes, bringing their number to 235 for that year.[24] These evening classes, comprising a mixed membership of (male) teachers, clerks and shopworkers, remained consistently more popular than the day classes until the later 1880s, when the emergence of alternative provision for technical education drew off increasing numbers of students from the more elementary classes, enabling the college authorities to raise the overall level of the evening class provision at a time when the evening class attendances for political economy were still significantly higher than the daytime attendances.

It was in the evening classes that Jevons was first set to work in 1863, nominally sharing the responsibility for the teaching of political economy with Christie, who took the day classes. Richard Christie had been appointed to the chair in history in December 1853, and in the course of the following year had added to this responsibility for a new chair in 'commercial science', dubbed the Faulkner Professorship of Political Economy and Commercial Science, after a recent benefactor of the college.[25] Christie was then further made responsible for the chair in jurisprudence in 1855, rather stretching his teaching, and there is in fact no record of any significant regular teaching in political economy before the arrival of Jevons in 1863.[26] Assigned to the evening classes, on Tuesdays from 8.30 to 9.30p.m., Jevons proposed that 'The

24 Thompson, *The Owens College*, pp.224–7.
25 This association of commercial science with the history chair was in line with the proposals made in 1836 for a General College, as were other early Owens appointments.
26 The Principal's report for the session 1862–3 records two day and eight evening students in political economy, presumably both taught by Christie, although the relevant calendar gives no indication of the courses concerned. *Calendar of Owens College, Manchester, 1863–4*, pp.53, 63.

Industrial Structure of Society will be described in some detail, and the simpler relations of Labour, Skill, Science, Property, Capital, Land, Trade, Money, Increase of Population, &c., considered'.

Eleven students took this course, using as their textbook Books One and Two of Smith's *Wealth of Nations*. Christie announced a day course in political economy for the autumn term 1863–4, based upon Mc-Culloch's edition of Smith, which was to meet twice a week – no students were however registered.[27] For the session 1866–7 Jevons switched to the day classes in addition to the evening classes, teaching six students in the former and twenty-six in the latter. Evening classes were also augmented at this time by the proposal of the Cobden Memorial Committee that the evening classes in political economy should be open, without payment of fee, to all masters of primary schools in Manchester.[28] By the session 1869–70, forty of the fifty-six attending the evening classes in political economy were Cobden students.[29]

Placed in charge of the daytime and evening teaching of political economy, Jevons gradually elaborated the course, using as his main text-book John Stuart Mill's *Principles*, adding only in the 1874–5 session his own *Theory of Political Economy* (1871). Twenty-four students registered for this course. Jevons's replacement, Robert Adamson,[30] took over the course as he found it, delivering a series of weekly daytime lectures on 'The Nature of Wealth, the Division of Labour, Capital, Interest, Land, Rent, Profit, Co-operative Associations, Trades Unions &c., the Theory of Value, Metallic and Paper Currency, the Foreign Exchanges, Banking,

27 Ibid., p.35. Christie also set questions for the evening class examinations of April 1863, such as: '1. Define political economy, considered as a science. 2. Define capital and state the advantages derived from its use. 9. Point out how money is influenced by cost of production and by supply and demand.' *Calendar 1863–4*, pp.cxl-cxli. Jevons's questions for the following year get off to a barely less laconic start, viz. '1. Explain the subordination of human wants', but there is overall a greater degree of economic precision in the questions set. *Calendar 1864–5*, p.cxlii.

28 Principal's Report, *Calendar 1866–7*, p.74. At this time there were 19 regular students at Owens (who were obliged to follow a course of systematic study leading to a Diploma), 94 occasional, and 282 evening students: *Calendar 1866–7*, p.97. The Cobden Memorial Committee gave an endowment of £400 for an annual prize in political economy, the balance of £1,500 being given to fund the Cobden Lectureship – Thompson, *The Owens College*, p.288.

29 *Calendar 1870–1*, p.88.

30 Adamson graduated in philosophy from Edinburgh in 1871, and then was employed as an assistant to the Edinburgh philosophy professors, and was also a member of the staff of the *Encyclopedia Britannica*. He held the post of Professor of Political Economy, Mental and Moral Science at Owens from 1876 to 1882, moving then to a chair of logic at Aberdeen.

Commercial Fluctuations, Taxation'.[31] The textbooks used for this course were also the same – Mill's *Principles of Political Economy*, Smith's *Wealth of Nations*, Jevons's *Theory of Political Economy*, and Jevons's *Money and the Mechanism of Exchange*.

Despite Jevons's best efforts in developing the teaching of political economy at Owens, the subject itself still had a marginal role in both daytime and evening teaching, a situation which was very much to do with its optional and 'recreational' character for its students. In 1858 Owens had been made a local examination centre for the University of London, and matriculation of its students for London degrees became a central purpose of the College. As the rubric stated, 'The College is instituted for the purpose of General Academic Education', with three distinct courses, in arts, science and engineering, for regular students. These were full-time courses over three years, preparing students for the ordinary London BA or B.Sc., teaching therefore being dictated by the London syllabus. The rubric for the London University Arts course suggested that it was

> suitable for persons preparing for the learned professions, to those who contemplate offering themselves as candidates for the Civil Appointments of Her Majesty's Government, and to persons whose aims in education are general rather than specific.[32]

This course was based around classics, English, ancient and modern history, mathematics, a modern language, with some science and, in the third year, logic, mental and moral philosophy. Adamson was primarily responsible for this last part of the London syllabus, teaching it in three daytime classes per week to political economy's one. This allocation of time underlines the occasional nature of political economy within the overall teaching structure at this time.

Nevertheless, during Jevons's period at Owens some significant changes to the organization of the college had taken place, most obviously associated with the limitations of the original premises in Quay Street, where Cobden's house had first been rented, and then later gifted, to the college as its premises. It is evident that these provisional arrangements hampered expansion in numbers, which in the later 1860s averaged just over one hundred daytime students; and so long as numbers remained at this level, little elaboration of the curriculum was possible. In 1867 an appeal was launched to extend the college, and £200,000 was eventually collected, providing for the purchase of land at the present Oxford Road site, and the commissioning of Alfred Waterhouse as the architect for the main buildings,

31 *Calendar 1876–7*, p.50.
32 Cited from the *Calendar 1876–7*, p.34.

completed in the early 1870s. The college thereby gained a more substantial public presence, underscoring the organizational restructuring of 1870–1 in which the college constitution was revised to provide the three-tier governing body of a broadly-based Court of Governors, a lay Council and a Senate composed of the Principal and Professors responsible for the conduct of academic business. This model structure, later adopted by all new universities, gave Owens College a secure foundation for development as a potential university institution, albeit one whose degree-level courses were still dictated by the syllabi of London degrees.

This limitation was removed in 1880 with the formation of the Victoria University, Owens College being the first constituent member of the new university. Under the terms of the new Charter, the reliance upon London University for BA and B.Sc. degrees was eliminated, and, in addition, the way opened for Honours degrees in specific subjects. Moreover, the regulations for the Ordinary Victoria BA degree advanced on those governing the London BA in distinguishing between four broad streams (classical, historical, English and modern languages, and philosophy), political economy appearing as one of six papers in the Final Examination for the 'mainly historical' Group B.[33] At the same time, Arts Honours Schools were established in classics, English language, history and philosophy, the final examination entry requirement for honours history stating that

> Candidates shall present certificates of having attended (1) during three academic years College courses of instruction in *History,* averaging not less than four hours weekly; (2) during three academic years College courses in *either* Latin and Greek *or* Latin with French and German, averaging not less than six hours weekly; (3) during the *first* and *second* years of his Honours course College courses in English Language and Literature, averaging not less than three hours weekly; (4) during the second or third years of his Honours course College courses in Political Economy and in the History of the English Law.[34]

33 Paper 1 was Greek or Latin; Paper 2 French or German; Paper 3 ancient history; Paper 4 modern history; Paper 5 English literature; and Paper 6 political economy, 'Production and Distribution of Wealth; Principles of Taxation (Adam Smith's *Wealth of Nations*)' – Regulations. Subjects for the Several Examinations for the Ordinary Degrees of BA and B.Sc., *Owens College Calendar 1881–2,* p.45. The London BA Final Examination subjects were as follows: (1) Latin and Roman History; (2) Greek and Grecian History; (3) a language; (4) Pure or Mixed Mathematics; (5) Mental and Moral Science. (1) to (3) were compulsory, choice being permitted only between the parts of (4) and (5) – *University College Liverpool, Calendar 1885–6* p.17.

34 *Owens College Calendar 1881–2,* p.55.

The situation in the early 1880s can therefore be summarized as follows: political economy was taught by Adamson in both evening and day classes, the latter being attended by ordinary BA students working for Paper 6 of their final examination, and second or third year honours history students seeking a certificate of attendance to qualify them to sit their finals examination in history.

Although there were not that many more students for these classes than there had been in the 1870s,[35] the syllabus became distinctly more demanding. Two classes were announced for daytime students in the 1880–1 session, the first dealing with economic theory, and the second with applied economics.[36] Adamson was primarily a philosopher, but it is evident from this rubric, and the examination papers set upon it, that the course was the most rigorous so far.[37] It can be supposed that he was assisted in this by the newly-established position of political economy in the Victoria degree structure; and that Jevons had in turn been hindered by the diversity of needs and abilities of the students that he taught. Even without any pressure from an increased student demand for the teaching of political economy at Owens, a change in the *type* of demand brought about by reforms to the institutional structure prompted alterations in the level and rigour of teaching in the subject. Adamson left Owens in 1882, being replaced in the political economy classes by J. E. C. Munro, an Irish barrister educated at Cambridge. Munro held the Cobden lectureship until 1890, but left the organization of teaching in political economy exactly as he had found it on arrival, apart from adding Sidgwick's *Political Economy* to the textbooks for the day course in 1883.

As noted above, the character of the evening classes began to alter in the later 1880s with the increased availability of technical and supplementary education and a consequent loss of students to courses in new technical and commercial colleges. The ensuing reduction in demand

35 Five in 1880–1; sixteen in 1881–2; eight in 1882–3.
36 'I. Economics. – A. Province, Method and Divisions of Political Economy. B. Theory of Production: Labour and Natural Agents; Capital, Invention, Organization of Labour, Exchange, including the Instruments of exchange, Money, Credit, Banking, and the theory of International Trade. C. Theory of Distribution: General conditions of Distribution: Property, Socialism, Communism: remuneration of Industrial Functions: Wages, Interest, Profit, Rent.
II. Applied Economics. – The Principles of Taxation.
During Easter term an additional lecture will be given weekly on some subject of Economic History or of the history of Political Economy.' The textbooks for these courses were A. and M. P. Marshall, *Economics of Industry*, and Jevons, *Money. Owens College Calendar 1880–1*, p.57.
37 *Owens College Calendar 1881–2*, p.clxi. Examinations were set for the Ordinary BA Final Examination, and for the University Certificate Examination in the evening classes.

for more elementary levels of educational provision enabled the staff of Owens College to elaborate their teaching, and create a graduated structure of courses and certification more demanding than hitherto possible. As is also evident from the impact of the Balfour Act of 1902 on the development of civic colleges into universities, the formation of the modern university as a teaching institution was facilitated by external developments which divested civic colleges of elementary and popular educational functions, functions which had initially been an important motive in their foundation, and which had over the years sustained their growth. Improvements to elementary schooling, and increased provision for vocational education, enabled the civic colleges to cast off the all-purpose role of providing instruction at diverse levels, and focus on degree-level work. It was this differentiation of educational provision, and the emergence of more definite points of transition between levels in the system, that enabled colleges and universities to develop new courses and recruit specialist teachers for them. The presence of student demand for new or additional courses was not therefore a necessary condition for the structural transition to higher education to occur; as the educational system became more diverse, the academic profile of university colleges became more distinct, in the case of the Victoria University, building upon the academic autonomy achieved in 1880; and in the case of other civic colleges, imitating the model that Victoria University had established.

It was for these reasons that the civic colleges were able to transform themselves into university-level institutions, in advance of any significant variation in demand from students; and as part of this process new subjects, such as political economy, could be added to the prospectus in advance of any notable alteration in the extent of established demand. Within this complex process of educational change political economy first retained its position as a supplementary subject for ordinary BA and honours history students; and second, elaborated its subject-matter and emerged in the early 1900s as an autonomous subject. Only after the newly-developed subject was properly in place is it possible to detect a significant and progressive shift in demand for teaching and certification.

Political economy at Owens, in purpose and substance, remained unchanged throughout the 1880s, so that the teaching delivered at the end of the decade was on much the same lines as that established by Adamson in 1880–1. During the 1890s, the subject underwent successive reforms, each change moving it away from its role as a component of other degrees, and towards the autonomy reflected in the creation in 1904 of the new Faculty of Commerce, with its B.Com. and honours economics degrees. A proper appreciation of how this happened requires that we chart in some detail these incremental shifts, so that we can adequately appreciate the slow transformation of existing courses, and establish that the emergence of economics as an autonomous subject of study required, above all, a clear conception of how the subject would be taught. Not until this perspective was in place was it possible for a coherent demand for certification in the subject to emerge, first on the part of students who wished to specialize in the study of economics; and second, on the part of employers for whom certification in the subject was perceived relevant in recruiting new staff. Indeed, the order in which these two last elements are placed should be reversed, in so far as the student demand for instruction is itself very largely derived from labour market signalling.

The first detectable shift in this long sequence took place in 1889–90, where in addition to the University Certificates which students could gain by sitting two examinations, new Technical and Commercial Certificates were announced 'in connexion with Technical Colleges and Schools, and other registered teaching institutions.'[38] Nine groups of technical and scientific subjects were open for examination, Group IX dealing with commercial topics:

A. Correspondence: Précis writing; arithmetic; and bookkeeping.
B. One of the following:
   French, German, Spanish, Italian (or any other modern language approved by the university for this purpose).
C. One of the following:
   (a) Outlines of political economy.
   (b) Commercial geography.
   (c) Commercial and industrial history.
   (d) Phonography.
   (e) One other modern language.[39]

In the following year (d) and (e) were dropped, and replaced with mercantile law and advanced bookkeeping and accounts. Political economy was in addition divided into three alternative options: principles of finance, foreign exchange, and banking.[40] Consequently, the evening lectures had to shift away from a general exposition of the principles of political economy, towards a more specialized treatment of individual subjects than provided by Munro. Elijah Helm, an occasional lecturer, assumed responsibility for the evening class, which now dealt primarily with taxation and banking. Additional classes were announced in commercial and industrial history, commercial geography and statistics, and advanced bookkeeping and accounts, the first and the third of these being taught by another occasional lecturer,

38 *Owens College Calendar 1889–90*, p.323.
39 *Owens College Calendar 1889–90*, p.326.
40 *Owens College Calendar 1890–1*, p. 220.

Mr Trevor.[41] Attendance figures given in the *Calendar* for the following year indicate that the most popular of these courses was Trevor's on bookkeeping, thirty-seven students attending the course, as opposed to eighteen in the political economy evening class.[42]

Munro left Owens in 1890 and the new Cobden Lecturer, with sole responsibility for political economy at Owens, was John Stuart Mackenzie, who had gained a First in the moral sciences tripos at Cambridge in 1889. Conforming to the established pattern, Mackenzie simply took over the classes as he found them, with some slight, but none the less significant, changes: for the 1891–2 daytime session he added a section on 'Relation of economics to ethics and politics; theory of state interference',[43] and added Keynes's *Scope and Method*, Marshall's *Principles*, and Walker's *Wages Question* to the list of textbooks for the course. He also took control of the evening classes, reverting to the more general approach of Munro, using as his textbooks Mill's *Political Economy*, Marshall's *Economics of Industry*, and Jevons's *Money*.[44]

There were further changes to the reading and course structure in 1892–3, but the appointment of A. W. Flux as Cobden Lecturer in 1893 (another Cambridge graduate) marks the beginning of systematic development in the teaching of political economy.[45] The syllabus for

41 *Owens College Calendar 1890–1*, pp.228–9. The Bookkeeping course consisted of ten lectures on single and double entry, the use of journals and ledgers, the preparation and illustration of accounts current, cash accounts, receipt and disbursement, income and expenditure, revenue accounts, partnership accounts, executors' and trustees' accounts, trading accounts and valuation, company accounts, the accounts of banking and insurance institutions, and audit – it therefore provided a thorough overview of all the commercial activities of accounting at that time.

42 *Owens College Calendar 1891–2*, p.390.

43 *Owens College Calendar 1891–2*, p.65.

44 Although Mackenzie had not sat the political economy paper for his Pt.II Moral Sciences, the introduction of Marshall's recently-published *Principles* by a Cambridge graduate is noteworthy. Marshall's teaching version of this text, the 1892 *Elements of the Economics of Industry*, was of course not available during this year, but it might be assumed that it was quickly adopted; the general title *Economics of Industry* continues to appear in the *Calendar* into the next decade, despite the fact that the 1892 book entirely displaced the earlier book of the same name written by Alfred and Mary Paley Marshall.

45 Flux had been joint Senior Wrangler at Cambridge in 1887, and then won the Marshall Prize in 1889. During the early 1890s he was active as an extension lecturer, teaching courses on economics, astronomy, electricity and magnetism, sound and light, and a course on spectrum analysis for a Cambridge summer school of elementary teachers in 1893. He continued his involvement in public lecturing after appointment in Manchester, and was secretary of the Lancashire and Cheshire Extension Society (*Manchester Faces and Places*, Vol.6 (May 1895), pp.125–6). In 1904 he published *Economic Principles*, the first 'Marshallian' English economics textbook apart from Marshall's own 1892 *Economics of Industry*.

the political economy day class was at first unchanged, although he added in the second and third terms one lecture a week on 'Economic history in the XVth. and XVIth. centuries', which attracted five students, presumably reading for honours history.[46] For the evening class, Flux repeated the course on wealth, value, production, distribution and exchange, which *via* Munro in fact dated back to Adamson; but this was flagged as a 'general course', a 'special course' of ten lectures being announced in the Lent term on 'Money and Foreign trade'.[47] This pair of lectures was retained for the following year, and a course of ten lectures on 'Government and taxation' added.[48]

The day classes remained unchanged in structure, while the scope and structure of the evening classes was subject to small cumulative changes, continued through the mid-1890s, although it ought perhaps to be noted that at no time did Flux have more students for the principal political economy evening class than Jevons had had in the 1860s and 1870s. For the session 1895–6 a two-year cycle was introduced, the session 1895–6 being taken up with 'The economics of industry' using Marshall's textbook of the same name, and the session 1896–7 with 'The economics of trade and finance'. The net effect of this alteration was to increase the time devoted, first, to an exposition of economic principles, and second, their application in an area relevant to those attending the evening classes. The arrangement of courses in this way also implied that students had to follow the cycle, beginning in one year and continuing with the next, so that students could enter the course only every second year.[49]

For the session 1897–8 further changes were made to the evening classes. A new set of twenty lectures, 'Outline of economics', was announced, linked to the Manchester and District Institute of Bankers and held in the rooms of the Bankers' Institute.[50] Two other evening courses were also delivered, the first, for Elementary School Teachers, covering 'The industrial and commercial arrangements of modern life',[51] and 'State

46 *Owens College Calendar 1893–4*, p.68.
47 *Owens College Calendar 1893–4*, p.256. In the *Calendar* for the following year fifteen students are reported as having taken this course. The advanced bookkeeping class continued however to be the most popular, with forty students.
48 *Owens College Calendar 1894–5*, p.276.
49 The daytime economic history lectures alternated each year between medieval (1272–1558) and modern (1558–1760).
50 Twenty students attended in this year, and fifty-six in 1898–9 – *Owens College Calendar 1897–8*, p.261.
51 'A plain exposition of important facts such as different forms of wage-contract, co-operation, profit-sharing, outlines of factory legislation, etc., together with explanation of the meanings of some of the more usual terms in use in trade, on the Stock Exchange, etc.' *Owens College Calendar 1897–8*, p.261. Eleven students were registered for this course.

insurance of working-men'; and the second, 'The limits of *laissez-faire*', which had been given during the previous session to daytime students.

The daytime courses were subjected to a similar revision and rationalization for the following academic year, the year in which the daytime students numbers moved decisively upward to twenty-nine in total as can be seen from the attendance statistics in Figure 1.

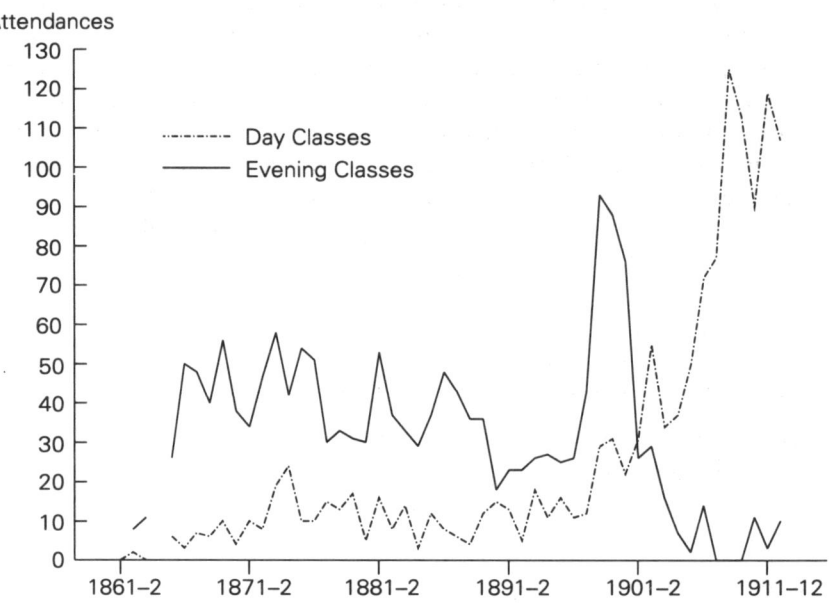

Figure 1: Attendance at political economy classes, Owens College, 1861–1912

Courses in 'Political economy and economic history' were presented in three groups. Group I met twice a week and followed a course in 'Theoretical economics', which was basically an elaborated version of the general political economy that dated back to Adamson and used the same textbooks, with the addition of Marshall's *Principles of Economics* and Bastable's *International Trade*; sixteen attended during the session 1898–9. Group II met once a week for a course of 'Descriptive economics', dealing with agriculture, industry, money and banking, government regulation and public finance; nine students attended in this session. Under Group III, 'Advanced courses', a weekly class in 'The theory of value' was announced for the Michaelmas Term, and one on 'Taxation' for Lent; four registered for these courses. No fixed time was given for these classes, nor any rubric or reading, from which it can be deduced that they represent a newly introduced course to be developed as they progressed. One economic history class was announced for the session, 'Economic history of England from 1702 to

1848', the nominated textbooks being Cunningham's *Growth of English Industry and Commerce*, and Toynbee's *Industrial Revolution*. The tripartite division was explained thus: 'Students taking Political Economy for Intermediate LL.B. Examination should attend Course I, and those taking this subject for the Final B.A. examination should attend Courses I. and II.'[52]

The 'Advanced courses' therefore went beyond any current requirement for Victoria degrees, and represent the first step towards the teaching of economics as an autonomous subject for full-time, day students. Tracking the manner in which this develops over the next few years is, it must be admitted, a rather tedious affair, but it is necessary in order to arrive at a clear understanding of the genesis of economics in Manchester as an independent discipline of university study.

In 1899 Flux was made Stanley Jevons Professor of Political Economy in addition to the Cobden lectureship, which he continued to hold. In the evening classes for the session 1899–1900 the Bankers' Institute lectures continued with great success, attracting sixty-seven students. Twenty-one students were registered for the Owens classes, which this year took the form of four short courses, as follows:

(a) Currency and exchanges (6 lectures)
(b) Commercial crises (3 lectures)
(c) British commercial policy (5 lectures)
(d) Railway rates (4 lectures)

Admission to (b) was free, since this was also announced as a short course of popular lectures open to the public without fee.[53] From this it can be inferred that the evening classes were moving away from the academic, examined and certified courses of the early 1890s, towards a more popular and recreational style of teaching. This adaptation did not suffice to preserve the evening classes, for they entered, even in this new form, a process of decline, having all but disappeared by 1914.

Curricular developments were now taking place entirely in the daytime courses. Revised regulations for honours history permitted an economic subject, examined in two papers, to be taken in lieu of two non-economic options. Paper 10 was made a general paper, covering 'English literature, archaeology, political economy and economic history, political science'; and the previous requirement that proof of attendance at political economy classes be provided for admission to final examinations was dropped. Although this reduced the general exposure of honours history students to political economy, it also meant that, for the first time, the subject was examinable within the history degree.

52 *Owens College Calendar 1898–9*, pp.91–2.
53 *Owens College Calendar 1899–1900*, p.284.

Teaching in political economy by Flux remained substantively the same, but was reorganized into five separate courses:

I. Descriptive economics (Fridays, 11.30a.m.)
II. Economic theory (Mondays at 12.30p.m., Saturdays at 11.30a.m.)
III. The industrial and commercial history of England from 1760 to 1860 (Tuesdays at 11.30a.m.)
IV. The principles of international trade, with special reference to the alleged decline of British commercial prosperity (Fridays at 10.30a.m. during the Lent Term)
V. The history of the English Poor Law (Tuesdays at 10.30a.m. during Michaelmas Term, and throughout session for history honours students).[54]

As before, Courses I and II were prescribed for LL B and honours history students, but there is an additional, and very significant, prescription:

> Students following courses for the Higher Commercial Certificate are recommended to take Courses I. and III. in their first year. Course IV. may be taken most advantageously by students who have already some acquaintance with Economics.[55]

A two-year, daytime certificate course in commerce had been introduced in 1899 for students who had to provide evidence of 'attainments of about the standard required for the Preliminary Examination of the Victoria University'[56] – that is, a general educational level equivalent to the first year ordinary BA examination.

Compared to the evening Commercial Certificate (which formally still existed), the new two-year day course was more academic in nature, with no accounting or commercial correspondence. For the first year, eleven hours of lectures were prescribed in modern languages, geography, law and economics, with students taking an optional additional course. The second year was roughly sketched as a combination of modern languages, commercial law and economics or economic history. As noted above, the regulations for this new course specifically directed students away from the basic class (II.) on economic theory, making this available to students as an optional choice instead, although, somewhat paradoxically, the Bankers' Institute lectures continued their great success with the 'Outlines of economic theory' course, drawing sixty-three students in 1900–1. Another change at this stage was that the venue of the general evening classes altered to the Board Room of

54 *Owens College Calendar 1899–1900*, p.96.
55 *Owens College Calendar 1899–1900*, p.96.
56 *Owens College Calendar 1899–1900*, p.71.

the Chamber of Commerce, following the same short course format established in 1899.

In 1901 Flux accepted a chair in political economy at McGill University, Montreal. He was replaced as Jevons Professor by Sydney Chapman, who had gained a first in the Cambridge moral sciences tripos in 1898 and in which he was one of the few students (ever) to take the political economy paper. During the sessions 1901–2 and 1902–3 his courses followed exactly the lines established by Flux, with the variation that the evening class lectures reflected his own interests.[57] Another small, but significant, alteration in 1902–3 was the exclusion of Mill's *Principles of Political Economy* from the reading for the economic theory course, temporarily rendering the selection of textbooks more 'Marshallian'; but then, in 1903, J. S. Nicholson's *Principles of Political Economy* was added to the list in Mill's place. This could be explained by the fact that, besides Mill, Marshall's *Principles* and Wicksteed's *Common Sense*, there were no other general treatises available in Britain;[58] but perhaps more important was the resolutely 'practical' cast of Nicholson's book, suiting it for use in the context of commerce teaching, besides Nicholson's general hostility towards neo-classicism.[59] Chapman was certainly no straightforward epigone of Marshall in the Pigou mould; the Manchester Faculty of Commerce that Chapman created did indeed develop specialized honours economics teaching, but on the back of practical commerce teaching of a kind that Marshall had criticized in his exchanges with Ashley on the role of accounting in education. Marshall's conception of the economic curriculum certainly had a long-term impact upon the teaching of economics, but for many years co-existed with the teaching of commerce degrees whose impact exceeded that of honours economics as the vehicle for the diffusion of economic education.

The session 1903–4 was the last of the old Owens College, and little

57 The four topics were: industrial organization, with special reference to the cotton industry; markets, their various forms and the conditions of their development; distribution of income; and British commercial policies – *Owens College Calendar 1901–2*, p.288.

58 For a discussion of Nicholson's *Principles* see John Maloney, *Marshall, Orthodoxy and the Professionalization of Economics*, Cambridge: Cambridge University Press, 1985, pp.75ff.

59 Nicholson had taken the opportunity afforded to him in 1893 as President of Section F of the British Association to attack Jevons's analysis of marginal utility. Interestingly, Flux responded the same year in his Evening Class, using Nicholson's attack to reaffirm the basic principles that Jevons sought to elucidate, although noting some of Jevons's mathematical deficiencies – see 'Extract from lecture introductory to session of evening classes for 1893–4 at Owens College, Manchester, on "Jevons and his work", by A. W. Flux, Cobden Lecturer in Political Economy', *Economic Journal* Vol.3 (1893), pp.339–42.

was changed in the general provision of economics teaching. A number of new appointments were made, however: lectureships in economic and political geography, commerce and economics, accounting, and banking were listed in the arts, science and law departments,[60] putting in place the staff needed to introduce a sufficient range of specialities to support degree-level teaching in commerce. This coincided with the reorganization for 1904–5 of Owens College as the Victoria University of Manchester, and the creation of a Faculty of Commerce with its own qualifications: the Bachelors and Masters degrees in commerce. The new faculty was to be the axis of economics teaching in Manchester up to the middle of the century, although an honours economics BA degree continued to be offered (and shared much of the teaching with that of the faculty).

The evolution of the new faculty is not our immediate concern here, since this takes us forward into the issues associated with the consolidation of economics teaching in Britain, rather than its permanent emplacement. Some consideration has nevertheless to be given to the initial organization of the faculty, since its dedication to commercial education at degree level provides a clear contrast to the modern accepted pattern of economic and business studies, and was to prove more influential in the teaching of commerce before the Second World War than either Cambridge or London.

The creation by Chapman of an adequately-staffed Faculty of Commerce was mainly facilitated by the recruitment of part-time lecturers from outside the university. Elijah Helm, Secretary of the Manchester Chamber of Commerce, reappears as a Special Lecturer on the cotton industry; D. Drummond Fraser, manager of the Manchester branch of the London, City and Midland Bank, is listed for 'The practice of banking'; A. E. Clear, Assistant Goods Manager, Great Central Railway is listed as a Special Lecturer in railway transport; Roger Carter continues as lecturer in accounting; while commercial and railway law are covered by two local barristers.[61] In combination with the existing staff in other faculties, this represented a solid basis for the initiation of teaching in commerce. Sixteen students registered for the first year of the new course, the total number of students rising to fifty-seven by 1913.

Eight subjects were prescribed for students, to be covered in at least

60 The new lecturer in commerce and economics (the title was altered in the following year to economic history and commerce) was W. G. S. Adams, an Oxford history graduate who had spent the academic year 1902 teaching economics at the University of Chicago; he was later first Gladstone Professor of Politics at Oxford. The lecturer in accounting was Roger Carter, and for banking, D. Drummond Fraser – both were to teach on a part-time basis at Manchester for some years.
61 *Victoria University of Manchester. Calendar 1904–5*, p.62.

three years, unless the student already held a degree, in which case two years was deemed sufficient:

(1) Political economy (2 hours per week)
(2) Geography (2 hours per week)
(3) Modern history (2 hours per week)
(4) A Modern language (3 hours per week)
(5) Organization of industry and commerce (2 hours per week)
(6) Accounting (1 hour per week for three terms for non-accountants)
(7) Commercial law (1 hour per week over one session)
(8) Special subject.[62]

Each subject could be sat for examination separately, rather than together as part of a single final examination. It was evidently anticipated that part-time students would be a major source of recruitment, and provision for this was made in scheduling all the principal courses for both day-time and evening hours.[63] Chapman himself lectured on 'Principles of political economy', the 'Organization of industry and commerce', and 'Railway economics'. The last were held in the evening only, were open to the public – and, according to the *Calendar*, were by far and away the most successful courses ever taught in terms of attendance, 856 students registering for lectures on 'Railway practice', and 921 for 'Railway history'. The faculty relied heavily for both students and part-time staff on the railway companies, banks, insurance, the law and accountancy, and this was reflected in the broad range of the syllabus, which was a model for later foundations. It was not however simply the range of subjects covered that was important; the teaching of economics remained at the core of the syllabus, and it was this feature that made Manchester, rather than Birmingham, where economic theory was a subject of minor importance, an alternative model to the Cambridge tripos for the joint development of teaching in economics and commerce.

The successful launch of the B. Com. degree in the Faculty of Commerce was followed with the rationalization of the Honours School

62 Special subjects could be drawn from sciences, languages, or from the faculty itself, for example, 'Railway economics and transport', 'Public finance', 'Insurance', 'Law of patents, designs and trade marks' – *Victoria University of Manchester. Calendar 1904–1905*, pp.254–5.
63 'Qualifying courses for degrees shall be arranged at such hours as to make it possible for students engaged in business to graduate in the Faculty, but candidates who have not attended approved courses of study in the University for at least seven hours a week each year for three years shall not be admitted to the degree without attending courses of study approved by the Board of the Faculty for one or more additional years.' *Victoria University of Manchester. Calendar 1904–5*, para.7 p.255.

of Economics and Political Science, which made use of some of the core courses prescribed for the B. Com. and added to them courses in political theory, history and philosophy. Comparatively few students completed this course in the years before 1914,[64] but its existence played an important role in the development of the Manchester Faculty of Commerce. Chapman, assisted by Meredith,[65] elaborated the core political economy course into a tripartite sequence of principles of political economy, economic analysis, and advanced and honours class, combined with a course on public finance taught by Adams. By 1910, the listing of staff for the faculty includes Chapman, C. F. Bickerdike, H. M. Hallsworth (future Professor of Economics at Newcastle) and R. B. Forrester (later Professor of Economics and Political Science, University College Aberystwyth). The Manchester faculty thus became sharply distinguished from its Birmingham counterpart, where economics teaching was only very weakly developed within the syllabus and the faculty. The emphasis laid on accounting by Ashley, who remained the sole significant representative economist at Birmingham, and the consequent dedication of staff resources to a chair in the subject when Manchester used part-time practitioners, hindered the joint development of complementary teaching in economics and commerce following the Manchester pattern. Student numbers and the course structure inhibited recruitment of young economists as teachers; and thus, as a consequence, commerce teaching could not directly benefit from contemporary developments in economics.[66]

There are a number of factors in the development of the Birmingham faculty that account for its significant deviation from the pattern laid out in Manchester, some of which will be examined below. Owens College was however only one constituent part of the Victoria University, and so far little mention has been made of the

64 Thirteen Manchester students gained a BA (Hons) Econ. before 1914, as compared with forty-six for the B.Com.; but this is placed in some perspective by noting that, on the one hand, only one student gained a BA (Hons) Econ. in Birmingham before 1940; while on the other, 101 passed Pt.II of the Cambridge Economics Tripos before 1914.

65 Hugh Owen Meredith, graduated in classics and history at Cambridge, taught at Manchester 1905–8, Wash Girdler's Lecturer in Cambridge as successor to Pigou 1908–11, and then Professor of Economics, Queen's University, Belfast 1911–45.

66 The importance of this economic core to Manchester's teaching is emphasized by the fact that in 1910 the two external examiners were Edgeworth and Cannan – *Victoria University of Manchester. Calendar 1910–11*, p.70. Ashley had different priorities to those of Chapman, but at the very least it is evident that the emergence of Manchester as a centre for the teaching of economics in no respect diverted the commerce curriculum in a less practical direction.

other two colleges, University College Liverpool, and Yorkshire College, Leeds. Neither of these institutions were at the turn of the century in a position to challenge Manchester's pre-eminence in political economy, but the reasons for this were dissimilar. Yorkshire College was handicapped by a general lack of resources, as well as a weaker network of the kind of cultural and business life that had sustained the development of Owens College. University College Liverpool on the other hand did possess a financial, cultural and commercial base broadly comparable to that of Manchester, yet here too teaching in political economy and commerce, although established by the turn of the century, remained at a low level in both quality and quantity. Liverpool enjoyed a position in the later nineteenth century as the leading port in the United Kingdom, as well as being the terminus of the passenger and goods trade with North America, and it was the commercial and industrial wealth associated with this that had provided the financial foundations for University College.

Besides the wealth of the city, there was, as in Manchester, a broad base of popular educational activity. The Mechanics' Institute, founded in 1825, was one of the largest and most successful, having over 3,000 members in the early 1840s.[67] In 1867 the Liverpool Ladies' Educational Association combined with similar organizations in Manchester, Leeds and Sheffield to sponsor a series of lectures by James Stuart, providing the initial impetus for the development of the University Extension movement. The local development of extension teaching in turn engendered a movement for the establishment of an institution of higher education in Liverpool, a Society for the Promotion of Higher Education in Liverpool being formed after a public meeting in January 1874.[68] By 1878 a platform had been created for the establishment of a college, and support lent to the proposal by the then Lord Mayor, a shipowner and Leader of the Conservative Party on the Town Council, reinforcing the broad base of the movement. The draft plan for University College, Liverpool put forward in November 1878 envisaged three arts and four science professors, plus lectureships in law and physiology, and estimated teaching costs at £3,000 per annum, requiring a capital of £75,000 to endow this level of expenditure. In the event, chairs were endowed individually with gifts of £10,000 each, a chair of 'Logic, mental and moral philosophy, and political economy' being endowed by

67 T. Kelly, *For Advancement of Learning. The University of Liverpool 1881–1981*, Liverpool: Liverpool University Press, 1981, p.32. In 1856 it was renamed the Liverpool Institute, and it oversaw the foundation in 1857 of Queen's College, which was affiliated to London University. Day classes were attempted in a number of subjects, but met with little success.
68 Kelly, *For Advancement of Learning*, p.37.

forty-one Scottish merchants of Liverpool.[69] John MacCunn of Balliol College, Oxford was appointed to this chair in December 1881, and the first classes began the following January.

Initially, students enrolled term by term for courses related to Cambridge Local Examinations, only a few intending to sit for a London University degree.[70] However, the merger with Victoria University in 1884 soon directed attention more towards degree-level work, and the addition of two more chairs, bringing the number of professors to ten, ensured a broader coverage of subjects. By the end of the first decade of the College, the impact of the Technical Instruction Act was beginning to be felt, further accelerating its development towards an institution teaching three-year degree programmes to full-time students.

The first teaching of political economy in the new institution was in evening classes, MacCunn announcing a course of twenty lectures over the Autumn and Lent terms for 1882–3.[71] Most of his time was devoted to moral philosophy, logic and psychology, together with some elementary political economy – which represented a standard grouping of subjects within the Cambridge Higher Local examinations. By 1884 MacCunn was teaching, instead of an elementary political economy course, a course of twenty lectures on English political economists, dealing in the first term with Smith, Ricardo and Malthus, and in the second dealing primarily with the theories of John Stuart Mill and J. E. Cairnes. MacCunn prescribed the main texts of the writers concerned, presumably in the absence of a British textbook on the subject.[72] In Manchester, an elementary political economy course already existed, having been established by Adamson in the early 1880s and surviving well into the 1890s. In Liverpool, no comparable teaching had developed by the middle of the decade, despite the ease with which the Manchester curriculum might well have been imitated.

For 1886–7 a 'Business curriculum' was announced, recognized by

---

69 Kelly, *For Advancement of Learning*, p.48. The six other chairs, including the King Alfred Chair of Modern History and Literature, were fully endowed by June 1882; and the total collected for teaching and equipment by this time was £109,171. Buildings and land on Brownlow Hill were acquired for £19,000.

70 The number gaining a London BA degree was at its highest, four in one year, in 1898 when fifteen gained a Victoria BA. Only sixteen London BA Degrees were awarded to University College students between 1882 and 1891.

71 *Calendar of University College, Liverpool 1882–3*, p.51.

72 Ingram's *History of Political Economy* did not appear until 1888, although a translation of Cossa's *Guida allo studio dell'economia politica* (1876) appeared as *Guide to the Study of Political Economy* in 1880.

over three hundred listed companies and associations.[73] The course however bears no comparison with the Commercial Certificate introduced in Manchester for 1889–90: it was a two-year course, students following in effect the first two years of a three-year ordinary BA or B.Sc. course. Political economy was only one of a number of options available in the second year, and none of the more usual commercial subjects were covered – not even geography was included. The course in political economy taught by MacCunn in the following year for this curriculum was scheduled on two evenings a week at 7.15p.m., indicating that the college authorities anticipated part-time students.[74] Furthermore, the *Calendar* also notes that these classes were open to the public on payment of the appropriate fee, further emphasizing the mixed nature of political economy teaching at this time.[75]

The situation altered with the appointment of E. C. K. Gonner in 1888: in the *Calendar* for the year 1888–9 he announces courses in commercial geography and commercial history and theory, directed primarily at the first and second years respectively of the college Business Curriculum.[76] In addition to this he also gave a series of twenty evening lectures entitled 'Work and wages', dealing with contemporary issues concerning wages, rent, profits, 'Dislocations of trade, and lack of employment', and trade unions.[77] Otherwise he offered a class in 'Economic and commercial science' similar in coverage to the Owens class in political economy, and clearly fulfilling the same purpose: providing teaching for a paper within the historical stream of the Victoria BA ordinary degree; and a course for certification by Victoria University honours history students, the first two of whom graduated in 1890.[78]

Gonner's original appointment had been made possible by a

---

73 These are listed on pp.24–8 of the *Calendar* for 1886–7.
74 *Calendar of University College, Liverpool 1887–8*, pp.63–4.
75 *Calendar of University College, Liverpool 1887–8*, p.119.
76 *Calendar of University College, Liverpool 1888–9*, pp.68–9. Gonner had been a pupil of Marshall at Oxford, and had been appointed to University College, Bristol as Lecturer in Political Economy, Modern History and English Literature – testimony enough to the character of teaching at this time. In 1892 Gonner was promoted to the Brunner Chair in Liverpool, occupying the post until his early death in 1922 – see the obituary for him by William Beveridge in *Economic Journal*, Vol.32 (1922), pp.264–7, and A. Kadish, R. D. Freeman, 'Foundation and early years' in J. D. Hey, D. Winch (eds) *A Century of Economics*, Oxford: Basil Blackwell, 1990, pp.25–6.
77 *Calendar of University College, Liverpool 1888–9*, pp.129–30.
78 In fact, only nine students ever graduated with a Victoria BA (Hons.) History from University College Liverpool, compared with three from Yorkshire College, and forty-eight from Owens. See *Victoria University Calendar 1903*.

temporary endowment, but in 1891 J. T. Brunner gave the college £10,000 to endow a chair of economic science, and Gonner was made first Brunner Professor of Economic Science in the same year.[79] Teaching, however, remained much the same until the later 1890s, with some variation in geographical subjects, and Gonner occasionally delivering lecture series on the history of political economy. Two classes in economics continued in being – an elementary course of economic theory using Marshall's *Economics of Industry* and Jevons's *Money*, and an advanced course whose rubric noted only that students would be taught to use statistics.[80] Added to this were the course in economic and commercial history (Cunningham's *Growth of English Industry and Commerce* Vol.II being the textbook), and two courses in commercial geography, the first of which used Gonner's own *Commercial Geography*.

During the academic year 1897–8 the college, together with the city Technical Instruction Committee and the Chamber of Commerce, initiated a two-year daytime School of Commerce. Like the Business Curriculum, it was aimed at school leavers aged 16 or 17, and represented a level of education intermediate between school and university, even as then understood. However, unlike the Business Curriculum, which had no formal commercial content, this course did seek to introduce such subjects. Three hours a week in each of the years was prescribed for commercial arithmetic, three and five hours for commercial practice, and two hours each in the second year for commercial law and economics. A workload of twenty-four hours a week was laid down in the programme published in 1899, eight of which were devoted to two modern languages; and it was further stated that

> Students who have attended the full two years' course, and passed satisfactory examinations, will obtain a diploma, which, it is hoped, will receive *substantial* recognition by the commercial community in the shortening of apprenticeship.[81]

It is not clear why the college would introduce a course at this level in the later 1890s, for by this time independent commercial schools were becoming established, serving the constituency identified above, a constituency quite distinct even to that served by Owens's own Commercial Certificates. In any case, the daytime course appears to

---

79 Kelly, *For Advancement of Learning*, p.74.
80 In 1898 the political economy course was divided into two sections, A and B, and to the second was added a new course in 'Descriptive economics' – *Calendar of University College, Liverpool 1898–9*, pp.100–1. This modification occurs at Owens, and must therefore reflect a structural modification within the Victoria University framework.
81 *Calendar of University College, Liverpool 1899–1900*, p.221.

have met with little success; in 1900 an evening course was added, although this too had a very moderate impact.[82]

This relatively low key reception of political economy and commercial subjects in Liverpool up to 1900 was not due to a general lack of interest in educational initiatives in the city. University College never wanted for financial resources in the way that most of its contemporaries did. When in 1900, spurred by the granting of university status to Mason College, Birmingham, pressure developed for independence from the Victoria University, £170,000 was raised by the autumn of 1902.[83] Gonner, it was true, remained rather a one-man-band, but his chair had been substantially endowed well before that of Flux in Manchester. The account given above of Owens makes clear that its pace of curricular and

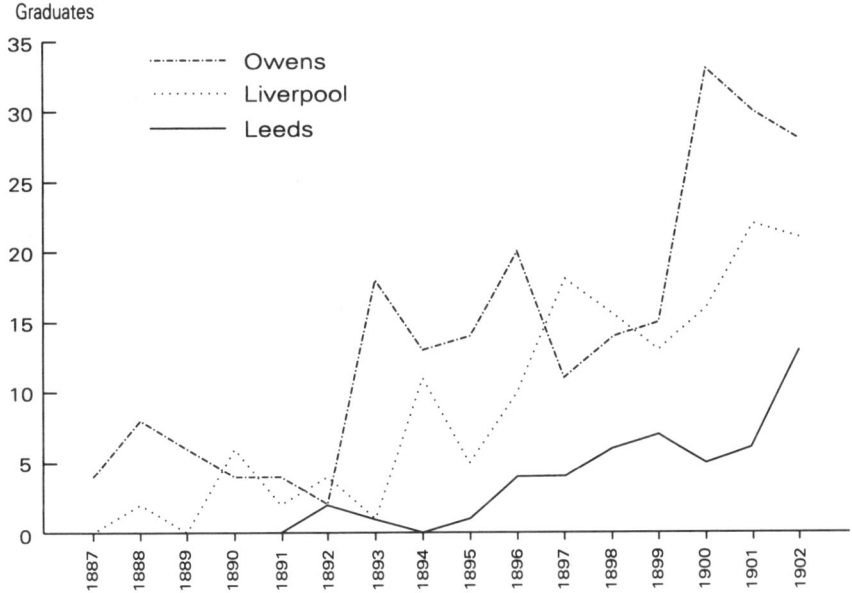

Figure 2: Victoria University BA degrees by college

82 Kelly, *For Advancement of Learning*, pp.115–16. The new evening course differed from the day course in having a tutor in accountancy in addition to the tutor for commercial arithmetic; the local accountant recruited for to teach during 1900–1 for the School was Sidney Dawson, later Professor of Accounting at Birmingham 1907–10 – *Calendar of University College, Liverpool 1900–01*, p.237.

83 For comparison, the government grant to University Colleges, originally set at £15,000 per annum, was raised to £25,000 in 1897 – Education Department, 'Reports from University Colleges Participating in the Grant of £15,000 made by Parliament for "University Colleges in Great Britain"', British Parliamentary Papers (1897), Vol.LXX, p.vii.

structural change gathered speed during the 1890s, a phenomenon that cannot be detected in Liverpool. Furthermore, if we compare the figures for Victoria BAs and BScs awarded over this period (Figure 2), we notice that there is a sudden expansion in Manchester at the end of the 1890s that is replicated in Liverpool, but in a distinctly weak form. At the level of the university as a whole, the transition to independent chartered status was not accompanied by a marked dynamic increase in academic activity, as was the case at Owens.

The staff situation in 1910 for the teaching of economics provides us with a useful comparative index of the respective colleges. As has been stated, by this time Owens had on its staff, besides the professor, three or four lecturers who can be clearly identified as academic economists of a new type, expecting to make their careers within the university system as teachers of economics. The Manchester Faculty of Commerce was therefore constructed around a core economics curriculum, with much of the more specialized commercial subjects being covered by local barristers, bankers, accountants and railway managers. This practice was followed in Liverpool – the 1907 *Calendar* lists five 'Special Lecturers in railway administration and shipping', three of whom are railway managers, and one a barrister.[84] However, full-time Liverpool staff in commerce and economics for 1910, besides Gonner, consisted of a lecturer in commercial theory (John Montgomery), and an assistant lecturer to Gonner, E. Hughes. That Hughes succeeded in this post as an assistant lecturer in geography, and was in turn replaced in 1912 by R. A. MacDonald (a Liverpool graduate), suggests that the post was very much one of a teaching assistant, rather than that of a junior member of staff. This situation did not alter greatly before the war, and then, on Gonner's death in 1922, his chair remained vacant until 1930, further underlining the low level of committment to the teaching of economics and commerce in Liverpool.

In principle, an honours degree in economics had been available at Liverpool from its inception as an independent university: the ordinances published in 1903 list economics as one of nine honours subjects, requiring attendance at lectures and classes of six hours in the first year, and four in the second and third years; together with certificates of attendance in approved courses in history and competence in French or German. The examination was heavily slanted towards economic history, in the second part of the examination two out of four papers being on a 'special economic period or subject.'[85] Six courses were offered:

A. General economics laws and growth of economic society. 'This course is the requisite first course in economic study. It treats of the

84 University of Liverpool, *Calendar 1907*, p.271.
85 University of Liverpool, *Calendar 1903–4*, p.176.

gradual growth of economic society through its different stages, and of its modern laws and conditions.' (Texts: Nicholson, *Elements of Political Economy*; Bagehot, *Postulates of Political Economy*; Hadley, *Economics*)

B. Descriptive economics. 'Existing English economic forms and institutions.' (No reading assigned)

C. Distribution of wealth, and theories of remuneration. (Texts: Hadley, *Economics*; Marshall, *Elements of Economics*;[86] Marshall, *Principles of Economics* (selected chapters); Leroy Beaulieu, *La Répartition*; Schloss, *Wages Systems*; Böhm-Bawerk, *Capital and Interest*)

D. Economic history. 'A general sketch of the economic history of England during the last four centuries'.

E. Economic history and modern political theory. Period, 1760–1815.

F. History and administration of the poor law.[87]

The first, introductory course was taken by BA Ordinary, LLB and honours economics students, while Course F was specifically for those taking history honours. Honours economics students took all of these courses, save E, to which no students are specifically directed by the *Prospectus*.

There is of course very little economic theory in this proposed honours economics course; it barely goes beyond a level of technicality available to Manchester evening students in the 1890s. In any case, according to available records, there were no graduates from Liverpool in honours economics before 1940. Perhaps this is not so surprising; Gonner was the sole representative of the subject at this time, and he continued to give geography courses in addition to those he gave in economics. In 1905–6 an additional course was proposed, 'Economic science in relation to history', which soon evolved into an 'Advanced economics' course, but it was evidently primarily aimed at the honours history students.[88] Only ten students graduated with a BA (Hons.) of any kind in 1908, as against fifty-three with ordinary BAs. The following year the figures are nine and fifty respectively – and so it can be concluded that the ordinary BA contributed most to the support of such political economy teaching as there was; and, in so doing kept it at the existing elementary level.

There was however development within the commercial curriculum; in 1906 a new category appeared in the Ordinances for the ordinary BA

86 I.e., *Elements of Economics of Industry*, the textbook replacing the 1879 *Economics of Industry*.

87 University of Liverpool, *Prospectus of Day and Evening Classes in the Faculty of Arts for the Session 1904–5*, pp.65–6.

88 University of Liverpool, *Prospectus of Day and Evening Classes in the Faculty of Arts for the Session 1905–6*, p.85.

degree, 'Subjects of examination for commercial students'. A three-year course was envisaged here, economics and a modern foreign language being present in all years, while geography, history, commercial theory and commercial law were taught in one or two of the years.[89] A new Bachelor of Commercial Sciences (B.Com.Sc.) was formally announced in 1909 on an equal footing to other degree courses, and in the same year the economics teaching was reformed, adding courses in 'Modern economic organization', 'Public finance', and 'Economic science in its historical growth'.[90] However, the first graduates with a B. Com.Sc. are recorded for 1924, and not before.

These developments do little therefore to alter our conclusion that political economy, while established early on in Liverpool, failed to stimulate the level of demand for teaching, either in evening or day classes, that would have made possible the recruitment of more staff, and a consequent elaboration in breadth and quality of the teaching. This is by no means untypical for the time, as will now be more briefly shown with the third member of Victoria University – Yorkshire College – concluding with a consideration of the experience of the Birmingham Faculty of Commerce.

Yorkshire College was originally conceived as a technical college for local science teachers, the original prospectus identifying engineering, manufacturing, agriculture, mining and metallurgy as the major subjects of study.[91] Opening in 1874 in rented premises with twenty-four registered students, only three chairs existed: chemistry; physics and mathematics; and geology and mining. This was as much to do with financial constraints as anything else, for the original modest target of £60,000 was soon reduced to £20,000, and by 1875 only £15,394 had been raised. The single most significant benefactor was the London Clothworkers' Company which, understandably enough, directed its funds into textile and allied departments, endowing a Chair in Textile Fabrics soon after the opening.

Total student numbers rose quickly, to 463 in 1879–80, and 994 in 1884–5. Only one-third of these were regular daytime students, the remainder being classified as teachers, occasional students, and evening students, of whom there were 259 in 1884–5.[92] In addition to this, at first the College authorities admitted students at the age of 14, only raising this in 1897 to the age of 16. Although an entrance examination

89 University of Liverpool, *Calendar 1906*, p.87.
90 University of Liverpool, *Faculty of Arts. Prospectus of Courses for the Session 1909–10*, pp.58–9.
91 1872 Prospectus cited in A. J. Taylor, 'County college and civic university: an introductory essay', in P. H. J. H. Gosden, A. J. Taylor (eds) *Studies in the History of a University, 1874–1974*, Leeds: E. J. Arnold, 1975, p.4.
92 P. H. J. H. Gosden, 'The student body', in ibid.

was set to all candidates, there was a greater than usual lack of clarity in the educational objectives of the institution; and even subsequent to the College joining the Victoria University, of 119 preparing for degrees in science and arts in the later 1890s, a total of only 20 Victoria BAs and B.Sc.s were awarded in 1898.[93]

Calendars for sessions preceding accession to Victoria University in 1887 are not available, but in that year a Business Course was announced similar in intent and level to that which Liverpool had adopted the previous year:

> In consideration of the great importance to youths who are intended for commercial life of a sound training in subjects which bear directly or indirectly upon their calling, the following Special Course of Instruction has been drawn up by the Senate and sanctioned by the Council. It has also received the approval, by resolution, of the Leeds Chamber of Commerce. It is hoped that students will enter for this course at 15 or 16 years of age. The time occupied in going through it will be two sessions, consisting of about one year and nine months. The fee will vary with the combination of languages selected, but can in no case exceed, inclusive of the registration fee £35 14s. for the two sessions. The course is in no way intended to supersede the technical training which is given in special departments for particular industries, but is intended to meet the wants of young men who are likely to be engaged in banks, merchants' offices, or in callings in which a more specialized training is not needed. Other branches of college work may be associated with the course here given, but this will not be recommended as a rule, as the subjects included are sufficiently numerous to occupy the full attention of a student.[94]

As in Liverpool, this is a 'business curriculum' only in the sense that it provides a modern curriculum; political economy occupied one hour a week in the first session only, languages between one and three hours, and mathematics five hours. More time was devoted in the two years to mathematics than to modern languages, unlike in Liverpool; and the language that occupied most time in Leeds was Latin, for which three weekly hours were prescribed, as against one hour for French, if

---

93 In this year Owens and University College Liverpool each accounted for fourteen BAs, as against six from Yorkshire College; in B.Sc.s on the other hand, Yorkshire College just outperformed University College from 1897, with a total of 110 science graduates as against 109 from University College.

94 *Yorkshire College, Leeds Calendar for the Fourteenth Session 1887–88*, pp.54–5.

selected as one of the two obligatory languages. Comments made by the Principal on the course indicate that it was directed at young clerks, and the syllabus itself betrays the intention of providing tuition supplementary to a school curriculum.[95]

Mention of the Business Course in the *Calendar* ceases from 1890; it can be presumed that systematic teaching at this level was taken over by the municipal authorities, able to fund such teaching from 'Whisky money', the duty on spirits appropriated to local authorities for technical education. A day course on bookkeeping was however added in 1889,[96] and this survived the demise of the Business Course with a small number of students; after hovering around eight or nine a year as a day course, numbers increased to thirty when it was transferred to the evenings in 1892.

The following year the evening class was divided into two, a general class (16 students), and an agricultural class (23 students), the latter covering 'Farm and Estate Accounts described. Cash Book and Ledger. Accounts of Labour, Crops, Stock etc., Balance Sheet. Profit and Loss Account'.[97] By 1900 the course had been absorbed into the second and third years of the Agricultural Course and taught by an assistant lecturer in mathematics and physics, according to a rubric identical to that of the previous evening classes.[98]

Two important facts can be detected from a perusal of the Yorkshire College calendars for the 1890s. First, political economy played a very minor part in the teaching, fading out entirely in the course of the decade. This cannot be attributed to the technical bias of the College, but rather to the lack of student demand. The Victoria requirement for honours history that students gain a certificate of attendance at a political economy course certainly applied, but there were only ever three honours history graduates from Yorkshire College – two in 1891, and one in 1900. The other function of political economy, as an optional but examinable course for ordinary BAs and LL Bs, was likewise in itself insufficient impulse for the continuation of regular

95 'Principal's Report for the Session 1886–7', *Yorkshire College, Leeds Calendar for the Fourteenth Session 1887–88*, p.177.
96 The course was taught by a local accountant, and covered: 'General principles involved in keeping accounts of business transactions. The three systems in common use – Single Entry, Double Entry, and Single converted into Double, practically illustrated, with the forms and uses of the several Books of Account employed in each case. The application of general principles to the different classes of business transactions. Commercial terms and phraseology.' *Yorkshire College, Leeds Calendar for 1889–90*, p.134.
97 *Yorkshire College, Leeds Calendar for 1894–95*, p.216; The course textbook was given as Woodman, *Book-keeping for Farmers*.
98 *Yorkshire College, Leeds Calendar for 1900–1901*, p.238.

teaching in the subject: there were few of the former, and only ever one of the latter, in 1902.

Second, the type of demand that existed for commercial courses was clearly of a different nature to that in other contemporary institutions. Bookkeeping is usually assumed to be a commercial subject related to employment in banking, insurance, or manufacturing. In Leeds, the demand for such skills derived more from farming than from textile manufacture. If this can be read as an indicator of the type of local demand for commercial education, then it is little wonder that political economy, with its bias to the world of trade and commerce, struck at first such shallow roots. This was however to change, for in 1902 John Clapham was listed as Professor of Economics.[99] The appointment, and the inauguration of the University of Leeds in 1904, gave scope for the development of teaching in economics and economic history along lines familiar in Manchester, but hitherto absent in Leeds, despite its membership of Victoria University. Once more we find that the elaboration of a recognizably independent curriculum in economic and commercial subjects anticipates demand for teaching. Quite why the College authorities chose to found a chair in a subject for which there was a marked lack of enthusiasm remains unclear; even more obscure is the process by which Clapham, an economic historian comparable in stature to Unwin in Manchester, was succeeded in 1908 by D. H. Macgregor, another of Marshall's students, later Drummond Professor of Political Economy in Oxford from 1921–45.

Clapham's first move was to instate a general economics class comparable to that of Owens, and introduce a two-year course of economics and economic history which, by 1903, was taught three hours a week.[100] In addition to this Clapham taught a course on commercial geography; and to this was added a new appointee in accountancy, who proposed a two-year course beginning with the principles of bookkeeping, but proceeding in the second year to the analysis of company accounts, cost accounts and depreciation. The new two-year course for which this was intended was the Diploma in Commerce, covering economics, economic geography, accountancy, mathematics, commercial law and at least one modern language.[101] To this was added in 1905 a three year B.Com. degree, which covered exactly the same subjects as the Diploma.

Despite the elaboration of courses for honours economics students, it is evident by 1912 that the principal area of growth was that of the B.Com. and Diploma. To the names of Macgregor and Shaw in the

99 Clapham had gained a first in history at Cambridge in 1895, and was a tutor at King's in history and economics from 1898 to 1902. He was subsequently Professor of Economic History in Cambridge from 1928 to 1938.
100 *Yorkshire College, Leeds Calendar, 1903–4*, pp.121–2.
101 *The University of Leeds. Calendar, 1904–5*, pp.133–4.

economics section of the *Calendar* are added in this year L. Rodwell Jones, as assistant lecturer in geography; and Henry Clay and Robert Dower, 'University Lecturers in Social Organization'. The commerce syllabus for 1912 also includes a new section, 'Social Organization and Public Service';[102] this presages a post-war development in which Commerce faculties were either the base from which the training of social workers developed (as in Birmingham); or in which the teaching of public administration came to overshadow the conventional B.Com. degree structure (as in Manchester). Despite its very shaky beginnings in the Yorkshire College, by 1914 the teaching of economics and commerce was well established in Leeds and following a path of development comparable to its better-known northern counterparts. The modest expansion in teaching that took place made it possible to recruit new, recently graduated staff, many of whom were to make their careers as economists within an academic context.

The Victoria University represented an important, but intermediary stage, in the development of the new civic universities of Manchester, Liverpool and Leeds. These gained independent status at almost exactly the same time as Birmingham, Bristol and Sheffield; but the similarity in the processes by which the original colleges arrived at chartered university status throws further light on those features of the movement already highlighted in the discussion of the Victoria University. It is logical to begin this concluding survey by considering the evolution of Firth College, Sheffield, since its effort to gain membership of Victoria University was rebuffed. In addition to this, Birmingham and Sheffield share important features in their initial endowment and development – neither so well-funded as Liverpool, nor yet lacking financial support like Yorkshire College, as new foundations of the 1880s with major individual benefactors they encountered similar difficulties in the establishment of a full range of subjects.

The moving force in the foundation of Firth College was a local ironmaster, Mark Firth, who, as Lord Mayor in 1874, sought to bring extension teaching to Sheffield. The required guarantee fund of £1,000 was quickly raised, and in January 1875 the first extension classes began, in economic science[103] and in English literature. The latter met at 12 noon Tuesdays, with a supplementary class at noon on Saturday. The economics lecture took place at 8 p.m. on Tuesdays, with a supplementary class on Friday nights, attracting 474 students. As emphasized above, the difference between daytime and evening teaching was that the evening lectures were directed at working men, while many of those

102 *The University of Leeds. Calendar, 1912–13*, p.230.
103 Taught by Moore Ede, who in 1878 was also to be active in promoting the development of University College, Liverpool – see Kelly, *For Advancement of Learning*, p.46.

attending during the day were middle-class women. The fees for the courses reflects this social difference: the course in English literature cost 10s.; whereas the political economy course cost only 5s.[104] As elsewhere, the early interest in political economy soon declined, while other lectures in English and geography retained their numbers; Moore Ede had 233 students in the following September to December course, and 130 in that of January to April 1876. Moore Ede dropped political economy in 1877 in favour of English history.

By this time Firth was pushing ahead with plans to build a permament college, with the intention of transforming it into a university as soon as practicable. Land was purchased and a building constructed, to plans approved by James Stuart of the Cambridge Extension movement. As a result Firth College, when it formally opened in January 1880, had a new building with two large lecture theatres and seven classrooms, suitable for extension teaching, but a definite obstacle to the development of regular college teaching. Both Principal and the first professor of chemistry were recruited from Owens College; and in addition there were professors in classics, modern history and a lecturer in modern languages.

Students were admitted to the new college without examination over the age of 17, and the day courses that they followed were linked to the London University examinations. Few however worked so consistently, preferring instead to take individual courses. Additional teachers were recruited in metallurgy and mechanical engineering, closely reflecting the principal local industrial interests and hence, *de facto*, consolidating the Firth College as a technical institution, despite the fact that this had not been the original intention, as had been the case in Leeds. This trend was further underlined in 1892 with the appointment of a Professor of Mining.

The predominant character of Firth College – chartered as University College, Sheffield in 1893 – remained that of a technical institution, in which commercial education had a very low priority. Prior to the appointment in 1897 of G. I. H. Lloyd to the new Department of Philosophy and Economics there was in any case nobody to teach political economy; and the association of philosophy with economics indicates that the College was by the end of the century still at a developmental stage that had long been passed through in Liverpool and Manchester. It was not until 1910 that an unequivocal appointment in economics was made, with the departure of Lloyd to be Professor of Economics in Toronto and the subsequent division of the department into its two constituent parts.

The new appointee was Douglas Knoop, pupil of Sydney Chapman in

104 Chapman, *The Story of a Modern University*, p.15.

Manchester, who became first lecturer in Economics, and then in 1920 professor. Here once more we encounter the generational changeover that took place in the first decade of this century: Knoop had graduated in 1905 with a first in economics and political science at Manchester, had been appointed an assistant lecturer in political economy at Manchester in 1909, and would not retire from his Sheffield Chair until 1948.[105] The consolidation of the discipline of economics in the British civic universities owed a great deal to this process by which senior academic economists, many of them students of Marshall from Cambridge, moved into their posts at the turn of the century, and then moulded the development of the discipline over the subsequent two or three decades. In so doing they displaced a previous generation of political economists whose concerns, while perhaps no broader, were certainly less focused on commercial education on the one hand, or economic analysis on the other. Corroboration of the importance of this process is evident from the development of the Faculty of Commerce in Birmingham and the role of its moving spirit, W. J. Ashley.

The origins of the Birmingham faculty are in their broad outlines fairly well known, not least because of the contrast drawn between Marshall's tripos and Ashley's faculty on the nature of the economics curriculum.[106] For Marshall, the inclusion of accounting in the Birmingham curriculum was inappropriate for the education of future business men, while for Ashley it came to have symbolic significance, the first University Chair in Accounting being established at Birmingham in 1903. As a consequence, the issue of teaching in accounting has come to have an unwarranted prominence, with the implication that here Ashley was breaking new ground. However, as we have seen above, accounting in one form or another had been a feature of curricula elsewhere since the early 1890s, and was not unique to Birmingham; and although Ashley clearly distinguished between 'accounting' as the transmission of an understanding of modern accounting methods to future businessmen, and 'accountancy' as the training of accountants, such a clear distinction is not evident in the syllabi of the time.[107] More important for the development of the faculty was that, besides Ashley as

105 Chapman, *The Story of a Modern University*, p.230.
106 The most accessible recent account of the establishment of the Birmingham Faculty is Alon Kadish, 'The foundation of Birmingham's Faculty of Commerce as a statement on the nature of economics', *Manchester School*, Vol.LIX (1991), pp.160–72.
107 Another important point here is that Ashley was inclined to invoke the 'American example' when advocating the teaching of accounting to business men, pointing to Harvard University and the Universities of Michigan and Wisconsin. At this time, however, the development of business education in American universities was in a very rudimentary stage of development, and the teaching of accounting techniques even more so.

Professor of Commerce and Public Finance, and the chair in account-ing, a third chair in finance was created in 1906; another first for Birmingham.[108] Combined with the establishment of a Chair in Com-mercial Law in 1913, the result was that the faculty failed to draw upon the pool of young graduates in economics during the first two decades of its existence – in contrast with Manchester, where a core of full-time economics staff was supported by part-time teaching in law, accounting and railway administration. By the mid-1920s, Birmingham was pro-ducing around six B.Com.s a year, as against Manchester's twenty-five, to which was added a regular, although limited, output of economics graduates.

Although the University of Birmingham was founded in 1900, this took the form, as elsewhere, of chartering an existing institution. Mason College opened in 1880 with purpose-built premises including administrative offices, lecture theatres, classrooms and laboratories.[109] The purpose of the college was explicitly to give instruction in scientific subjects, the Constitution stating that

> The College has been built and endowed by Sir Josiah Mason, to provide for a thorough systematic education in Science, with a distinctly practical application to the industries of the Midland district, and particularly those of Birmingham.[110]

By 1881 four humanities professors had joined the college, forming a new 'Department of Art', and bringing the total number of chairs to eleven. However, no teaching in political economy is recorded until 1893–4, when nineteen students are reported as attending an evening class on political economy.[111] The class soon lapsed, however, and it was only with the appointment of J. H. Muirhead in 1898 as Professor of Mental and Moral Philosophy, and Political Economy, that regular teaching was initiated.[112] This was oriented to the London BA examin-ation, and used as its text Marshall's *Economics of Industry*; originally offered as one lecture and one class a week, this was extended in 1899 to two lectures a week, for which the demand was so great that Muirhead

---

108 This chair lapsed and was then re-established as the Mitsui Chair of Finance in 1923, endowed with £5,000 – *Economic Journal*, Vol.33 (1923), p.434.

109 Building and site cost £80,000, while the total endowment of the College is estimated at £200,000: E. W. Vincent, P. Hinton, *The University of Birming-ham: its History and Significance*, Birmingham: Cornish Bros, 1947, p.63.

110 *Calendar of the Mason Science College, 1880–81*, p.21.

111 *Calendar of the Mason Science College, 1895–96*, p.440.

112 Birmingham's Social Science building is prominently named after Muir-head; curiously, this building bears no other visible sign of its function than the name of the founding 'Social Science' Professor.

recommended the creation of a special chair for political economy.[113]

With the chartering of the University in 1900, Muirhead was re-designated as a Professor of Philosophy, dropping the short-lived political economy course. Instead, the Faculty of Commerce was formed in 1902. This was very much at the behest of Joseph Chamberlain, who played a leading role in the creation of the university, and who forcefully supported the establishment of organized commercial education. A draft curriculum had been put forward by the Chamber of Commerce in 1899, placing emphasis on modern languages, commercial geography, commercial law and commercial arithmetic.[114] Apart from the prominence given to accounting in all three years of the new B. Com. degree, this Chamber of Commerce proposal prefigures the main subjects and emphases in the new curriculum. Only one course of economic theory was included, initially in the second year, and then switched to the first year. The rubric for this course clearly identifies it as an elementary course broadly comparable with the political economy class at Owens in the 1890s:

> This course will take a rapid survey of the whole of the wealth-producing and wealth-distributing activity of society. It will seek to disentangle the larger forces at work, to direct attention to the complex relations of cause and effect, and to indicate the general causes and criteria of national prosperity. It will thus supplement the courses on Commerce by (1) emphasizing the general considerations only incidentally touched on therein, and (2) connecting commerce with other sides of national life.[115]

The rudimentary nature of the economics actually communicated to the students is evident from the minutes of the Faculty Commercial Seminar, which met on a regular basis from November 1902 and in which students presented papers, and members of staff made comments. The first paper which could be said to have used elementary economic analysis appears in 1905;[116] and while a paper presented in 1906 prompted students to draw some diagrams on the blackboard, it

113 B. M. D. Smith, 'Education for management: its conception and implementation in the Faculty of Commerce at Birmingham', Faculty of Commerce and Social Science, University of Birmingham *Occasional Paper*, No.5 (1965), p.13.

114 Smith, 'Education for management', p.6.

115 *University of Birmingham. Calendar for the Session 1903–4*, p.321.

116 The paper was on payment by piece as a method of remuneration; Ashley did congratulate the student 'on one of the best papers ever read at a meeting of the Seminar', but the structure of the syllabus was such that students did not receive anything more than elementary economic training. Meeting of 18 March 1905, Faculty of Commerce Commercial Seminar 1905–1907 [Birmingham University Library Archives 9/iv/22].

transpired that none of those present clearly understood the function of elasticities in the determination of new equilibrium prices following an alteration in supply.[117]

The strategy pursued in Birmingham by Ashley focused strictly on commerce, for which, he considered, a systematic training in economics was not necessary. The Birmingham faculty turns out to be unrepresentative of the teaching of commerce: not only was most of the teaching of economics elsewhere in Britain before 1940 done within commerce courses, many of its exponents were comparatively young men with an appreciation of modern economic analysis. Without the presence of at least one or two members of this new rising academic generation it was not possible to develop economics teaching to a point where it assumed distinct and autonomous outlines. Appointments of this kind were not made in Birmingham, or for that matter in Liverpool. The faculties remained small,[118] as was the range of subjects that they could offer and new recruitment was slow. It could well be the case that this itself provided an impediment to the successful early development of economics teaching, for in the absence of such teaching it is not possible to say, with any degree of certainty, whether the supply of such teaching would in fact have prompted local demand.

Ashley was only 42 when the faculty was founded; in the same year Marshall was 60. He was, therefore, a comparatively young man; his death in 1927, soon after those of Marshall and Edgeworth, was in fact premature. More telling is a comparison with his opposite numbers in Manchester and Leeds – in 1902 Chapman was 31, and Clapham 29. This age difference is not great, but it gave them quite different experiences of political economy as a university discipline: Ashley gained his first in history at Oxford in 1881, Chapman his double first in moral sciences at Cambridge in 1897–8. Both Clapham and Chapman had of course been students of Marshall at Cambridge, but it would be wrong to see the transition in the teaching of economics as one driven solely by the propagation of Marshallian economics. For one thing, it is evident from the above that elementary courses in economics remained remarkably unchanged through the period 1880–1910. If a text by Marshall were to be assigned, then it was almost certainly going to be *Economics of Industry*. Adoption of this textbook brought with it the structure of the elementary Cambridge course for which it was prepared, generating a common theoretical basis wherever it was used.

117 'The effect of the interchangeability of materials on manufactures and markets', meeting of 20 January 1906, Faculty of Commerce Commercial Seminar 1905–1907 [BUL 9/iv/22].
118 Among a series of economic historians at Liverpool, the appointment of Ronald Coase to an Assistant Lectureship in 1934 stands out as a startling exception to this rule.

Upon this elementary core there was however erected a commercial curriculum that did not coincide with Marshall's conceptions of advanced teaching in economics. Furthermore, apart from their readiness to teach subjects like railway economics, both Clapham and Chapman had public differences with the Marshallian tradition that clearly separates them from the likes of the proselyte Pigou, Marshall's chosen successor in Cambridge. Marshall's pedagogic programme, as embodied in the economics tripos, provided a basis for moving the teaching of economics beyond the routine elementary nostrums; but it seems to have had a limited impact on his older students, who do not seem to have perceived the need to ensure the subject's disciplinary isolation.

This distinction, between a new view of economic science increasingly shared by younger academic economists, and the broader, practical aspects of most curriculae, is important in our understanding of the long-term development of economics as a discipline in British universities. It is customary to see the Cambridge Tripos as the model embodying the Marshallian organon, a model which was then diffused throughout the academic system. If we date this process from 1906 (the year of the first Pt.II Tripos graduates), a passing acquaintance with the teaching of economics in Britain up to the 1950s will reveal a curious 'delay' in this diffusion process. This apparent tardiness is however simply a fault in a perspective which assumes that theoretical innovation will quickly translate into pedagogical diffusion, disregarding the complex dynamics of student demand, institutional constraints, and the availability of appropriate teaching. Indeed, it might be suggested that the teaching of economics within a traditionally commercial framework was the condition for the expansion of academic economics, facilitating a disciplinary development which would not otherwise have been possible. The very different dynamics in Manchester on the one hand, and Liverpool and Birmingham on the other, lend clear support to this view.

226

8

THE CITY, THE FABIANS AND THE FOUNDATION OF THE LONDON SCHOOL OF ECONOMICS

Alon Kadish

In 1888 the London Chamber of Commerce decided to initiate a scheme of commercial education which, it was hoped, would serve to raise the standards of recruits to various clerical and junior executive positions in the City. It was a period of growing concern over the performance of England in international markets and it was generally assumed that the growing competitiveness of many of the newly industrialized nations was largely due to their superior arrangements for commercial training. France had the *Ecole Commerciale* (1863) and the *Ecole Superieure de Commerce* (1869), the latter founded by the Paris Chamber of Commerce, and Germany its *Realschule*, whereas in England 'every foreign observer continues to be puzzled by the contrast between the boundless and ever increasing business transactions of the British Empire, and the lack of provision for the technical training of those who are charged with them'. Sidney Webb, who some years later attempted an explanation of this phenomenon, argued that it was mainly the result of

> the ingrained belief of the English business man that there is not, and never can be, any 'commercial education' comparable with that which a man 'picks up' in the actual business of daily life. The most intelligent merchant never dreams of seeking for his son any special 'commercial education': he either sends him to Oxford or pitchforks him straight into his office.[1]

Over the years various non-governmental bodies tried to provide solutions of one sort or another. In 1856, the Society of Arts, for instance, established examinations in a variety of commercial subjects, for which a number of educational institutes, schools, polytechnics, etc., subsequently undertook to prepare students. But these efforts were largely voluntary and uncoordinated. In 1880 the Society of Arts

---

1 *Journal of the Society of Arts*, 6 August 1897, pp.938–43. Webb's observations were made in the course of an international congress on technical education.

proposed to discontinue all examinations on commercial subjects, and it was only after remonstrations from 'certain provincial institutions' that this decision was reconsidered and the examinations re-established.[2] Even within the Chamber of Commerce there were those who clung to a more conservative view of education. During a debate on the Report of the Commercial Education General Subcommittee which recommended the commercial education scheme, a member of the Council 'remarked that he was afraid that the scheme was one for instruction and not for education and did not sufficiently provide for the training of the mind.'[3] And, on an earlier occasion, Sir John Lubbock, while explaining the scheme to the Council, pointed out that it, in fact, constituted 'a compromise between the commercial and the scholastic members of the Committee', and that in his view too much prominence had been given to Latin.[4]

The committee entrusted with the drafting of the scheme recommended that the Chamber of Commerce too should award certificates by examination. In order to encourage candidates to take the examinations, the Council was urged to impress upon the various City companies the need to guarantee immediate employment to holders of its certificates. It was further argued that the adoption of such an employment policy would encourage parents to invest in suitable courses of training for their sons.[5] Rather than go to the length of instituting a new examining body, the Council chose to approach the College of Preceptors which, in turn, undertook 'to act as the Chamber's agents in instituting examinations . . . throughout the districts and the schools where the College of Preceptors have organized examinations'.[6] In addition, the Oxford and Cambridge Board for Local Examinations found the Chamber of Commerce certificate of a high enough standard to recognize it as an equivalent to the Board's examinations.[7]

The scheme established two grades of certificates: the junior certificate for candidates not older than sixteen years; and the senior certificate for candidates not older than nineteen, which could be taken in parts (for which separate certificates were given) or in total. While the arrangements made by the Chamber proved sufficient for the junior certificate, the same could not be said of the senior certificate,

2 'Report of the Council, p.xiii, examinations', in *Journal of the Society of Arts*, Vol. 28 June 1895, pp.735–7.

3 Guildhall Library, London Chamber of Commerce, 14, 459, Council Minute Books, Vol. I, 1891–4, 12 July 1888.

4 Ibid., 12 April 1888. Latin was eventually made an optional subject: see ibid., 17 July 1890.

5 Ibid., 14 February 1889.

6 Ibid., 8 November, 22 November 1888.

7 Ibid., 11 April, 25 July 1889.

and an insufficient number of candidates presented themselves for the examinations.[8] Consequently, in addition to the instruction offered by the various institutes which had undertaken to prepare candidates for the examinations, early in 1895 the Chamber initiated a course of evening lectures on 'The history of European commerce', which were delivered by W. Cunningham to a class of some fifty listeners,[9] mostly clerks of subscribers. In December the previous year, the Chamber of Commerce and the London County Council Technical Education Board (TEB) had been invited by the Recreative Evening Schools' Association to help organize a scheme for 'education on the most practical lines in commercial subjects.'[10] Following consultations, and on the basis of the success of Cunningham's course the TEB invited the Chamber of Commerce in May 1895 to hold future evening courses under the joint auspices of the two bodies.[11]

The TEB was founded to manage the 'Whisky money' which, on the basis of a report specially prepared by Hubert Llewellyn Smith (at the time Secretary of A. H. D. Acland's National Association for the Promotion of Technical Education),[12] had been allocated to county councils for technical education by the 1889 Education Act. It consisted of twenty members of the London County Council and fifteen outsiders, mainly representatives of various educational bodies and a number of expert officers, and was chaired (until 1898) by Sidney Webb. Unlike ordinary LCC committees, it enjoyed considerable fiscal autonomy and, once its annual budget was approved, was virtually free to make use of it as it chose. From the outset, Webb had aimed at furnishing London with a comprehensive education system. Higher education was to be provided for by the projected teaching university of London.

The TEB wanted to ensure that, if the university were founded, appropriate arrangements would be made for higher technical training, a purpose which it had agreed to help subsidize with a grant of £10,000 recommended by Llewellyn Smith.[13] In addition, the TEB was most anxious for the university to offer advanced evening classes for part-time students, with the same level of teaching and use of laboratory facilities as regular day courses. Furthermore, in a letter to the Prime

8 See ibid., Vol. II, 1895–1902, 11 June 1895. In 1895 there were 58 entrants for the junior examinations, but the only senior examination with sufficient entrants to allow the examination's being held was in bookkeeping.
9 *Chamber of Commerce Journal (Supplement)*, May 1895.
10 GLC Record Office, TEB, 16, Minutes of the TEB 1895–7, 14 January 1895.
11 London Chamber of Commerce, Council Minute Books, Vol. II, 9 May 1895.
12 See H. Ll. Smith, 'The teaching of London: a scheme for technical education', *Contemporary Review*, Vol. 61, May 1892, pp.741–53; B. Webb, *Our Partnership* London: Longmans, Green & Co., 1948, p.76 ff.
13 TEB, 59, Report of the TEB for the year 1894–5, May 1895, p.5.

Minister stating the TEB's position concerning the establishment of a teaching university, it was categorically stated 'that only on the condition that this provision should be made for the class of students in which it is more particularly interested, could it be expected that any large contribution should be made by the Board towards the cost of the maintenance of the University.'[14] Should the university choose to ignore the Board's appeal or choose to relegate evening students to the status of 'external students', the Board would regard its decision 'as a serious blow to its work', and would probably be forced to divert its 'contributions for higher scientific and technological instruction to places where this could be made accessible to the working population.'[15] In view of the eventual discontinuance of the deliberations concerning the foundation of a teaching university, the TEB was soon forced to seek other venues for higher technical instruction. In the budget of 1894–5 it approved a £1,000 grant to University College, London, and a £500 grant to Bedford College, on the condition that both colleges would offer some advanced instruction in technical subjects. The question of higher commercial education, however, remained unresolved.

A solution to this problem facing both the Chamber of Commerce and the TEB was provided by Sidney Webb. In September 1894 Webb set up the Hutchinson Trust in order to supervise the use of some £10,000 left to the Fabian Society for the promotion of socialism.[16] Webb decided that it would be a mistake to spend all or even most of the money on the Society's current activities. Instead, he set his heart on founding a research centre, which would specialize in the 'investigation of problems of municipal and national administration from a collectivist standpoint', and would publicize its findings. To do this, it would have to train a body of scholars competent to undertake original research,[17] and would therefore need to combine training in research with actual research. In addition, some means would have to be found for the dissemination of the school's work. Webb was confident that within ten years such a school 'might change the whole political thinking of England.'

With the Trust's eventual approval of the plan for a research centre (8 February 1895), Webb appears to have gone a step further, adopting it as a possible solution to the problem of advanced commercial education and thereby extending both its functions and its financial base. From the outset he managed to maintain the Trust's autonomy

14 Ibid., and Report of the TEB for the year 1895–6, May 1896, p.15.
15 Report of the TEB for the year 1895–6, p.16.
16 A. Kadish, *The Oxford Economists in the Late Nineteenth Century*, Oxford: Oxford University Press, 1982, p.247 ff.
17 London School of Economics, Hutchinson Trust Minute Book I.

vis-à-vis the Fabian Society and to keep its deliberations confidential, in case the other members of the Society insisted on a more
conventional interpretation of the terms of the Hutchinson bequest
and objected to Webb's virtual appropriation of the money. Most
members of the Society were eventually placated,[18] and, more importantly, the source of the original fund remained generally unknown,[19]
enabling Webb to introduce the projected school to the LCC's
Financial and General Purposes Subcommittee (6 May 1895) as financed 'out of certain private trust funds which have been made available
for the purpose, with a view to co-ordinating and developing the
teaching in these subjects [economics and political science], including
commerce.'[20]

In his presentation to the Financial and General Purposes Subcommittee, of which he was at the time Acting Chairman, Webb based
his argument on the Council's inability to implement its resolution of
28 November 1893 to provide for commercial training. The matter was
of some urgency.

> Latterly the Board has been more than once approached by
> members of the Chamber of Commerce and others, as to the
> importance of something being done to provide higher and wider
> instruction in commercial subjects, in order to prevent the English
> clerk from being ousted by his better educated German rival.

The Science and Art Department (i.e. Acland) had accepted the TEB's
(i.e. Webb's) argument that subjects adapted to London's special
circumstances, including banking, economics, commercial law, history,
geography, insurance, and, in fact, any subject 'except ancient Greek
and theology',[21] should be added to the list of those supportable by the
'Whisky money'. Hence training London's clerks, which numbered
over 100,000, fell within the TEB's jurisdiction.

The Chamber of Commerce had already admitted the need to extend
and systematize the type of higher commercial training initiated with
Cunningham's course, and the projected London School of Economics
and Political Science offered a way of doing so. The co-operation of the

18 Some of the money was to be used for the Society's educational activities
and for its general overheads: see N. and J. MacKenzie, *The First Fabians*,
London: Quartet, 1979, pp.215–16. For G. B. Shaw's objections, see letter to
B. Webb, dated 1 July 1895, quoted in M. Cole, *The Story of Fabian Socialism*,
London: Heineman, 1963, p.71. Another hostile Fabian was Ramsay Mac-
Donald. See LSE Archives, 'Reminiscences of former students, members of
staff and governors, Edward R. Pease', September 1945.
19 E.g. in the School's first published *Register*, London 1934, p.218, Hutchinson was enigmatically mentioned as 'an early benefactor of the School'.
20 TEB, p.16, Minutes of the TEB 1895–7, 6 May 1895.
21 B. Webb, *Our Partnership*, p.80.

Society of Arts had already been secured. It would allow for the free use of its hall and, in return, the new School would offer courses in some of the subjects the Society examined on, including commercial geography and, an addition to its 1895–6 list, economics.[22] Similar co-operation was promised by the Chamber of Commerce, provided that the School developed its 'special commercial side'. However, Webb stated that this could not be done without the TEB's help.

All the TEB was asked by its Chairman to do was to subsidize courses agreed with the Chamber of Commerce and held in the Chamber's rooms in Botolph House, Eastcheup. In adopting Llewellyn Smith's report, the LCC had agreed to expend £2,000 annually on higher commercial education. So far no action had been taken in the matter. Now, however, the foundation of the LSE offered a solution, and the subsidy asked for was a mere £500. Not surprisingly, it was granted, and in later years it was increased to £1,200. In 1896 it was further agreed that since the grant was conditional upon the delivery of courses approved by the Chamber of Commerce, the TEB should have a representative on the School's governing body.[23] However, in view of the governing body's smallness, it was agreed that since Webb was both Chairman of that and the TEB, he was in the best position to co-ordinate the use made of the LCC's grant, which, after all, he was largely responsible for.

Thus, the Hutchinson bequest intended for the furtherance of the cause of socialism, and the TEB's grant made conditional on the approval of the Chamber of Commerce, combined to bring the London School of Economics into being. Its first director, W. A. S. Hewins, had been a successful Oxford extension lecturer who had failed to induce Oxford to recognize the importance of his subject – economic history. By the early 1890s it became clear that the extension was unlikely to live up to his and his contemporary Oxford economists' expectations. By his own admission, 'In the early days of the Oxford movement some of us expected to see by this time [c. 1896] the establishment of thorough and systematic courses in the larger industrial centres.'[24] Instead they found that local interest in economics could not be sustained beyond elementary courses which, consequently, could only be repeated at relatively large intervals at any one location (with the sole exception of London, where extension work was carried out by the London Society

---

22 *Journal of the Society of Arts*, Vol. 43, 28 June 1895, Vol. 44, 26 June 1896.
23 The governing body consisted of Wm. Clarke, W. R. Pease, and Webb, i.e. the Hutchinson trustees.
24 W. A. S. Hewins, 'The teaching of economics', *Journal of the Society of Arts*, Vol. 45, 4 December 1896, pp.42–52.

for the Extension of University Teaching).[25] It was Hewins's belief that, whereas it was in the national interest for the majority of the population to acquire some knowledge of elementary economics, demand was dependent on the creation 'of public institutions in which advanced work could be carried on'. While 'no spontaneous demand for scientific training in economics can be said to exist, the indifference is largely due to the absence of any satisfactory provision for the subject in our educational system.'

There was also the problem of the individual economist's limited employment options. Contrary to earlier expectations, Oxford did not appoint its extension lecturers to university lectureships, thereby denying them the security of income and the prestige without which the extension movement found it impossible to retain the services of even its most popular lecturers. Without a university appointment, no 'English economist could live on his salary in the manner required of him, and at the same time provide for old age and the ordinary incidents of family life. The result is, that much ability, which might be exercised in economic work, is diverted into more profitable vocations.' The LSE was meant to solve both problems – providing for a systematic study of economics and creating an institute in which economists could dedicate themselves to the teaching and study of their subject.

Hewins had initially been brought in by Sidney Webb to advise on the organization of the extension of the Chamber of Commerce's initiative. As the scheme developed, he was eventually offered the directorship of the LSE, which he readily accepted.[26] As part of his duties, Hewins undertook to recruit a staff of economists and teachers of related subjects, most of whom had previously been unable to obtain a permanent academic appointment, or had been unhappy with the conditions under which they taught. At the same time, he was fully aware of the importance of the City connection. He agreed to examine for the Society of Arts,[27] and had made certain that the Chamber of Commerce was happy with the choice of courses offered by the School.

The LSE's first session was advertised by the Chamber of Commerce as an extension of its own educational activity.[28] At a meeting at which the School's work was to be introduced to the members of the Chamber,

25 See J. Burrows, *University Adult Education in London. A Century of Achievement*, London, 1976, and idem., 'The teaching of economics in the early days of the University Extension movement in London 1876–1902', *History of Economic Thought Newsletter*, no. 20, Spring 1978, pp.8–14.
26 Webb's first choice, Graham Wallace, turned the offer down on 28 March 1895.
27 'Report of the Council, XV. examinations', *Journal of the Society of Arts*, Vol. 44, 26 June 1896, pp.677–80.
28 *The Chamber of Commerce Journal*, September 1895.

its President, Sir Albert K. Rollit, explained that, whereas no one could question the importance of commercial training, examinations on their own were insufficient. Since 'the Chamber had felt that as there might be many students who had the time to attend lectures and classes, it was desirable to have not only examinations, but teaching and training, teaching not merely through lectures, but also by systematic instruction in classes.' The new School was in effect only a temporary solution on the way to the eventual incorporation of the study of commerce 'as a branch of culture in a re-organized Teaching University of London, which was very much wanted'.

The School's programme advertised in August 1895[29] consisted of courses which were declared useful as preparation for the public examinations held by: the Civil Service (Class I and Indian); the Council of Legal Education; the Institute of Bankers; the Institute of Actuaries; London University (Mental and Moral Science); and the London Chamber of Commerce (Commercial Education), while the School itself did not offer a degree or an equivalent thereof.

The courses held under the auspices of the Chamber of Commerce (and subsidized by the TEB) were: a twenty-lecture course by H. J. Mackinder, future Director of the School, on 'Influence of geographical conditions on commercial development, trade routes, etc.'; a twenty-lecture course by W. A. S. Hewins on 'The history of English commerce'; a twenty-lecture course by J. E. C. Munro of Owens College, Manchester, on 'The law in relation to the exchange and distribution of wealth'; a twenty-lecture course by H. S. Foxwell of St John's College, Cambridge, and Professor of Political Economy at University College, London, on 'The history and principles of banking in England'; and a six-lecture course by Major the Honourable George Peel on 'Foreign banking systems' and 'The Bank of France'. The rest of the courses, held in the hall of the Society of Arts, included: a twenty-lecture course by Hewins on 'The state in relation to industry and commerce'; a three-lecture course by W. Cunningham on 'Economic effects of alien immigration'; a six-lecture course by W. M. Acworth on 'Railway economics'; a four-lecture course by E. Cannan, an Oxford contemporary of Hewins, on 'The history of rating'; a six-lecture course by E. J. Harper on 'The rating question'; and a twenty-lecture course by Graham Wallace on 'The English Constitution since 1832'. In addition, day and evening classes were arranged in economics, statistics, commercial geography and history, commercial and industrial law, and political science.

As far as the Chamber of Commerce was concerned, the School clearly justified its support. By October 1896 its Education Committee

29 *The London Technical Education Gazette*, vol. I, no. 10 August 1895.

could report of 74 candidates for the senior certificate, of which 49 passed the examinations.[30] By the following October the numbers rose to 110 and 86 respectively,[31] and by November 1897 it was resolved that the Chamber's senior certificate scheme should be incorporated into the School's programme.[32] There remained the relatively minor problem of the inconvenience of holding courses in Eastcheap, because of the noise from the street produced by 'organ grinders and street musicians',[33] a problem solved by the School's move to 10 Adelphi Terrace, where courses were held from October 1896.

Following the School's first session, Sidney Webb submitted a confidential report to the TEB,[34] on the basis of which the Board re-emphasized in its Annual Report the importance of the School's contribution to commercial education:

> London contains not only far more clerks than any other city, but also probably a larger proportion of clerks to the total population than is to be found elsewhere . . . Great efforts are being made by the heads of the banking world to induce the very numerous bank clerks to study banking economics and banking law. The insurance clerks, and those of the accountants, actuaries and auditors require specially applied mathematics, the principles of insurance, statistics, etc. The large staff of railway officials need a special department of their own dealing with railway economics and statistics. Finally it must be remembered that London includes several thousands of civil service and local government clerks, who need special training in statistical methods, economics, and what may be called 'comparative public administration'. Higher technical instruction of this specialized kind is costly, and can never be made to pay its way at fees within the reach of what is, in the mass, a poorly remunerated class. There is, however, no direction in which better technical education is likely to be more serviceable to the community.

In order to cater for this need, the TEB should, in Webb's view:

> quietly and unofficially ascertain what subjects were deemed most necessary by such bodies as the Chamber of Commerce, the Institute of Bankers, the various associations of accountants, actuaries, auditors, etc., those representing the insurance and

---

30 Chamber of Commerce, Council Minute Books, Vol. II, 8 October 1896.
31 Ibid., 7 October 1897.
32 Ibid., 4 November 1897.
33 Ibid., 12 November 1896.
34 GLC, TEB 79/4. Parts of the report were incorporated into the section on commercial education in the TEB's Report for 1895–6.

railway companies, the local government officials, and others acquainted with the needs of different sections of the great army of 'clerks'. We should, I think, avoid the mistake of inciting professional associations themselves to take up educational work. Whatever instruction is needed had, almost certainly, better be given as a part of the work of some definitely organised educational institution, acting in co-operation with the professional associations concerned.

As for extension courses, these, too, should wherever possible be incorporated as part of the curriculum of existing educational institutions. Hence the LSE emerged from the Report as the body in which 'the Board might most usefully extend its work', thereby ensuring that the School would receive most of the sum earmarked by the LCC for annual expenditure on higher commercial education.

On a later occasion,[35] Webb elaborated on the manner in which the LSE fitted into a comprehensive scheme for commercial education. He defined three levels of training:

1. The 'education of the youth before he enters business life', which should be provided by schools, 'which should reject all connection with the university, which should altogether exclude its influence, which should decline to follow its traditional curriculum, and which should arrange a course of studies deliberately based on the needs of boys who will become clerks in City offices at 15 or 16'.
2. Evening instruction for young clerks who should be encouraged by their employers to develop professional qualifications.
3. Perhaps 'most important of all . . . higher commercial education, required by the officer of the commercial army, if not by every auditious member of the rank and file.'

According to Webb, the LSE had been 'founded by a little committee, who believed it possible to create a demand among men engaged in the practical business of life, for instruction in the concrete applications of economics to the affairs of commerce, finance, and public administration'. The School had in fact set out to combine the two advanced levels enunciated by Webb. In keeping with the philosophy that clerks and business men would not respond to an offer of a general commercial education but would attend specialized courses, the LSE offered a number of courses aimed at relatively narrowly defined sectors. Its courses on railway economics, for instance, led the Great Western and the Great Eastern companies to pay the fees of over one hundred of

35 The 1897 International Congress on Technical Education, *Journal of the Society of Arts*, 6 August 1897.

their employees who attended these courses in the first year.[36] By 1898–9, in addition to the full-time three-year courses in economics and political science, the LSE offered a two-year course in statistics, a 'Higher Commercial' course, and special courses for railway and municipal officials.

The connection with extension work was also emphasized. From the outset the School hoped to attract extension students who sought advanced training but whose numbers at any one extension centre were insufficient to create a local demand for such courses.[37] Furthermore, the LSE itself operated as a kind of extension centre. Upon the payment of fees, anyone could attend the lectures of any single course as well as any of the classes. The general lectures especially were supposed to operate as feeder courses for the more specialized and advanced courses.[38] Altogether the public was offered a choice of a programme of systematic studies, single advanced courses of a specialized nature, and general lectures.

As for the LSE's more general scientific and academic orientation, it was clear from the beginning that it intended to abandon the traditional Oxford and Cambridge approach to higher education, and adopt instead a more pragmatic attitude to the problem of dealing with the nation's current needs. In an early interview,[39] Hewins presented the School's case by contrasting it with the work done by the universities in training future social investigators:

> Take our universities at the present time . . . these questions which the School of Economics and Political Science has been formed to deal with, have largely been left untouched by the universities . . . If a person wishes to devote himself or herself to economic investigation, we want to provide that person with the means of getting the best possible training in the subject, and also to enable that person to get on the right line in carrying out the investigation. Suppose an undergraduate at the universities at the present time, or anybody else, wishes to devote himself to this sort of study, he has to pick up his training as well as he can, and is left more or less free to follow his own inclinations . . . What we are going to do is to provide a thorough and efficient three years' training.

36 Report of the TEB for the year 1896–7, p.32.
37 See the *Westminster Gazette*, 7 June 1895; Kadish, *The Oxford Economists*, pp.253–4. On the operation of extension courses as feeders to the LSE, see S. Webb, 'The organisation of economics teaching in London', *The University Extension Journal* (London), April 1896.
38 Hewins in the *Daily Chronicle*, 5 October 1895.
39 *London*, 3 October 1895.

And in an age deeply troubled by its awareness of the growing complexity of economic and social problems, the founders of the LSE had little doubt that theirs was a national mission.

The training Hewins envisaged consisted of: first year – economic theory, economic history, statistics, and political science; second year – specialization in 'the particular department of work for which his [the student's] previous experience seems to have fitted him'; third year – training in 'actual methods of research'. 'We are going to see', Hewins added, 'that the student does research and that his work leads to direct and practical results. The research branch of the work will almost be like apprenticeships.' For instance, a complete course in economics offered for 1897–8 consisted of first-year elementary courses which included: economic theory by Cannan, using A. T. Hedley, *Economics, or An Account of the Relations between Private Property and Public Welfare* (1890) as a textbook. The course's principal object was described as using 'elementary economic theory' to throw light 'on questions of general interest, such as the effects of competition and modern attempts to aid or impede it, the growth of population, monetary changes, protection, etc.'; the outlines of English economic history by Hewins; and elementary methods of social investigation by Hewins, covering 'the relation of statistics to economics and the elementary uses and methods of statistics'. The second year's advanced courses were in economic theory (Cannan) and economic history (Hewins). And for his third year's work, the student was expected to choose a subject for research with the Director's approval, and work on it under the supervision of one of the teachers.[40]

The orientation of the School's non-vocational teaching, then, was entirely towards empirical, practical research. Like other virtually self-taught economists of his generation whose scientific work was largely shaped by their interest in current social and economic problems, Hewins did not believe in the need for an extensive preparatory training in economic theory. As far as he was concerned, 'by attending University Extension courses of lectures, reading the books recommended, and writing papers in connexion with the courses, a man may get a very good grasp of the elements of economics'.[41] A similar view was expressed by Webb, who maintained that the standard elementary courses given by the extension, the polytechnics, and similar institutions offered sufficient preparation for a systematic LSE training in research.[42]

40 The London School of Economics and Political Science, 'Arrangements for the summer term 1897', 'Arrangements for the session 1897–1898', Bodleian Library, Per 26333 YE.25.
41 Hewins in the *Westminster Gazette*, 27 September 1895. Compare with W. J. Ashley, *What Is Political Science?* Toronto: Rowsell & Hutchinson, 1888.
42 S. Webb in the *Sketch*, 11 November 1896.

Research undertaken by the School's teachers and students was to take maximum advantage of its location within close proximity of many valuable topics. According to Llewellyn Smith, who had done his apprenticeship on Charles Booth's project, London resembled 'an enormous laboratory'; the School was 'surrounded on all sides by masses of facts.'[43] The LSE, therefore, enjoyed a clear advantage over older institutions. In Hewins's view:

> The universities . . . could train men up to the point at which some of the subjects could be undertaken with a fair chance of success, and the work itself would do the rest. Oxford might turn out men well qualified in all branches of economics which require careful historical training; Cambridge its statisticians; Victoria University, men well versed in the economics of modern industrial and commercial questions . . . In the case of London alone no selection of appropriate subjects was necessary because nearly every branch of economics could be studied with greater advantage here than in any city in the world. In no city had there ever occurred so splendid an opportunity.[44]

Research was to culminate in some 'practical work', in which the student would 'take up some business, study thoroughly all the economic and social aspects of it, find out from the workers how it affects them, and, finally, compile a report similar to a Blue-Book on it.'[45]

In order to attract research students, the LSE succeeded in founding a number of scholarships and studentships, the first of which were the LSE Research Studentships, awarded 'to promote the execution of definite pieces of original work relating to past or present economic or political conditions and to enable students to become trained investigators', and the Russell Studentship, Bertrand Russell's gift of his Trinity Fellowship.[46] In addition to £100 per annum for two years (similar to the LSE studentship), the latter offered the opportunity, at the end of the two years, for the holder to deliver a short course of lectures on his subject which could then be prepared for publication.[47] The School was co-educational from the outset, and attracted a high

43 The *Borough Polytechnic News*, October 1895.
44 Hewins at the Society of Arts, in *Chronicle*, 4 December 1896.
45 *Pall Mall Gazette*, 22 May 1896.
46 Cole, *The Story of Fabian Socialism*, p.71.
47 The *London School of Economics Register*, p.217–18; *London*, 31 October 1895; *The Times*, 18 January 1897. The Russell Studentship was awarded by an examination which contained four papers in economics: theory (including history of theories); economic history; the principles of social investigation; and a general paper – and four papers in political science – ancient constitutions; modern constitutions; the theory and history of the English constitution; and a general paper.

proportion of women from the Oxford and Cambridge women's halls[48] who at first appeared to dominate the School's research activity.[49]

One focus of research was local government, a subject close to the Webbs' heart. The first work published under the auspices of the LSE in a series called 'Studies in economics and political science', edited by Hewins, was E. Cannan's *The History of Local Rates in England* (London, 1896), which was based on his lectures in the School's first session. In his Introduction Cannan, who (with H. S. Foxwell) was in charge of the School's elementary and advanced courses in economic theory during its early years, outlined some of the main characteristics of the LSE's approach to the study of economic problems:

> Laborious students whose investigations have interested scarcely anyone but themselves have been known to seek comfort in the assertion that truth is valuable for its own sake. I do not believe that this is the case. A great deal that is true is not worth knowing. The most inveterate bore is often the most truthful man. All history should, I think, have some practical aim. Some moral, some lesson of guidance should be offered by it. Even if this is not true of all history, it is surely true with regard to economic history. It would be absurd to study a subject so dry, not to say odious, as local rates except with a view to practical aims. We do not study such subjects from a love of truth in the abstract or to while away a wet Sunday afternoon, but because there are practical controversies about them and we hope that we may learn something which may be of assistance in these controversies.[50]

Local government was often dealt with in the School's courses, and in 1899 a prize of ten guineas was offered in a competition for the best description of the organization of a local governing body.[51] It was also argued that the School's courses could not fail to improve the performance of local government officials. But local government was only one sphere in which the LSE set out to forward the cause of progress. Progress was understood as requiring to an ever increasing extent,

48 Of the first (1896) holders of the LSE Studentship, three were women: Lilian Tomm, later Professor Lilian Knowles, and Ellen Marianne Leonard, both from Girton; and Edith Deverell from Somerville: *The Times*, 11 August 1896.

49 S. Webb in the *Sketch*, 11 November 1896. Of the first 300 students, 75 were women.

50 E. Cannan, *History of Local Rates in England*, London: Longmans & Co., 1896, p.1. For Cannan on the usefulness of economic theory, see E. Cannan, 'The practical utility of economic science', *Economic Journal*, Vol. XII (December 1902).

51 The *Echo*, 29 March 1899. The prize was won by the Deputy Town Clerk of Middlesborough.

conscious collective action along scientifically determined lines.

The School set out to examine scientifically the best courses of progress and to train an army of reformers – administrators and teachers, rather than politicians. Indeed, following the Tory victory in the general election of 1895 and the poor performance of both the Liberal and the Labour Parties, the LSE's type of work seemed the most promising course of action left to radical liberals as well as Fabian collectivists.[52] At a lecture following the election Hewins stated that:

> They had heard a good deal since the last General Election of what some people regarded as a revolution in public opinion, the result of which was that everything was going to the dogs; but a little exact knowledge of the history of the past would clear away such cobwebs from their brains. No effort in the direction of progress was ever lost, and although their aspirations had not been realised, research would show that things were improving and had been improving for generations. However feeble their efforts might be, good work would in the end help to bring about a nobler state of society than at present existed. If people understood the economic history of the country, they would be in a better position. If they made the best of the opportunities which were now so numerous, they might be perfectly certain that long before they got to the end of their studies they would be in a position to suggest a remedy for the evils of which they complained.[53]

The Webbs were convinced that anyone who studied economics was bound to become a Fabian socialist.[54] Hewins and fellow liberals held a similar view of the connection between the School's work and reform. Not surprisingly, the LSE rapidly gained a progressive 'no-nonsense' reputation: 'To the students of facts whose gospel is the blue-book, and to whom statistics are the sword of progressive faith, the London School of Economics is a very temple of light.'[55]

The more partisan view of the School's purpose expressed by S. Webb in the privacy of the Hutchinson Trust meetings was, as a matter of policy, given minimal public airing.[56]

52 See Kadish, *The Oxford Economists*, p.257; MacKenzie, *The First Fabians*, pp.219–20.
53 Hewins at the Battersea Public Baths, *Daily Chronicle*, 19 November 1895. See also *Westminster Gazette*, 21 January 1898.
54 Sir S. Caine, *The History of the Foundation of the London School of Economics and Political Science*, London: G. Bell & Sons, 1963, p.29. See also H. Samuel in LSE Archives, Reminiscences of Former Students, etc.
55 *New Age*, 22 September 1898.
56 Lord Snell, one of the School's first students and secretary to Hewins, in Reminiscences of Former Students etc., Nuffield College, Oxford, Fabian Papers, A2, Webb to Pease, 9 June 1895.

Initial hopes of attracting and training potential working-class leaders were soon abandoned. Following its first session, Hewins pointed out that the small number of artisans who attended courses was probably due to their being 'rather too advanced . . . and [demanding] more mental effort than the man engaged closely all day in manual work can well give.'[57] And a plan to hold a summer meeting in 1896 to attract 'Co-operators, Trade Unionists and Scientists from the provinces',[58] was replaced by a call for a conventional summer extension-type meeting. By then the Webbs themselves had come to place their hopes for the future of socialism on the progressive members of the middle class.[59] Even attempts to attract members of the Fabian Society with an offer of reduced fees were eventually abandoned due to lack of interest.[60] In a letter to the Manchester socialist weekly, the *Clarion*, John McKillop, one of the first holders of the Research Studentships, warned that:

> People will soon be voting for Socialist candidates in sufficient numbers to put them into power, and they will expect results . . . We want working class legislators and administrators, but they must have sound knowledge, or results that are desired will not follow their work . . . Why cannot I. L. P. and S. D. F. and other organisations and branches take up the work of preparing suit-able men to meet this demand when it comes? I would suggest that as far as London is concerned, this might be done by each branch selecting its most suitable members and sending them to the London School of Economics and Political Science . . . The School should be crowded with Socialists, but this is not the case.[61]

Hence the School's early reputation for political activism was not so much influenced by the Fabian connection as by the politics of the staff. In addition to their relatively radical liberalism, some of the School's first teachers, especially the economic historians, including Hewins, Foxwell, MacKinder, Acworth, Cunningham (who lectured occasionally at the LSE), and later Mrs L. Knowles and Percy Ashley, came to question the orthodoxy of free trade.[62] Imperialism appears to have held a distinct fascination for many historians of Hewins's generation who, to begin with, had been critical of orthodox liberalism. English imperialism as described in Seeley's *The Expansion of England*

57 Hewins in *Echo*, 18 January 1895.
58 Kadish, *The Oxford Economists*, p.255–6.
59 E.g. B. Webb, *Our Partnership*, p.125.
60 Hutchinson Trust Minute Book, vol. I, 29 July 1895; E. R. Pease in *Reminscences of Former Students*.
61 *Clarion*, 31 May 1896.
62 Free-traders on the early staff included E. Cannan, C. P. Sanger, and later F. W. Hirst.

seemed an obvious example of the type of inexorable and impersonal force of progress which shaped the course of human history.[63] Economic imperialism was, furthermore, regarded by some radical liberals as an extension of state intervention ensuring world-wide peace and prosperity.[64] Economic historians such as W. J. Ashley and W. Cunningham, who had been greatly impressed by German historical scholarship, added to the arsenal of the imperialists' arguments the German defence of the use of economic intervention in the interests of *Staatsbildung*. In the case of Hewins, neo-mercantilism began to emerge as a characteristic of his work around 1895. Consequently, he came to reject the foreign policies normally associated with classical economics. Free 'competition and the doctrine of *laissez-faire* were not, in his opinion, the cause of England's industrial greatness; that greatness and prosperity being rather the inevitable outcome of the previous existing colonial policy.'[65]

Since neo-mercantilism did not entail a rejection of radical reformism, no ideological split emerged between Hewins and Webb. In an address to the Political Economy Circle of the National Liberal Club in 1898, Hewins professed a clearly collectivist view of state action:

> Labour and Capital were in hostile camps and was it safe, he asked, to trust the commercial and industrial welfare of the country to men about whom there was no certainty that they would act with regard to the interest of the State as a whole rather than their own? . . . the outcome in the course of time would be a demand for the state regulation of wages, which they would find it impossible to resist.[66]

In publicly adopting definite positions on a variety of current controversial issues, such as minimum wages, Hewins and most of his colleagues, whether neo-mercantilists or free-traders, acted in defiance of Marshall's advocacy of the economist's scientific impartiality. From the outset, the LSE had regarded itself as the embodiment of an alternative to the Marshallian view of economics as well as to Marshall's position on the proper course of economic training. And this was in spite of the fact that as soon as the School's academic character became accentuated in anticipation of the organization of the University of London and the establishment of a BSc (Econ.) degree, courses in economic theory (i.e. Marshall's *Principles*) were introduced. Webb had categorically

---

63 E.g. Hewins's summary of his course on the economic implications of imperialism in the *Manchester Guardian*, 22 June 1899.
64 E.g. H. Samuel, *Memoirs*, London 1945, p.33.
65 *Weekly Times and Echo*, 23 February 1896. See also Kadish, *The Oxford Economists*, p.260.
66 *Manchester Evening News*, 30 June 1898.

stated: 'I was in revolt against one Professor of Economics; I wanted a lot of Professors', and that Acworth and Cunningham had been brought in 'to counteract Marshall'.[67] The School's official position as stated by Hewins was that there was 'enough theory in the air to last for a time, and now we want to get at the facts';[68] on 'economical subjects we have hitherto had plenty of unwarranted generalization. We confidently predict that this new school will do much towards exposing flimsy sophistries by the light of carefully ascertained and scientifically arranged facts.'[69] By disassociating himself from theory, Hewins believed he was in fact ensuring scientific objectivity. The School, he stated, would not attach itself 'to any particular section of economists. Personally, he thought, that day had passed for writing treatises dealing with economic science as a whole [e.g. Marshall's *Principles*]. Rather we must expect monographs on special subjects; the ages of faith had passed, and it was now the time for special investigation.'[70]

Hewins often contrasted the LSE curriculum with the status of the study of economics elsewhere in England, and especially with Oxford and Cambridge. At Oxford it was largely neglected, but with Cambridge, 'where economic studies are much better organised than anywhere else in England',[71] comparison was somewhat more problematic. Marshall had been trying for some years to develop economics with economic theory as its main focus. Hewins could not object to Marshall's efforts to develop the study of economics as such. His argument with Marshall was over the latter's definition of the nature and scope of economics, and the purpose of economic teaching. A purely or mainly theoretical approach was far too narrow and one of the main reasons for the subject's unpopularity:

> I believe the opinion is still very widespread that by economics we mean a neatly rounded set of general propositions which can be comprised in a small crown octavo text-book, and learnt like the multiplication table. So far as that is the case, it is easy to understand the objections to the subject felt by the great manufacturer on the one hand, and the artisan on the other. But, as Jevons pointed out, it is important to realize that economics is not one subject but several. It includes . . . the pure theory, which can be carried to a very high degree of abstraction, the analysis of the actual structure of the modern world of business, the more or less

67 S. Webb in 'Reminiscences of Former Students, etc.' See also *London*, 29 August 1895.
68 Hewins in the *Daily Chronicle*, 5 October 1895.
69 Hewins in the *Echo*, 18 January 1896.
70 Hewins in the *Westminster Gazette*, 21 January 1898.
71 Hewins, 'The teaching of economics', *Journey of the Society of Arts*, Vol.45, 4 December 1896, pp.42–52.

inductive work of the historian and the statistician, the art of finance and administration, and many other branches.[72]

Accordingly, the object of teaching economics was 'not to enable people to pass examinations, but to impart useful knowledge',[73] and the 'claim of economic training to public support must be based upon its practical usefulness.'

There were two ways of developing the study of economics in England. In the existing universities, one was forced by the system's nature to try and change examinations and institutions by presenting a theoretical ideal of the best possible course of teaching. The LSE, on the other hand, was not impeded by antiquated views and vested interests. In developing its programme it was able 'to find out precisely what people wanted by consulting the heads of the civil service, municipal bodies, and so on, as to the points in which their subordinates over whom they were set, failed at the present time'. The next step was to work out the best way of meeting those needs and devising an appropriate examination system. And, finally, it was up to the School to reach out 'by personal negotiation and other means' and 'get in touch with . . . potential students, and persuade them to make use of the lectures and classes' by demonstrating the usefulness of the training offered.[74] Appropriately, many of the School's first teachers were either scholars who had previously failed to obtain a permanent teaching position in one of the older universities or university colleges (Hewins, Cannan), teachers in other universities who were either unhappy with the way their subject was being taught (Foxwell, Mackinder) or simply welcomed the opportunity to lecture occasionally on subjects not included in their institutions' curricula, and various scholars (G. Wallas, A. L. Bowley) and specialists (A. W. Acworth, H. Hall) whose subjects were not normally included in the curricula of more traditional institutions of higher education.

So long as the School sought to attract well-defined professional groups to its commercial training, the planning of appropriate courses was a relatively simple matter. Following its first year of operation, Hewins was able to report of a student body which included 'civil servants, local government officials, railway officials, young men and women engaged in business, bank managers and clerks, teachers and other persons engaged in public work.'[75] In time the differentiation between the city-oriented courses and the training for research diminished, with one type of course blending into the other. In a sense

72 Hewins in the *Journal of the Society of Arts*, Vol.45, 30 July 1897, pp.930–3.
73 Hewins, 'The teaching of economics', op.cit.
74 Ibid., and *Daily News*, 21 January 1897.
75 Quoted in 'The teaching of economics', op.cit.

it could be argued that the research students were also there for a relatively well-defined practical purpose. Thus Hewins could claim in 1897 that 'there was a scientific conception and unity of purpose pervading the whole school ... The students were not mere vague enthusiasts but people with a more or less definite training, who knew what they wanted, with a view to improving their own efficiency.'[76] The School allowed each student to follow a course of studies which included both general principles and specialization, thereby avoiding the pitfalls of too general an education on the one hand, and too early a specialization on the other.[77]

By the time the LSE became part of the teaching University of London, most of the narrowly vocational courses had disappeared.[78] Nevertheless, the School's policy of offering a variety of options within one comprehensive programme remained. A degree course within the Faculty of Economics and Political Science (including Commerce and Industry) was still deemed suitable for:

(i) those whose main object has been to acquire a sound training in economics and political science and the methods of investigation appropriate to those subjects, with a view to tutorial or professional work, or research, or because they appreciate the importance of a knowledge of these subjects in relation to general education;

(ii) those who recognise the utility of such general scientific training, combined with some detailed knowledge of some group of subjects, in relation to business and professional life, e.g. bankers, merchants, railway officials, etc.;

(iii) those engaged in public administration, central or local; 'persons engaged in or about to engage in the public service whether in this country, in India or the colonies' and 'persons engaged or about to engage in public life or in the administration of public law, as Members of Parliament, Magistrates, etc.' (Gresham Report, p. xliii).[79]

The comprehensive nature of the programme was ensured by including amongst the obligatory first-year courses both economic history and statistics, the British constitution, European history AD 600–1915, mathematics, and economic and political geography; and by allowing second- and third-year students to specialize in specific areas such as banking and currency, international trade, transport, and

76 *Daily News*, 21 January 1897.
77 Hewins's report to the TEB, quoted in the *School Guardian*, 1 April 1898.
78 Caine, *Foundation of the LSE*, p.49.
79 From the *Calendar* for 1900–1, in W. H. Beveridge's Introduction to *The L. S. E. Register*, p. ix.

insurance, through courses which covered the history, theory, and current organization of each area.[80]

One final feature which the School could justly boast of was the British Library of Political and Economic Science, lauched by Sidney Webb as an independent venture,[81] but which has been commonly identified with the LSE. It was represented as more than a mere teaching aid, but rather as a vital component of the School's work. In a thinly concealed jibe at Cambridge, the *Daily Chronicle* reported in April 1896 that:

> in the moral sciences . . . [e]ach student collects his own books, uses his own eyes, and begins not where his predecessor ended, but where his predecessor began. The proposed Library of Political Science represents, like the London School of Economics, to which it is to be attached, a definite protest against this, a definite attempt to introduce a 'Novum Organum' into the study of the difficult and shifting facts of political and social life.

The reporter likened the library to 'a properly equipped laboratory' for the subjects taught at the School. Some years later, J. Bryce, addressing an annual dinner of the Economic Students' Union of the LSE, compared the library to a museum, 'a collection of specimens' without which no serious work in any experimental science was possible.[82]

The contrast between the LSE and the older universities, especially Cambridge, of which the School's founders had been so conscious, was not lost on its supporters. The *Manchester Guardian* stated as early as January 1896, that 'before its foundation it was not possible anywhere in England to gain a systematic and thorough course of instruction in political and economic science'.[83] And, later the same year: 'The London School may yet become the university of a science which in England has too long been neglected or left to private study'.[84] By the late 1890s, when it became clear that London would, after all, have its teaching university, those who had supported the LSE's combination of commercial education and political economy looked forward to the establishment of a university programme and degree on similar lines. At last as 'a nation we are beginning to realise that university education must not only be in relation to the literary professions and to ordinary culture, but to almost every possible vocation.'[85] More tellingly perhaps,

80 See LSE, Misc. Coll. 523/2. Adopted 31 May 1901.
81 Mackenzie, *The First Fabians*, p.227.
82 *The Times*, 13 February 1899.
83 The *Manchester Guardian*, 10 January 1896.
84 Ibid., 19 September 1896.
85 *Commerce*, 19 October 1898.

the LSE was seen by some to break the Oxford and Cambridge monopoly on the training of Britain's future rulers. No less an authority than J. Bryce, addressing the School's students, stated that possibly 'Plato had a school like the present in his mind when he said all kings should be philosophers, and philosophers kings.'[86]

The success of the LSE inevitably affected the approach of other English universities to the question of the status and nature of economic studies. A. W. Flux, a senior wrangler (1887) who, whilst at Cambridge, had been described as 'one of the distinguished band of mathematicians who have followed Professor Marshall in devoting their attention to economics',[87] was appointed Cobden Lecturer in Political Economy at Owens College, Manchester, in 1893. In 1898, following his acceptance of the Stanley Jevons Chair at Manchester, he described[88] how, when he had first come to Manchester, he had found that schemes for high commercial training

> had been already discussed, and were held as it were, in reserve, awaiting the appropriate moment for more public discussion. I think I may be allowed to express now my feeling of bitter disappointment which I experienced when London was shown to have taken a decisive step in a matter in which, as it seemed to me, Manchester ought by right to lead.

Like Hewins he believed that the issue touched the very *raison d'être* of the university:

> For what reason are colleges such as ours established in great centres of industry if it be not so that the higher educational needs of the neighbourhood may be more effectually met? In a great mercantile centre such as Manchester, should not the educational apparatus of a university college be adapted to the service of the mercantile classes, as well as to the manufacturing classes, who are served by the Chemical, Physical, and Engineering Departments of the College ... the association between the College and the Chamber of Commerce is so valuable that I should like to see it emphasised in every reasonable way.

Flux did not envisage the introduction of straightforward vocational courses in commerce of the type initially offered by the LSE. He also retained his faith in the value of a sound theoretical training in acquainting future business men with the general principles of business life in the same way as a degree in history, for instance, was thought to

86 The *Observer*, 25 February 1900.
87 *Cambridge Review*, 27 April 1893.
88 The *Manchester Guardian*, 4 October 1899.

prepare men for a political career. The purpose of change was, in his view, to attract mainly the future captains of the business world, rather than the whole range of ranks in business and public administration to which the LSE chose to cater. However, he too was prepared to admit that not all prospective students had time for a full degree course:

> the College proposed to give in the future greater attention than hitherto to students whose life-work is to be done in a merchant's or banker's or other business house. Special facilities, too, are to be provided for those who are unable to give sufficient time for the completion of a degree course, but who can devote two years or perhaps only one year, to that stage of their education for which a university college can provide.[89]

Even Marshall who had initially dismissed the LSE's early programme as reflecting the interests of the lecturers available rather than a systematic approach to the teaching of economics,[90] found it necessary, when presenting his case for an economics tripos, to adopt some of Hewins's and Webb's positions. Addressing the Cambridge Senate,[91] he stressed the importance of fostering good relations between Cambridge and the business community. Some of 'the younger academic foundations', he observed, 'are making vigorous efforts to remove the reproach that English Universities, while consistently devoting a considerable part of their energies to preparing professional men for their duties, have neglected the special interests of business men.' Cambridge must face the risk, therefore, that 'the rising generation of wealthy business men became the loyal sons of the newer and not the older Universities', and that, while the provision of 'a good education for business men' could not be described as the primary object of the suggested tripos, it was nevertheless important as a secondary aim, 'for its own sake' and for the sake of the university.

In the case of Marshall, who intended the tripos as a training mainly for professional economists, this may have been largely lip-service. But it was one point on which his scheme was forcefully supported by H. S. Foxwell, who had taught at the LSE since its foundation and whose view on the nature of economic studies was virtually identical to Hewins's:

89 Cf. LSE *Calendar* for 1900–1, quoted in *The LSE Register*, p. viii: 'The lectures and classes at the School will still be open to those who are not "internal students" and cannot, for various reasons, pursue a full University course.' It should be noted that the commerce degree in London was not established until 1919.

90 A. L. Bowley in 'Reminiscences of former students, etc.'

91 *Cambridge University Reporter*, 10 March 1903. Report of the Economics and Political Science Syndicate, 4 March 1903, discussed in the *Reporter*, 14 May 1903.

According to the view of the study which prevailed a generation ago, it was enough to furnish men with a system of abstract principles, the application of which to actual affairs was supposed to be safely left to common sense. Experience has shown that this method simply turned out *doctrinaires*, men quite unfitted for the ordinary business of life ... But nothing was more evident ... [than] that the power of applying principles to actual affairs was extremely rare, and could only be developed in economists by making their study more realistic. Men of undoubted ability constantly showed themselves unable to handle principles which, in the abstract, they evidently understood, because they were not trained to observe the details, distinctions, and complex relations of the historical situation to which theory had to be applied.[92]

He did not, he hastened to add, wish to see Cambridge establish technical commercial instruction as part of its curriculum. But rather an approach to economics which would 'cultivate habits of mind which would aid the business man to deal with the problems of his after-life'.

The LSE, then, did not only provide an institutional alternative to economists and economic historians who either could not find a suitable position in one of the existing universities, or who were unhappy with the manner in which they were forced to teach their subjects. It also embodied from its very inception a different approach to the study of economics, and to its relation to current problems and needs, of which its link with the Fabian Society was of only minor importance. This different view of the nature of the study of economics, the importance of which was acknowledged by older institutions, was only slightly modified with the foundation of the teaching University of London. More significant changes, such as the establishment of the commerce degree (1919), were yet to come and remain to be studied.

92 The *Cambridge University Reporter*, 14 May 1903.

SELECT BIBLIOGRAPHY

Augello, M., Bianchini, M., Gioli, G. and Roggi, P., (eds) *La cattedre politica in Italia. La diffusione di una disciplina <sospetta> (1750–1900)*, Milan, Franco Angeli, 1988.

Barber, W. J. (ed.), *Breaking the Academic Mould. Economists and American Higher Learning in the Nineteenth Century*, Middletown, Wesleyan University Press, 1988.

Checkland, S., 'The advent of academic economics in England', *Manchester School*, Vol.19 (1951) pp.43–70.

Copeland, M. T., *And Mark an Era. The Story of the Harvard Business School*, Boston, Little, Brown and Company, 1958.

Harvie, C., *The Lights of Liberalism: University Liberals and the Challenge of Democracy 1860–86*, London, Allen Lane, 1976.

Kadish, A., *The Oxford Economists in the Late Nineteenth Century*, Oxford, Oxford University Press, 1982.

Kadish, A., *Apostle Arnold. The Life and Death of Arnold Toynbee 1852–1883*, Durham N. C., Duke University Press, 1986.

Kadish, A., *Historians, Economists and Economic History*, London, Routledge, 1989.

Kelly, T., *A History of Adult Education in Great Britain*, 2nd edn, Liverpool, Liverpool University Press, 1970.

Le Van-Lemesle, L., *Les problèmes de l'institutionnalisation de l'économie politique en France au XIXe siècle* series *Oeconomia*, (1986).

Maloney, J., *Marshall, Orthodoxy and the Professionalisation of Economics*, Cambridge, Cambridge University Press, 1985.

Reader, W. J., *Professional Men: The Rise of the Professional Classes in Nineteenth-Century England*, London, Weidenfeld and Nicolson, 1966.

Roach, J., *Public Examinations in England, 1850–1900*, London, Cambridge University Press, 1971.

Sass, S. A., *The Pragmatic Imagination. A History of the Wharton School 1881–1981*, Philadelphia, University of Pennsylvania Press, 1982.

Sugiyama, C., and Mizuta, H., (eds) *Enlightenment and Beyond. Political Economy comes to Japan*, Tokyo, University of Tokyo Press, 1988.

Waszek N., (ed.) *Die Institutionalisierung der Nationalökonomie an den deutschen Universitäten*, St. Katherinen, Scripta Mercurae Verlag, 1988.

Welch, E., *The Peripatetic University: Cambridge Local Lectures, 1873–1973*, Cambridge, Cambridge University Press, 1973.

INDEX